2-23

MANAGEMENT OF VALUES
The Ethical Difference in Corporate Policy and Performance

Charles S. McCoy
Pacific School of Religion
and Center for Ethics and
Social Policy, Berkeley

Pitman
Boston · London · Melbourne · Toronto

To
Carroll, Marsha, Priscilla, Sherry, Stephanie, Beth,
and, of course, Margie,
who have taught me what is really valuable in life

Pitman Publishing Inc.
1020 Plain Street
Marshfield, Ma. 02050
Pitman Publishing Limited
128 Long Acre
London WC2E 9AN

Associated Companies
Pitman Publishing Pty. Ltd., Melbourne
Pitman Publishing New Zealand Ltd., Wellington
Copp Clark Pitman, Toronto

© **1985 Charles S. McCoy**

Library of Congress Cataloging in Publication Data

McCoy, Charles S.
  Management of values.

  Bibliography: p. 355
  Includes index.
  1. Business ethics.   2. Industry — Social aspects.
3. Performance.   I. Title.
HF5387.M4   1985   ·   174'.4   84-16487
ISBN 0-273-01988-0

All rights reserved. No part of this publication may be reproduced, stored in a retrieval system, or transmitted in any form or by any means, electronics, mechanical, photocopying, recording and/or otherwise without the prior written permission of the publishers.

Manufactured in the United States of America
10   9   8   7   6   5   4   3   2   1

CONTENTS

PREFACE viii

FOREWORD xii

Part One
A NEW PERSPECTIVE

One
PERFORMANCE AND ETHICS 3
The "Bottom Line" as Measure of Performance 5
The Management of Values 10
The Close Relation between Ethics and Performance 18
Suggestions for Group Study 24

Part Two
VALUES AND POLICY

Two
ETHICS IN CORPORATE POLICY 29
The Rising Interest in Ethics 31
Misunderstandings and Problems of Ethics 35
Recognizing Ethics—Individual and Corporate 40
Suggestions for Group Study 48

Contents

Three
CORPORATE CULTURE AND MORAL AGENCY   *50*
Our Organized Society   53
Dimensions of Corporate Culture   58
The Corporation as Moral Agent   68
Suggestions for Group Study   74

Four
FROM SOCIAL RESPONSE TO CORPORATE ETHICS   *76*
The Crisis of Ethics and Policy   78
Challenge to Innovate   86
Dealing with the Web of Social Values   91
Suggestions for Group Study   96

Five
A COMPREHENSIVE ETHIC FOR CORPORATE POLICY   *97*
Criteria for Corporate Action   101
The Ethics of Corporate Self-Interest   102
The Ethics of Multiple Responsibility   109
The Ethics of Social Vision   113
Comprehensiveness and the Context of Policy   116
Suggestions for Group Study   120

Part Three
MANAGING VALUES FOR PERFORMANCE

Six
POLICY PROCESS AND CORPORATE PERFORMANCE   *125*
Action: Decision Making as Policy Process   130
The Politics of Corporate Policy Formulation   136
Evaluation: Ethics in Policy Formation   139
Suggestions for Group Study   148

Seven
SOCIAL VALUES AND POLICY ETHICS   *149*
The Changing Environment of Values   153
Social Values Systems Analysis   159

Contents

Three Social Values Systems	165
Postscript	175
Suggestions for Group Study	176

Eight
INSTITUTIONALIZING CULTURE, VALUES, AND ETHICS 177
Developing Corporate Culture and Value Commitments	180
Integrating Values into Corporate Structures	187
Relating Values to the Policy Process	191
Suggestions for Group Study	202

Nine
COMMUNICATION, PARTICIPATION, AND COMMITMENT 203
Communication: Information and Values	206
Participation: Management and Human Nature	217
Commitment: Imagination and Innovation	222
Suggestions for Group Study	230

Part Four
CONCLUSION

Ten
THE ETHICAL DIFFERENCE 233
The Testimony of James Burke	236
Evaluating Corporate Performance	238
Ethics and Performance: A Summary	239
Suggestions for Group Study	246

Appendices
MATERIAL FOR GROUP STUDY

A
SUGGESTIONS FOR USE OF STUDY MATERIALS WITH GROUPS
Charles S. McCoy   *251*

Contents

B
THE SOCIAL RESPONSIBILITY OF BUSINESS IS TO INCREASE ITS PROFITS
Milton Friedman *253*

C
CASE STUDY: PENN SQUARE BANK
Tim Metz and G. Christian Hill, condensed from article in the *Wall Street Journal* *261*

D
THE PARABLE OF THE SADHU
Bowen H. McCoy *266*

E
THE CHAMPION WAY
Champion International Corporation *275*

F
ETHICS AND BUSINESS: A PROGRESS REPORT
Kirk O. Hanson *280*

G
CASE STUDY: AETNA LIFE TRIES TO HELP A NEIGHBORHOOD
Based on an article by Robert Johnson in the *Wall Street Journal* *289*

H
BOOK BRIEF: RONALD INGLEHART'S THE SILENT REVOLUTION
Prepared by Fred N. Twining *291*

I
CORPORATE POLICY STATEMENT ON PEAKED-OUT EMPLOYEES
Prepared by Fred N. Twining and Charles S. McCoy *298*

Contents

J
BOOK BRIEF: CHRISTOPHER D. STONE'S WHERE THE LAW ENDS
Prepared by Fred N. Twining   *304*

K
CASE STUDY: BANK DEVELOPS SOCIAL POLICY LOAN COMMITTEE
Charles S. McCoy and Fred N. Twining   *312*

L
CORPORATE RESPONSIBILITY CREED
Wells Fargo & Company   *314*

M
BOOK BRIEF: ROBERT W. ACKERMAN'S THE SOCIAL CHALLENGE TO BUSINESS
Prepared by Fred N. Twining   *316*

N
SPEECH TO THE ADVERTISING COUNCIL
James Burke   *325*

O
CASE STUDY: EASTWEST BANK LOAN POLICIES TO DEVELOPING COUNTRIES
Fred N. Twining   *342*

NOTES   *345*

BIBLIOGRAPHY   *355*

INDEX   *371*

PREFACE

It was a spring evening in 1968 at the San Francisco airport. I had arrived at 10:25 to board a Delta flight to Atlanta, running late for what I thought was a 10:40 departure. I had failed to note that since my last trip on that particular "red-eye" special the departure time had been shifted to 10:30.

I hurried through the entrance and headed for the counter. Three Delta attendants stood there chatting with each other. As I approached, one of them glanced at me. His eyes opened wide. "Atlanta?" he asked, at the same time reaching to get his colleagues' attention.

"Yes," I responded and then saw the departure time on the monitor. It suddenly occurred to me that I was about to miss my first flight ever.

Without further question or even a look of reproach, one attendant reached for the telephone. The other two stepped through the gap in the counter, one taking my luggage and the other motioning me to follow. We took off at a rapid pace. When we reached the gate a few minutes later, a fourth attendant was waiting for us.

"We caught them just in time," she said, conducting me down the ramp to where the door of the plane was reopening. My four escorts turned me over to the flight attendants and with cheery smiles wished me a good trip.

Although I fly Delta less often than I did years ago, I would still choose Delta over other lines if schedule and price were equal. The

Preface

experience that evening impressed me, and I suspect that this book about corporate values and performance had an important point of origin then.

In the 1970s a group of us in Berkeley began studying the ethics of organizations. Although building on previous experience and insights, we knew we had much to learn. The extent of that learning went far beyond our early expectations as we worked with policymakers in corporations, governmental agencies, community groups, and hospitals.

We found that culture, values, and ethics are crucial for organizations. The resulting performance is, in one sense, immediately visible, as I found out in the case of Delta Airlines. But the processes by which corporate values are developed and nurtured can be discovered only by patient, in-depth work over a period of time. Even though we became acquainted with many organizations through our projects, it was in a relatively small number of cases where we worked closely with the policymakers of a particular organization for 8 to 12 months that we learned the deeper meanings of ethics in the organizational policy process.

In discussions about organizational practices and needs, we encountered widespread concern for ethical values. The president and chief executive officer of a bank told us that business cannot operate without moral responsibility and commitment at every level. We saw him working to make sure that these elements were important in the organization he directed. Mario Obledo, then secretary of health and welfare for the state of California, said at one of our consultations on health policy ethics that the paramount task of every policymaker is ethics, *ethics, ETHICS*. I have seen few executives who took this responsibility with greater seriousness and sensitivity than he. We met a host of middle-management executives in business and government who believe deeply that societal organizations ought to serve humane goals. Their ethical commitments led them often either to become cynical or to try to change the policy-making system instead of continuing the struggle over particular issues.

Interesting and exciting things, we discovered, are happening in organizations. First, we encountered executives as interested as we were in finding out what ethics means within organizational systems beyond the itch of individual conscience. A growing group of top executives, we found, is moving toward new insights into what it takes to run large organizations: technical expertise and adminis-

Preface

trative skill, certainly, but also the ability to integrate values into corporate culture and policy. Second, we learned that thoughtful policymakers are convinced that ethics and performance are closely related. Although there is no consensus about the nature of that relation, many executives know that ethics makes a difference. Excellent performance requires that managers and workers possess a common vision of what the company is about and how the company is contributing to the quality of life for themselves and for society. Excellence demands developing a corporate culture with value commitments and giving attention to ethical judgment as well as efficient production. Above all, excellence necessitates managing with sensitivity to the environments of value inside and outside the company.

This book builds on what we have learned from operating policymakers about the relation of ethics and performance. It makes sense to speak of the *ethical difference* in corporate management. The insights of the executives we encountered can help other managers and managers-in-training understand organizational ethics. As the discussion widens, it will generate further insights important for business, society, and the world.

At the end of each chapter there appears a section entitled "Suggestions for Group Study." The suggestions are provided to assist persons using this book in discussions of corporate culture, ethics, and the management of values. Specific suggestions are made for each chapter and will prove especially helpful to persons leading group study sessions. The materials referred to are found in the appendices at the end of the book. Teachers will want to supplement these suggestions with additional resources drawn from the bibliography and elsewhere.

Many people have contributed to these pages. Francis F. Bradshaw, who taught me at Chapel Hill and later was president of Richardson, Bellows, Henry, and Co., first aroused my interest in the problems addressed. Richard P. Cooley, Ernest Arbuckle, Ralph Crawford, and Richard Rosenberg, of Wells Fargo Bank, provided encouragement and assistance in the early stages of our work on corporate ethics. Arjay Miller, formerly of Ford Motor Company and later dean of Stanford University School of Business, compelled us by his probing questions and comments to sharpen our perception of executive decision making. Thomas Tusher and Frank Brann of Levi Strauss added significant insights. Mario Obledo and many of his lieutenants in the California Department of Health and Welfare

Preface

helped us understand the political dimensions of policy. Robert Ray Parks, rector of Trinity Church in New York, continues to provide realistic and accurate views of policy-making in organizations and society. Andrew Sigler, Robert Longbine, Pat Stoddard, Don Powell, and Harry Dodds, of Champion International, exemplify the best in management concern, believing that corporations can be humane in their internal policies and good citizens in the surrounding society.

Some of my colleagues deserve special mention and thanks. Edwin M. Epstein of the University of California, Berkeley, has provided invaluable editorial suggestions and scholarly critique. Bowen H. McCoy of Morgan Stanley & Co.; Kirk Hanson of Stanford; Laura Nash of Harvard; and Sherry McCoy of Medi-Physics, have given helpful criticism and comments. William Roberts of Pitman Publishers has been supportive all along the way. Jim Donahue, Phil Mullins, Kevin Hanley, and Rick Vanasse have assisted in projects and contributed in many ways to these chapters. Randall Hepner assisted with reading proof and checking references. My special appreciation goes to Fred Twining, who has read several versions, collected helpful material, corrected many errors, drafted several of the study supplements, and been a good friend and source of encouragement over many years. I express gratitude also to President Neely McCarter and to the trustees of Pacific School of Religion for a leave that provided time to complete this manuscript.

Others too numerous to mention, who participated in various projects, have provided ideas and illustrations that appear in these pages, probably in forms no longer recognizable to them. They have all contributed, although they can in no way be held responsible for the results.

Most of all, I thank Margie. She read every draft, discussed all the ideas with me, and helped make the entire manuscript more clear. She is my light and my love.

Drawing on many resources and experiences, the Berkeley Center through its projects has pioneered in the field of corporate ethics and recovered forgotten insights about collective moral agency. In addition to the persons acknowledged above, these efforts have been informed by Plato and the Greeks, by the Bible and the Jewish-Christian heritage, and by a wide range of human experience. This endeavor belongs, therefore, to the long and exciting enterprise of understanding and shaping our organized world.

PITMAN SERIES IN
BUSINESS AND PUBLIC POLICY

CONSULTING EDITOR
EDWIN M. EPSTEIN
University of California, Berkeley

CURRENT BOOKS IN THE SERIES:

John D. Aram, *Managing Business and Public Policy: Concepts, Issues and Cases*
R. Edward Freeman, *Strategic Management: A Stakeholder Approach*
S. Prakash Sethi, Nobuaki Namiki and Carl L. Swanson, *The False Promise of the Japanese Miracle: Illusions and Realities of the Japanese Management System*
Charles S. McCoy, *Management of Values: The Ethical Difference in Corporate Policy and Performance*

Part One

A NEW PERSPECTIVE

One

PERFORMANCE AND ETHICS

We were discussing Milton Friedman's views on the purpose of business and its social responsibilities. The group included a practicing corporate executive, a business administration professor, several graduate students, and me, a teacher in the field of ethics.

"There's no doubt in my mind," Joe, the executive, was saying, "that making a profit is one primary aim of most business enterprises. I've been a successful corporate executive for over 20 years, and the so-called bottom line is always central when we decide what to do and evaluate results. But there is a lot else we consider. From my experience, I cannot make sense of such statements as 'The business of business is business' or 'The only purpose of a corporation is maximizing profits.'"

"But isn't that what a business is for?" a student asked. "Friedman says it clearly: 'The social responsibility of business is to increase its profits.'"

"I know that's what he says," Joe rejoined, "but his argument is not as clear as the title of his article."

"From the standpoint of teaching ethics, I agree," I said, "but I'd like to hear what you mean from a manager's perspective, Joe."

"He's right in saying there's some loose thinking about social responsibility and that executives must pay attention to the way the owners want the business run," Joe continued. "But Friedman thinks that the 'interest of the employer' provides a clear criterion for performance. Only a professor who believes his categories define reality could talk like that." Joe glanced at the two professors present and gave us a quick smile.

4 / Performance and Ethics

"Friedman bothers me, too, at that point," Paul, the business administration professor, interposed, *"by assuming that the people who are the founders and operators of organizations have single objectives. He says that hospitals and schools have only service as their purpose, but that does not apply to proprietary hospitals and schools, where profit is also an important goal. And though persons usually establish businesses to make money, they must provide, or appear to provide, products or services valued by society in order to turn a profit."*

"The people who own and manage corporations have varied purposes," Joe added, sitting forward in his chair, *"and it is the mix of motives and interests inside the corporation that makes the criteria of performance less clear than Friedman supposes."*

"In addition," I said, *"there are the factors Friedman mentions that complicate business policy more than he seems to realize. He speaks of making 'as much money as possible while conforming to the basic rules of the society, both those embodied in law and those embodied in ethical custom.' That statement really muddies the waters of his supposed clarity. Suddenly, in an aside, he introduces the entire environment of social values and tradition within which a corporation operates. Societal rules and ethical customs not only provide criteria for evaluating business performance but also undermine any attempt to speak of the 'market system' as the result of 'purely economic' factors."*

"Friedman opens up an important area of discussion and glosses over it too easily," Paul added.

"Then his title, 'The Social Responsibility of Business Is to Increase Its Profits,' is misleading and perhaps contradictory, isn't it?" asked a graduate student. *"Friedman affirms social responsibility but reduces it to maximizing profits. By doing that, he seems to think he has dealt with ethical criteria for business performance. As an afterthought he mentions law and ethical custom. Without appearing to realize it, therefore, he brings back the problem of relating corporate performance and ethics in all its complexity."*

"That says it well, as far as my experience goes," Joe concluded.

Laissez-faire capitalism has never existed in anything like a pure form in the political economies of the industrialized nations — not even in the 1870s when John D. Rockefeller was building his Standard Oil empire in Cleveland. Even then, Rockefeller could not operate his business with no other value in mind than maximizing profit.

Times have changed since those days, and today corporations operate with many more constraints and higher social expectations than was the case then. A much wider spectrum of interests and values must be taken into account in formulating business policy. It is for this reason that choosing the values and setting the priorities by which to evaluate corporate performance are among the most important and difficult tasks facing management. What is emerging from the experience of seasoned executives is that a new perspective is needed.

THE "BOTTOM LINE" AS MEASURE OF PERFORMANCE

Some people still hold that the only valid criterion of performance is the *bottom line*. By this, they mean profit or loss in terms of money. Some defenders of business — executives, economists, and so on — say that this is the only measure really used and the only correct way to evaluate performance. In their view business is supposed to make the largest profit possible and increase earnings every year. Higher profits are a sign of success; lower profits are an indication of poor performance. Critics agree that the sole aim of business is to make money and that the measure used for performance is indeed the bottom line. In view of this agreement there would be no issue were it not for two difficulties: first, the bottom line as a measure of corporate performance is not at all clear; and second, business executives in fact use various criteria rather than this one alone.

Short-Range versus Long-Range Performance

What does it mean to use the bottom line as the measure of performance in a business? To judge success or failure by the amount of profit generated would seem to be the unambiguous answer. But are we talking about profit now or later? Making a low profit this year in order to increase earnings even more next year usually makes good business sense. The measure of performance, then, is not the bottom line for this year or for this quarter but a cumulative view of profit, requiring planning, projections, and risk. This simple measure begins to be complicated by considerations of short-term versus long-term profits and by the necessity of including criteria of performance related to managing so as to achieve results in the future.

A recent book that chronicles the problems of the U.S. automotive industry in the 1970s and early 1980s places blame on those who put immediate profit ahead of quality. It was the "bean counters," as engineers derisively refer to financial men, who cut corners excessively and injured the quality of American cars, writes Brock Yates. He quotes W. Edward Deming, a quality control specialist, as saying, "Populating management with financially oriented people has ruined the country."[1] According to Yates, exclusive attention to the bottom line can be harmful to business even on a short-range basis, as the experience of the automotive industry in the 1970s illustrates.

The necessity for taking more than profit into account becomes even clearer when the long-term view is taken. A business may ignore almost all values other than making money in a very short-term operation. The short-term operator trying to make a fast buck often makes a shrewd appeal to the greed of potential clients. Occasionally, a new invention or a special position in the market provides opportunity for maximizing profits on a short-term basis. Even then, the entrepreneur in a favorable situation must have a product or a commodity that fills, or appears to fill, the needs and values of some consumers. But those who appeal to greed or take advantage too obviously of market circumstances may be regarded as unscrupulous and find it difficult to do business again with the same people. Over a long-range period, business must respond to the values and needs of consumers, it must function within socially accepted limits of business practice, and it must operate realistically in terms of economic values in order to make a profit. When one takes the long-range view of performance, values beyond the bottom line are a requirement — not an option to be considered. To the extent that ethics is seen not as following rigid rules of behavior but as knowing the values necessary for operating a business and finding ways to make them effective parts of business practice, we can speak very specifically of the ethical difference in management.

Varied Values and Goals

If the bottom line is *not* adequate as a measure of performance in the actual practice of business managers, what are the purposes that modify or eclipse the single-minded pursuit of profit? Some of these additional values will meet general approval. Other motives and goals may draw more mixed reactions.

The automotive industry is not the only sector of the corporate world where enormous pressures exist to show immediate profits. One factor leading to the failure of the Penn Square Bank of Oklahoma, according to some commentators, was the push to show substantial growth and quick returns, with the result that too many inadequately secured loans were made. The careers of executives are sometimes made or broken by comparing the earnings this quarter to the ones in the same quarter last year. Management may feel compelled to forego future profits in order to ensure a current financial statement that maintains the appearance of upward movement. Retaining power and enhancing the prestige of the company's leadership this year may take precedence over a better bottom line during the next five years.

This does not mean that profits are ignored. But it does emphasize that power and status also provide criteria by which performance is evaluated. The matter is more complex than the bottom-line advocates would have us believe.

Values representing responsibility to various social groups and goals also play an explicit role in many businesses. Johnson & Johnson's *Credo* puts four purposes ahead of making money. The chief executive officers (CEOs) at Johnson & Johnson are convinced that this ordering of values ensures the kind of performance that includes profitability. The Bank of America pioneered placing branches in ethnic neighborhoods and, in the process, became the largest bank in the United States. Wells Fargo Bank lends money back into agricultural areas because it has branches there — although a higher return could be made by lending elsewhere — and has acquired an enviable reputation for integrity and responsibility along the way. Levi Strauss tries to operate with social and ethical concerns woven into its business policies. Many corporations place a high value on the quality of the environment around them and contribute money and executive talent to civic improvement. Other companies will forego business if shady practices are required.

David McClintock's *Indecent Exposure* (Dell, 1982) provides a fascinating account of a sleazy struggle within Columbia Pictures. Top managers of the company become entangled in a fight with the directors over how to deal with an executive guilty of forgery and fraud. The characters in this sordid drama are caught up in an interesting conflict of values, with control of the corporation at stake. Profit takes a backseat to jealousy and power.

Instead of a single purpose — profit, service, or some other — controlling business policy and providing the measure of performance, there are multiple value commitments and goals shaping the actions of executives and the corporations they administer. Some of the values are short range; others are longer term. Some are quite narrowly self-interested; others are more broadly based in the well-being of the wider community. Some values are compatible; others are in conflict. Central tasks of management involve identifying clearly what the real interests and values of a corporation are, sorting them out in regard to priority, and getting them embodied in policy.

Making decisions and shaping policies in a business, whether large or small, involve choosing among competing purposes and values. It could be a choice between the value of product quality and the value of a bigger profit margin, between higher pay and increased capital outlay, between more employee involvement and faster decisions, between budgetary controls and strategic considerations, between time spent on improving technical processes and time spent improving overall corporate culture. The alternative may be immediate profit versus development toward greater potential earnings or influence. At other times choosing will involve deciding how much to contribute toward building a better arts program in the corporation's home city, whether and when to establish additional branches, how to invest surplus capital, or whether negotiating a labor contract that costs the company more outweighs risking a strike. What becomes dramatically clear when the perspectives of actual policymakers are examined, rather than the dogmas of economic theorists, is that a wide variety of values and purposes enter into the formulation of business policy.

Weighing Values and Setting Priorities

In 1981 the Business Roundtable published a "Statement on Corporate Responsibility." Drawn up by a panel of prominent executives, the statement says in part:

The "Bottom Line" as Measure of Performance / 9

Many companies now include the whole spectrum of corporate social objectives in strategic planning. This requires planners to consider not only economic and technological trends and events but also social and political; to study not only the expectations of shareholders, employees, customers, and suppliers, but also those of the community and the public. Such an approach encourages a broad, systematic corporate overview and an evaluation of a wide range of performance expectations. (The Business Roundtable, October, 1981, pp. 9–10)

Instead of exclusive focus on the bottom line and maximizing profits, managing requires evaluating multiple factors and alternatives, making policy in accord with values decided as having priority, trying to achieve purposes desired and to avoid unwanted results, and developing criteria of performance in line with a complex set of trade-offs among many goals and values. When the shaping of policy and the measurement of performance are viewed as involving the weighing of values and choosing among alternative courses of action, it becomes clear that managerial skill must include attention to the values of the company, setting priority among the values and goals sought and making sure that these priorities are observed in policy-making and implementation. The reflection and development of criteria required in the exercise of this managerial skill have become known in Western society as *ethics*, whether called by that name or another. Ethics, therefore, is not something foreign to management but something at its core. Whether or not aware of it, managers are always considering the ethical implications of what they do and making use of their reflection to set priorities and weave diverse interests, values, and purposes together into coherent policy.

It will come as no surprise to perceptive business executives that they have been making difficult ethical judgments throughout their careers. Balancing values and setting priorities are unavoidable at every level of management, but they are most intense and inescapable for top executives. The real question is, How well and with what precision of insight does ethical reflection take place? Effective managers are aware that ethics and performance are closely related. To understand more clearly how they are related is the insight needed now.

THE MANAGEMENT OF VALUES

Once we recognize that a variety of values confronts the business executive rather than the single value of the bottom line, a new perspective emerges on ways to measure performance in corporations and what excellence in managing for effective performance requires. With the help of insights from corporate managers and from those who have studied "good" companies, we shall explore what this new perspective is and how it works.

Productivity as we have known it in modern industrialized societies has at least six well-known sources: labor; capital; technology; raw materials; markets; and managerial ideas, energy, and skill. A seventh source, usually ignored in the past but increasingly recognized as implicit and important all along, is emerging into view: the corporate culture, including the climate of values and the organizational ethics, that shapes, directs, and empowers the other six.

Over the past three centuries the climate of values in Western societies — in combination with the resources of labor, technological innovation, increasing capital, skilled management, and expanding markets — has resulted in levels of productivity and improved standards of living unparalleled in human history. The gains of major sectors of industrial societies, however, have not been without problems. Not all the values sought were realized and certainly not for every person or social group. New values emerged as industrialized, middle-class, more democratic societies came into being. Many persons in the industrial nations shared minimally in the rising standard of living. Massive immigration threatened older groups in these societies and made values of justice and equality difficult to achieve. With improved communication and travel the improved quality of life in the industrialized nations evoked rising expectations around the world but did not provide the means for meeting these expectations. So now an increasing number of questions are being raised about the effect of development policies on developing nations; about the enrichment of powerful, elite groups in these nations without providing substantial help to the poorer elements; and about the problems of exploitation. New values of ecology, protection of the natural environment, and social justice for oppressed groups have emerged. The imperative to build a humane global community in the age of nuclear peril has become clear. Attention to the climate of values and purposes shaping the policies of major organizations and nations is increasingly viewed by perceptive leaders not as a luxury but rather as a crucial necessity for human survival.

As the importance of culture, value commitments, and ethics has become visible, leading executives and management scientists have sought ways to give this dimension of productivity more emphasis and to delineate the relations among organizational policy, performance, and values with greater clarity. The experience of policymakers in corporations is being explored and documented, and their insights into the crucial character of corporate culture and values for managerial excellence are being confirmed as well as their convictions about the close relationship between ethics and performance.

The Way toward Excellence

When Thomas Peters and Robert Waterman investigated the secrets of excellent corporate management, they came up with some conclusions that are in part surprising and in part, as they admit, obvious. In their best-selling book *In Search of Excellence: Lessons from America's Best-Run Companies,* these two management consultants provide a report on the characteristics that successful U.S. corporations have in common. For those acquainted with recent literature dealing with problems of organizational management in the United States, there are two unusual aspects to the book. First, Peters and Waterman investigated corporations in the United States rather than in Japan. Second, they come up with conclusions that are basically optimistic.

Out of their research the authors identify eight traits shared by the companies they regard as "strong" and "excellent." What they conclude is that behind such "hard" indicators of corporate success as growth or return on capital are the "softer" factors of culture and values. "The excellent companies," the authors affirm, "seem to have developed cultures that have incorporated the values and practices of the great leaders and thus those shared values can be seen to survive for decades after the passing of the original guru."[2]

Building especially on the work of Chester Barnard and Philip Selznick, Peters and Waterman assert that the central task of management is shaping values. The "real role of the chief executive is to manage the *values* of the organization," they say. "While good companies have superb analytic skills . . . their major decisions are shaped more by their values than by their dexterity with numbers."³

Values that are embodied in culture are central for excellent performance. A corporation is infused with values that endure beyond the tenure of particular leaders by means of a strong culture. For example, Peters and Waterman report that Delta has been more successful than other airlines because it has a very efficient route structure, and IBM does well because it builds on the market it has created. Why, the authors ask, did such companies make decisions that turned out well? There is a difference, the authors say, and the difference is that strong leaders have impressed a distinctive culture and value system on the internal environments of excellent corporations.

Peters and Waterman see clearly the central importance of culture and values for corporate performance. Although the eight traits of excellent companies they name are mainly described by anecdote and how appropriate these traits may be for other firms remains unclear, the book and the interest it has evoked indicate that managers are undergoing a major shift in defining the nature of effective management. The principles that the authors propose depart sharply from the rules of rational management usually taught in business schools. By contrast with the rationalistic emphasis recently dominant, Peters and Waterman describe ways to motivate and reward human efforts most effectively that relate to the work of Elton Mayo and Douglas McGregor. *In Search of Excellence*, therefore, suggests the need for an innovative philosophy of management.

The authors' view of the role of the CEO, however, remains somewhat individualistic and not integrally related to corporate culture and value commitments. Their insights must be supplemented by those of James O'Toole. In *Making America Work*, O'Toole emphasizes the centrality of culture and values for the national economy as well as for particular corporations. He perceives that the role of management must be understood in terms of organizational culture and values rather than viewed individualistically.

It has been assumed, writes O'Toole, "that individual managerial behavior is at the core of such problems as institutional inflexibility, bureaucracy, resistance to innovation, insensitivity to employee needs, and social irresponsibility. This is truth, by half."[4]

The reason for this inadequacy is that psychologists have dominated the study of organizational behavior and given attention primarily to individual behavior. "The missing element," O'Toole continues, "is *the organizational context* in which managers find themselves. This is the half of the analysis concerned with the institutionalized social relationships that maintain the functioning of the corporation. This is the organization structure and ideology that compose the *culture* of the firm."[5]

A third perspective tying ethics to the central functions of management appears in the work of Kenneth Andrews on corporate strategy. As custodians of corporate objectives and architects of corporate performance, the CEO and senior management carry out their complex task by means of corporate strategy, which, as Andrews defines it, "is the pattern of decisions in a company that determines and reveals its objectives, purposes, or goals, produces the principal policies and plans for achieving those goals, and defines the range of business the company is to pursue, the kind of economic and human organization it is or intends to be, and the nature of the economic and noneconomic contributions it intends to make to its shareholders, employees, customers, and communities."[6]

Andrews also underscores the importance of the environment of values in which business operates. Value commitments and choices based on careful evaluation, he points out, are inevitable throughout corporate action and the development of strategy — in the appraisal of opportunities, in the evaluation of corporate competence and resources, through the personal values and aspirations of policymakers, and in carrying out obligations to various groups. Ethics is especially prominent in the last component, as management deals with "the moral and social implications of what once was considered a purely economic choice." Andrews continues, "The emerging view in the liberal-professional leadership of our most prominent corporations is that determining future strategy must take into account — as part of its social environment — steadily rising moral and ethical standards."[7]

When we combine the insights represented by Peters and Waterman, O'Toole, and Andrews, it becomes apparent that the paramount task of executive leadership is the *management of values*. This does not mean facile manipulation of values but rather managing with the clear understanding that evaluation and choice permeate the entire policy process. Effective performance and managerial excellence require skill in production, marketing, control, planning, and personnel development; at the same time, ethical insight, judgment, and action are equally essential in all sectors of management.

Managing values, in part, requires identifying and clarifying the criteria by which policy will be formulated and evaluated. In part, managing values means developing ways for measuring performance that go beyond the immediate bottom line. Long-term criteria of performance must supplement and be given more weight than short-term measures. Even so, it should be remembered that the sole criterion of performance is never maximized profits. The evaluation of performance involves careful review of the varied purposes of the corporation, clarity about the means permitted by the character of the corporation for achieving those purposes, and full awareness of the resources and restraints making up the environment of the corporation. Corporate interests include survival as well as profit, building a reputation for integrity as well as increasing sales, and serving the community as well as the stockholders. Managing values necessitates combining these varied purposes in corporate policy and action. Ethical reflection to weigh alternative values and set priorities is needed in order to develop criteria by which to shape, implement, and evaluate policy.

Appraising the Environment

When the way toward excellence is recognized as the ability to manage values — not in the sense of manipulating them but rather in the sense of taking them into account throughout company operations — the internal and external environments understood as filled with values become crucial for effective performance. Examples abound illustrating what can happen when these environments are incorrectly appraised and values are inadequately managed.

The automotive industry in the United States exemplifies corporate management excellence in many sectors of operation but deficient in accurately appraising the changing values of the U.S. public. If the increasing sales of small, economical, fuel-efficient foreign cars had not been enough to alert top management to changes under way, then surely the oil crisis and embargo of 1973 should have jarred even the most isolated persons at the boardroom level of the major automakers. Although limited adjustments were made, some of these because of activist and governmental pressure, the real effort appears to have been on the public relations front. Rather than responding to the changing values of American society, the push was on to persuade the domestic buyer to return to the older values of bigness and comfort. This policy proved inadequate — not because it involved faulty engineering and design or bad fiscal management, but because it failed to adjust to social change through effective management of values.

Ethics for business executives is far more than concern about bribery and expense account fudging. Corporate ethics involves, among other things, the ability to monitor the environment of values related to company operations and to integrate this awareness into the process of making and implementing policy. Corporate ethics requires remembering that persons, societal groups, and governments regard corporations as moral agents and that a central task of management is shaping corporate policy and action in that light.

Thomas Donaldson explains the point clearly: "People perceive the corporation as a moral entity. Indeed, they credit it with the unmistakable mark of morality: a duty to acknowledge standards which transcend laws." To illustrate this view, he tells the following story:

> Consider the much discussed case of Chisso, a Japanese industrial corporation. Following a lengthy series of trials, Japanese courts concluded that Chisso must compensate thousands of victims whom it had indirectly poisoned with mercury. The company had discharged mercury into the ocean, knowing it posed a danger to local residents. The mercury contaminated local fish and then accumulated in the bodies of local residents who ate the fish. Many years later the accumulation triggered an explosion of bizarre and crippling birth defects.
>
> But, remarkably, Chisso had broken no law. Throughout, it remained secure in the knowledge that its emission levels fell within Japanese government guidelines, even though it suspected the guidelines were inadequate. Arguing on behalf of the victims, attorneys claimed that despite honoring legal

niceties, Chisso had disregarded its moral responsibilities. The court agreed, and Chisso was forced to make massive payments.[8]

Performance is related to ethics in the evaluation of consequences as well as in the appraisal of the environment of values and in choosing purposes and setting priorities for policy. Ethical consideration within a corporation, whether accomplished on a subconscious or a fully conscious level, is central to all effective policy-making.

We have seen several aspects of ethical reflection that can be helpful for shaping policy and evaluating performance. Let's take a more comprehensive look at ethical elements permeating corporate policy process.

Operative Corporate Ethics: A Preliminary View

Management is, of course, already taking values into account and doing ethical reflection in relation to corporate policy. There is growing recognition that the quality of corporate culture and value commitments is crucial for performance. Insight into the management of values is emerging.

To understand corporate ethics as it actually takes place in policy-making, there is no better place to go than to the executives who make policy. In a series of projects, beginning in 1973, my Berkeley colleagues and I have been investigating ethics in organizational settings. Through individual interviews and group discussions we have worked with executives in exploring the values used in making corporate policy, the sources of operative criteria for performance, and the relation of ethics to corporate culture and decision-making processes.

These policymakers regarded themselves and their colleagues, for the most part, as persons with high moral standards, although they knew that there are exceptions and that there was plenty of room for improvement. They viewed the organizations in which they worked as having traditions of social responsibility. But they recognized problems of social injustice and believed it important to deal with these issues. They were not accustomed, however, to discussing ethics with one another. Nor was there a corporate ethic except as it was embodied in the culture of the organization and the value commitments embodied in individual activities. After interviews with individuals and a series of group discussions, policymakers were able to discuss ethics in relation to policy and to recognize the ethical reflection already taking place on a less conscious, inarticulate level. Eventually, they could begin to share their value judgments, relate survival and profitability to other corporate purposes, reflect critically on inclusive criteria for performance, and develop ways to integrate ethics into the policy process.

The value commitments of corporate executives draw heavily on the Western religious tradition. As *The Connecticut Mutual Life Report on American Values in the '80s* reports, most U.S. business leaders are members of a religious community, regard themselves as religious, and find religious faith meaningful in their lives. Although corporate executives know this about each other, the pluralistic climate of our society means that the religious faith and ethics of their colleagues are assumed. These matters are rarely referred to and usually regarded only as background for executive character. This background is also important for corporate character and culture through the influence of strong figures who shaped the organization in the past as well as through the value commitments of the current group of executives. Recognition of the religious background of managers explains in part the agreements and the differences in purposes, values, and motives to be found among corporate policymakers and provides important resources for developing corporate ethics.

Among executives involved in our projects over the past decade, we discovered that their operative ethics has the following primary elements: (1) self-interest; (2) multiple responsibility; and (3) social vision. Self-interest is always a central concern in the actions of corporate managers. They regard it as their task to develop policies that reflect the interests of the corporation. But this notion of self-interest includes long-term performance as well as short-term profit. The interests of the corporation relate its survival to its reputation for integrity. Building a good work environment contributes to employee morale and also to productivity. These executives, including especially CEOs, want their policies to reflect responsibility, not only to shareholders but to the many other stakeholders in company policy inside and outside the corporation. Specific groups to whom they acknowledge responsibility include owners, directors, employees, clients, minorities, women, students, and the elderly, as well as government and governmental agencies at various levels, other corporations, and community social and cultural groups. These executives are also prepared to discuss whether such a list should be extended and how to improve the quality of corporate responsibility. In addition, these executives utilize criteria for policy based on social vision and the effects corporate actions would have on society. This set of three ethical principles reflects criteria actually operative in corporate policy and provides a basis for understanding the management of values and developing a comprehensive corporate ethic.

As will become clear in subsequent chapters, discovering the criteria for shaping policy and evaluating performance in a company provides only a beginning for developing corporate ethics. The next task is to examine these criteria carefully. Are they the ones intended? How are the criteria actually used? Do they fit the character of the business organization (1) as inherited from its past and (2) as the present community of managers wishes to pass it on to the future? Further, there is the work of integrating the criteria into the processes by which policy is developed and implemented. It is far easier to write codes of conduct and to publish ideal standards than it is to make them operative throughout the company. Finally, there must be ways to measure performance by the criteria agreed upon, to evaluate the actual results in terms of what was intended, and to improve the criteria, implementation, and patterns of evaluation. Lifting ethical reflection to a more conscious level does not diminish the problems of business leadership, but it can lead to more effective management of values and to better performance.

THE CLOSE RELATION BETWEEN ETHICS AND PERFORMANCE

What are the components of effective performance in business? What characteristics distinguish excellent management? What combination of factors leads to corporate success? How are effectiveness and excellence in performance to be understood and defined clearly in today's corporate world? How are value commitments, ethical reflection, and a strong overall corporate culture important for corporate performance? These are crucial questions for executives wrestling with the problems of corporate policy and operation, for practicing managers at all levels, and for those concerned with managerial training.

Business leaders know that the answers to basic questions like the ones above are always going to be difficult, many-sided, and incomplete. The answers are difficult to come by because they must work in actual practice as well as in theory. The answers will inevitably be many-sided because multiple factors working well together are necessary for effective performance. All answers are going to be incomplete because every real situation has unique, unexpected elements and will not stand still for long-term analysis. Insight and training are indispensable for good management but must be supplemented by sound judgment and the experience of responding under the pressure of operating conditions. And, too, every experienced manager knows that, beyond complexity and change, there will always be unforeseen occurrences and luck influencing the outcome of decisions and the resulting performance.

The views about the close relation of ethics and performance presented here are drawn primarily from experienced executives and from seminars on corporate values with senior managers. Throughout, we shall remain close to the perceptions of practicing policymakers, to their ways of posing problems, and to their insights into viable solutions. Resources from the management sciences and from ethics are used to illumine and extend what has been learned from managers themselves.

Reginald Jones, former CEO of General Electric, has said: "Public policy and social issues are no longer adjuncts to business planning and management. They are in the mainstream of it. The concern must be pervasive in companies today, from boardroom to factory floor. Management must be measured for performance in noneconomic and economic areas alike. And top management must take the lead."[9]

Corporate performance and ethics, as Jones suggests, are integrally related. If Peter Drucker is correct that performance provides the basis of managerial legitimacy, then the criteria by which performance is measured are central, not peripheral, for managerial practice. Ethical reflection and evaluation provide the criteria of performance and determine what economic and noneconomic measurements will be used and how to use them. Corporate performance is shaped in crucial ways by the quality of ethical consideration, discussion, and action at all levels of management and by how well top executives perform in managing values.

The discussion and illustrations have suggested this close relation between performance and ethics. It remains to spell it out in greater detail.

Criteria for Performance

The most basic statement of the relation between corporate performance and ethics involves these elements: (1) any evaluation of performance requires criteria; (2) the choice of these criteria by which to measure performance involves reflection on the values, goals, and priorities worthwhile for shaping action; and (3) this process of reflection, sorting, clarifying, choosing, and using in action is ethics, whether or not recognized and so named. In this perspective it becomes clear that performance and ethics cannot be separated from one another.

When ethics and performance are misunderstood or not understood clearly, the relations between them become obscured and are often overlooked or forgotten. On the one hand, those concerned primarily with policy-making and performance may give inadequate attention to the criteria governing their activities; on the other hand, primary concern with ethics may focus on rational codes or principles and ignore the importance of relating purposes and values to actual policy-making and realistic performance. For example, ethics is sometimes reduced to moralistic judgments that outsiders demand be followed or even seek to impose. When this is the case, it may be difficult for corporate executives to understand the relevance of these demands from external sources for the operational policies of the corporations they manage. There may be no disagreement about overall purposes and principles but rather about how to use them as criteria for evaluating policy and performance. Even demands by outsiders with which corporate managers agree must, if such demands are to become operational, be integrated into the complex elements shaping policy.

Or again, performance may be understood in truncated and limited ways. Emphasis may be given to short-range goals at the expense of long-range purposes or to a single criterion of performance rather than to utilization of a spectrum of values that corporate policy is intended to fulfill. An understanding of performance is never complete unless the criteria for measurement have been carefully considered and clarified.

Viewed in this way, the close relation between performance and ethics becomes obvious. What may be even clearer is that business ethics as we are exploring the subject does not involve theoretical discussions about how corporations "ought" to behave. Nor will it require teaching executives how to engage in philosophical thinking or moral reasoning like academic ethicists. Instead, the process undertaken here is designed to assist business executives in becoming more aware of and improving the ethical reflection in which they are already engaged and thus enhancing the performance of the corporations they lead. The focus is on the management of values in the real world of corporate operation.

Dealing with values requires continual monitoring of the surrounding environment, weighing alternative courses of action, balancing and (when possible) integrating conflicting responsibilities, setting priorities among competing goals, and establishing criteria for defining and evaluating performance. Along with these goes learning ways to bring this ethical reflection directly and fully into the processes by which policy is made, implemented, and evaluated. Increasingly, skills in dealing with values as integral components of performance and policy-making are being recognized as central for effective management in a society and a world undergoing rapid change.

Building on Executive Insight

"We don't need 'do-gooders' telling us how we ought to run our business," said the executive of a large midwestern corporation. He is, of course, in a fundamental sense correct. The community of persons running an organization knows it and how to operate it better than outsiders. Once that is made clear, however, it is also true that external perspectives may help managers see things their routines have obscured or led them to overlook. It is possible to build on executive insight, extend it, and sharpen it in ways that will increase its possibilities for enhanced performance.

Ethics, as presented here, is not something imported from academic seminars into executive suites. Scholars in the field of ethics do not have a monopoly on ethical reflection. Humans of any age and any context faced with conflicting moral demands and the necessity of setting priorities are involved in ethical reflection. Certainly it is also the case with those engaged in the complex process of making and implementing corporate policy.

The success of this book will be measured by the extent to which it helps executives understand with greater clarity and precision the ethical dimensions of management. Building on this deepened appreciation of ethical reflection and perception, executives can use the insights gained to improve corporate performance.

The question is never one of bringing ethics to corporate contexts or teaching something to executives about which they know nothing. The issue instead is what kind of ethics permeates corporate policy process. Does it embody the standards intended and does it help produce the results desired? What is the quality of ethical reflection used in choosing corporate goals and shaping corporate action? How perceptively and accurately are the intended purposes of policy being carried out, and what criteria are used to evaluate performance? There is much to be done about corporate ethics, but it is a matter of building on what is already present and of relating ethical reflection at all points to the actual operations of corporations, that is, to their performance.

Resources for Relating Ethics and Performance

Academic treatments of ethics most often deal with individual ethics or with ethical theory. Ethics for the professions, for business, or for government is then proposed by academic ethicists as the use of ethical theory by individual agents in those organizational settings. Business ethics, for example, is a kind of "applied ethics," taking the theory of academics and applying it to "real-life" contexts and problems. This way of putting it gets things backwards. Ethical reflection is taking place in the actual situations of choice and action throughout human society. Academic ethics must take these situations of human moral wrestling as the primary material of ethics and bring resources that enhance the quality of judgment and action. Just as the natural sciences at the opening of the modern era had to abandon the method of applying abstract theories to experience and begin with the human experience of nature as the basis of theory, so ethics today is finding it necessary to begin with the human experience of moral action in community and use that experience as the basis of ethical theory.

The long tradition in Western thought dealing with the ethics of social collectivities and organizations has been given far too little attention in recent years by ethics and the social sciences. Social scientists who work in the field of organizational theory and behavior usually ignore values and ethics in the futile attempt to be completely "objective" and "value free." The result has been the separation of ethics from the management sciences. This specialization has usually led to the irrelevance of academic ethics and the social sciences for organizational policy and to lack of clarity among policymakers about the ethical dimensions of their daily activities. The value judgments, the setting of priorities, the development of criteria for performance, and so on, are central elements of the ethical reflection constantly taking place as an integral part of organizational process and policy.

In the chapters that follow, we shall seek to understand corporate policy-making with a wholeness that academic specialization has fragmented. This will require what can be termed *the triadic approach* (see Figure 1.1). In this perspective the resources for relating ethics

FIGURE 1.1 *The Triadic Approach to Policy Ethics*

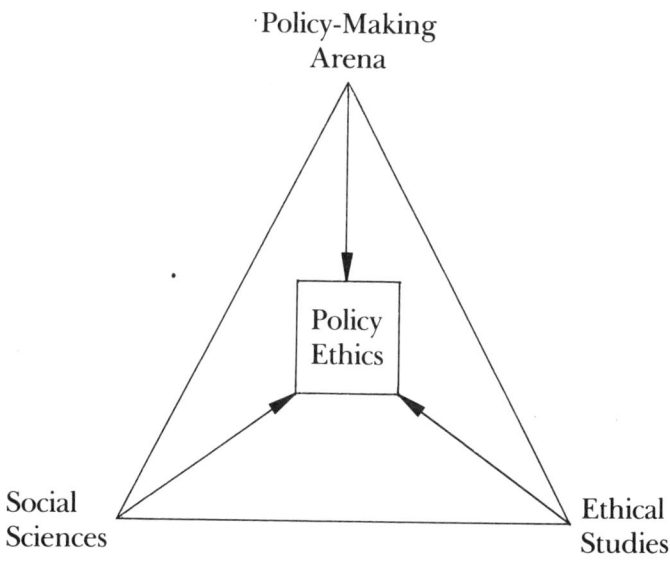

and performance are drawn, first, from the experience and insight of persons in the policy-making arena itself; second, from the knowledge and analytic tools of the management sciences; and third, from ethical studies. The process of understanding how to manage values effectively in a corporation begins with the difficult judgments and choices required for developing and implementing policy, but it must be expanded and enriched by social science and ethics. The *management of values,* as we shall call management that deals with the ethical dimensions of policy and performance, can make a crucial difference for business organizations today when done well. No less important in government, labor unions, churches, educational institutions, and all the organizations shaping society than in business, managing values is much too important for the future of humanity to be neglected, especially in organizations wielding the power of modern corporations. Through insight into the relation of ethics to performance, we shall provide resources for effective management that can be helpful to corporate executives and to students in schools of business who aspire to careers in management.

SUGGESTIONS FOR GROUP STUDY

1. Read the instructions in Appendix A on the use of the chapters in this book as a basis for group study and discussion. You will find there a number of ideas on how to relate the text material, the "minicases," and the experiences of group members to the operating world of business. You should find this process stimulating and rewarding.
2. Read the article by Milton Friedman on "The Social Responsibility of Business Is to Increase Its Profits," which is reproduced in full in Appendix B. This article first appeared in the *New York Times Magazine,* September 13, 1970. It was reprinted in Raziel Abelson and Marie-Luise Frequegnon, eds., *Ethics for Modern Life,* 2d ed. (New York: St. Martin's Press, 1982), pp. 318–24.
3. Review the conversation at the beginning of the chapter by assigning parts to members of your group. Have them continue the discussion based on their own understanding of the issues involved. Then see if the group can come to a consensus on the validity of the various viewpoints expressed.

4. Read the case study on Penn Square Bank in Appendix C. Discuss the way this bank made loans in relation to Friedman's notion that the only purpose of a business is the maximization of profits. What criteria beyond the "bottom line" appear to have been used by Penn Square management?
5. Look back at the report on the Chisso corporation of Japan in this chapter. What issues concerning the relation of ethics and corporate performance does the Chisso experience suggest to you?
6. Years ago, "Engine" Charlie Wilson, then president of General Motors, stated, "What is good for General Motors is good for America, and vice versa." Use the material in this chapter and your knowledge of what has happened to the U.S. automobile industry in recent years as the basis for discussing the validity of Wilson's statement and its implications for ethics in the management of the companies involved.

Part Two

VALUES AND POLICY

Two

ETHICS IN CORPORATE POLICY

"Ethics is not something we deal with in business operations," Tom told me. "All the people I work with are, I'm sure, thoroughly ethical in their business practices, and we certainly are not going to check on people's private morals unless there were some clear impact on their professional capabilities. But we can't afford ethics in our loan policies. That would be giving the store away. We have to go for the bottom line. There's no other way."

Tom is a senior executive in a bank well up in the top 20. We were sitting in his office, high in the firm's skyscraper headquarters. He was the first of several top managers that the corporation's CEO had asked me to talk with as preparation for a corporate ethics seminar.

"Let's see what Bill says about ethics and business. It's time for our interview with him now," Tom continued. He got up from his desk and led me out of his office and down the corridor. "Bill manages our entire real estate loan division. He is the hardest-nosed person here when it comes to profits."

Bill's secretary greeted us, went to his door to announce us, and then escorted us into an office with a spectacular vista of harbor and bridges from its windows.

"Would you make any kind of loan that would produce a big profit?" I asked Bill when we had been introduced and the three of us were settled comfortably around a coffee table at one end of his office.

"That's what we're here for, to make money," Bill responded, "and I always take that into account. But that doesn't mean we would make any *kind of loan to turn a buck. For one thing, we have our reputation to consider.*

We've been around a while, so people respect and trust us. Without that, we'd be dead in the water."

"So you do have other criteria for making loans besides maximizing profits?" I queried, pressing the point further.

"Sure, that's always necessary," he agreed, "but then, it would be a matter of long-range versus immediate profit."

I asked several questions about the difference and how it could be used as an effective criterion for policy. Then Tom raised the most interesting issue of the conversation.

"I hear there's lots to be made financing casinos in Vegas, Reno, and Atlantic City," Tom said. "We must have quite a bundle invested in those places."

Bill's eyes narrowed slightly as he turned toward Tom. "We don't have a dime in casinos anywhere, and we won't as long as I'm running this division."

"Why is that?" Tom asked, somewhat puzzled.

"Two reasons, basically," Bill replied without hesitation. "First, I don't think it fits in with what this company stands for. And second, those places poison the social atmosphere all of us live in. No way."

I expressed interest in this view and said that I hoped we could explore it further, perhaps as a case study in the projected seminar.

Back in his office, Tom confessed to me that Bill's response about casino loans took him by surprise. He was unaware that the company made no such loans, regardless of the probable profit from them, and he doubted that the other top executives were aware of this policy by which the firm operated.

"Maybe," I suggested, "you and Bill and others here are making all sorts of value judgments without discussing them among yourselves very often or being aware, usually, of the criteria shaping your policy-making process."

"That's possible," Tom answered thoughtfully and gave me a wry smile. "It's worth looking into. If it's so, we may have more ethics here than I thought."

"Yes," I said, picking up on this notion, "not only can you afford ethics in your loan business; it may be more accurate to say that you never leave home without one set of ethics or another. If ethical reflection is the process of selecting the values used in making policy, you and your colleagues who manage this corporation are clearly deeply engaged in ethics. You can discuss this process or you can let it operate covertly as with Bill and casino loans. The real choice is whether to fly blind or to be clear about the ways you set priorities and determine the values that control corporate policy. I would think you'd want to manage values as carefully as you manage financial affairs."

"I'm beginning to see why our president wants us to discuss ethics. Other

examples like the casino loans may turn up in our interviews," he said as we walked toward the elevator when I was leaving.

Tom and Bill illustrate two views of ethics found among corporate policymakers. When the subject is first mentioned, they view ethics in business operations with some suspicion, perhaps because of experiences with social activists and religious moralists. Yet when they reflect upon it, they recognize that they exercise ethical judgment and engage in ethical reflection, whether or not they use those names. Their attitudes, and that of the president of the bank, provide interesting introductory perspectives on ethics in corporate policy:

1. Interest in ethics is on the increase among corporate executives and also in business schools, where new generations of managers are being trained.
2. There is, however, considerable wariness about ethics among many executives, based upon widespread misunderstanding of ethics and its meaning for business.
3. Ethics must be related to the value judgments actually being made by business management and formulated in terms of the processes of policy-making in corporations.

Ethics as a set of strident demands by activists, as moralisms for individual behavior, or as rational analysis by ethical theorists makes little sense for the complex patterns of interaction in large, contemporary organizations. Needed instead are the exploration and explanation of ethical reflection and value judgment as these take place within the development and implementation of corporate policy. That is what the bank president was looking for, and it is what Tom and Bill and their colleagues began to understand more clearly as they discussed the meaning of ethics for their business practices.

THE RISING INTEREST IN ETHICS

Across the entire spectrum of professions and institutions in the United States, ethics is receiving increased attention. In the education and practice of lawyers, physicians, clergy, engineers, government officials, law enforcement personnel, social workers, the military, even members of the intelligence and covert operations community, and others, the importance of moral responsibility is being emphasized. Evidence of the trend can be seen in the appearance of articles and books, in the rising number of courses on ethics offered in professional schools, and in the proliferation of discussions and seminars on ethics among leaders in a wide variety of organizations.

Nowhere is the increased concern with ethics more apparent than in schools of business administration and management and among thoughtful executives in leading corporations. Courses on ethics are proliferating rapidly in business schools. Discussions are increasing in number and in depth of concern in management seminars. An interesting array of new books on business ethics, values, and culture is being published. And issues of ethics and closely related themes are gaining attention among management scientists in all fields. The interest in business ethics seems to be surviving even though academic ethicists usually know little about business and often speak a language that borders on being unintelligible to corporate managers.

"Although executives tend to call the subject anything but 'business ethics' (for example, issues management or the business environment)," one observer comments, "their renewed attention is legitimate. By whatever name you call it, the moral aspect of business is showing up in more sales training classes, board rooms, and company policy statements. . . . The recent emphasis on corporate culture, and the recognition that successful companies are the ones with 'good values,' have helped push ethics further into the corporate spotlight."[1]

Why the Growing Concern with Ethics?

Explanations for this attention to ethics in the business community are varied and not always convincing. Daniel Callahan of the Hastings Center, for example, explains the widespread interest in this way: "When a profession redefines itself and society redefines its role as well, there is a heightened emphasis on ethical issues. When a profession is secure and there is agreement about its role, issues of ethics become minor."[2] Societies and social groups, however, are always in the process of redefining themselves and their roles. Professionals in all areas have continuing problems with insecurity and identity. One might argue with more plausibility that insecurity rather than security generates resistance to ethical reflection and that a firm sense of identity provides a better basis for moral concern than do times of identity crisis. The reasons for the mounting interest in ethics may be more obvious and direct.

First, concern with moral issues in the business community clearly derives in part from well-publicized stories of bribery, fraud, and questionable practices by corporations and corporate executives. Management and directors, especially those with ethical commitments, fear that accounts of wrongdoing in the media, whether or not correctly reported, will undermine public confidence in business. The successful operation of a commercial enterprise is usually dependent on a high level of trust in the surrounding community. Adverse publicity hurts, and corporate leaders want to avoid it. Thus, the interest in ethics comes from a perceived need among executives to maintain a good public image of business.

Second, concern with ethics among business leaders derives in part from the heightened standards of performance applied to most societal institutions, corporations as well as others. As Michael Blumenthal, former secretary of the Treasury, has pointed out, "People in business have not suddenly become immoral. What has changed are the contexts in which corporate decisions are made, the demands that are being made on business, and the nature of what is considered proper corporate conduct."[3] This changing environment and the higher standards can be seen most clearly in the proliferation of agencies and statutes regulating business, in the increased number of public interest groups aggressively pressing their concerns on corporate leaders, and — since the 1960s — in the youth protest movements challenging business values.

Third, the rising interest in ethics derives not only from external pressures. It comes in part from the genuine concern of many executives for the well-being of society. Managers are family members and citizens. Most of them were reared in one or another religious community. Their consciences and ethical convictions have been shaped by the same traditions that inform social activists. They have children who raise questions about the impact of business. Because of the social location of corporate leaders, they may not evaluate issues in the same way as consumer advocates or activist clergy, but they all share similar cultural values.

And fourth, corporate executives want to be good at their jobs. Increasingly, it is becoming clear that excellence in managing and performance demands attention to corporate culture and values and that policy-making requires ethical insight and moral courage as well as technical know-how and organizational skills. Most managers know with their guts, even if they are uncertain about using the language of ethics, that there are no shortcuts for learning how to deal effectively with values. Experience and time can be helpful. So also can the study of business ethics if such study is closely related to the realities of business practice.

The Need for Relevance

Whatever the reasons, ethics is widely discussed and taught today in business contexts. It becomes important that ethics be understood and formulated in ways that will be effective in corporate management and in the training of future executives.

Business ethics must be related to the activities, judgments, and purposes of business enterprises. This may seem too obvious to deserve comment, but, for various reasons, it needs to be said. Business ethics cannot first be shaped by academic theorists and then, in a secondary sense, be applied to the context and problems of business. This is approaching the matter backwards. Ethics with meaning arises from human contexts of action, responsibility, and conflicting values. These contexts give rise to ethical reflection and may be enriched from academic sources, including ethical theory. But academic perspectives will be helpful only if they are related to and based upon human experience in actual contexts of interaction and moral decision.

Making ethics relevant to business operations can be viewed as accommodating ethics to business needs so as to remove any cutting edge of judgment. Just the opposite is the case. To the extent that ethics loses its cutting edge of criticism, it becomes irrelevant and useless to those confronted with responsibilities for shaping policy in organizations. *Relevance* in the sense intended here refers to ethics that emerges from, is related to, and can contribute to the actual reflection, decisions, and actions of business enterprises. In the same way, navigation must focus on the actualities of steering a ship or boat, rather than being controlled by the purposes of academic theorists. Theory can be helpful if it emerges from, and relates to, the real conditions of navigating vessels.

As presented in this book, business ethics has developed out of projects with policymakers in corporations and other organizations. How these leaders understand ethics, as brought out in discussions over many years, shapes what is found in these pages. As policy-making executives engage in interaction and mutual learning with persons in ethics and in business administration, genuine progress can be made toward developing policy ethics applicable to the corporate processes in which the executives are the principal actors.

MISUNDERSTANDINGS AND PROBLEMS OF ETHICS

To understand ethics as it emerges in the experience of corporate policy-making, it is first necessary to overcome some widely held misconceptions. This ought not to be surprising in an area such as ethics and morality where there are strong convictions and powerful personal involvements.

Corporate leaders, though concerned with business ethics, often exhibit uneasiness about discussions of the subject until they discover what kind of ethics is meant and who is involved. Too often the focus of proposed discussions on ethics has been on well-worn topics like bribery, price-fixing, and padded expense accounts or on confrontation with social activists rather than on dialogue concerning difficult current issues.

Executives in all types of organizations, as we have encountered them in our projects, are very interested in the ethical dimensions of organizational policy, even though they are often reluctant to discuss ethics with their colleagues. The reasons for this reluctance can be summarized as follows:

1. Some think that ethics means enforcement of predetermined moral rules.
2. Others are convinced that ethics refers to academic abstractions having little relation to business operations.
3. Another group regards ethics as applying only to moralistic judgments of individual behavior.

4. Many managers have been taught that ethics is "doing good" apart from sound business practices, and, as a result, they may be unable to recognize the ethical reflection and judgments in which they are constantly engaged.
5. Executives often lack the language enabling them to discuss ethics with the same ease and precision they bring to economic and administrative matters.

It will be helpful to look at each of these problems more closely.

Ethics as Enforcement of Rules

The "police" concept of ethics lies behind one misunderstanding of ethics. The purpose of ethics in this view is to place a guard over us to monitor our actions and to arrest us if we do anything wrong. Ethics is understood as enforcing a set of rules for conduct and punishing violators. Some people feel the judgmental power of an ethical police force, working either through their conscience or through an external monitor of behavior. Most of us let up on the accelerator when the highway patrol appears and feel a twinge of uneasiness when we encounter the police. There are also moralists who believe themselves to be the guardians of the rules and given the task of denouncing violators.

To the extent that we are social beings our consciences have been shaped by the moral climate of our community. We are well aware of the police function of enforcing communal laws and mores. That, however, is the result of a long process of social consensus — not ethics.

The police notion of ethics has problems. First, it mistakes enforcement and punishment for ethical reflection and action. The concern of ethics is deciding what is right and wrong, better and worse, among alternative courses of action. Rules, laws, and codes are part of ethics as the end product of ethical reflection, but ethics involves much more. Appropriate ways of enforcement and punishment are matters for ethical consideration, but they are not substitutes for ethics. Second, the police concept mistakenly locates ethics in external enforcers. Instead, ethics deals with the internal evaluation of action by persons and communities who are themselves involved in social interaction. This evaluation may be an appraisal of their own action or the actions of other persons and communities. It is, however, evaluation performed according to criteria and standards developed by those doing the evaluating, not by an outside enforcer. We can no more do someone else's ethical work for them than we can repent for other people's sins. Third, the police concept overlooks the fact that the legitimate law enforcement agencies represent the moral consensus of which we are a part. These agencies are not external but internal to our society and are the result of society's ethical reflection.

Ethics as Rational Abstractions

A second problem with ethics for business organizations is the abstract nature of what is regarded as ethics by academic theorists. A professor of economics in a prominent school of business administration said: "We wanted more emphasis on ethics in the curriculum, so we invited a professor of philosophy in for some lectures. He spent the entire time explaining Kant's ethical theory to us. Few people there had the background to understand much of what he told us. And no one could see its relation to ethics in the setting of business."

Texts on business ethics often discount the views of practicing business professionals as naive. Then, after discarding as "inadequate" the thinking of persons actually engaged in business ethics, the academic author provides the "correct" understanding from philosophical theory. Chemists, for example, base their work on actual experiments with solids, liquids, and gases, not on theories unrelated to experience. Ethical theory (sometimes called *metaethics* — the analysis of moral concepts and language) will inevitably seem abstract if developed in isolation from human interaction in real contexts such as business, government, family, community, and so on. Both philosophical and theological ethics can contribute little to business ethics if they are preoccupied only with ethical theory or ethics purely for individuals rather than with the experience of ethical reflection and judgment in organizational and social policy settings. Though escape from the wastelands of rationalism and individualism is not easy, many ethicists have been attempting to overcome their isolation from areas of social dynamism. Ethics is now moving toward usefulness as an instrument of effective management.

Ethics as Moralism

Many people do not want to discuss ethics because they have acquired the mistaken notion that ethics has to do only with individual honesty and sexual behavior. The fault for this misunderstanding usually rests with those who taught us "ethics" for purposes of social control when we were very young. As a result of these early experiences, persons with no further exposure to moral reflection find it difficult to imagine a wider understanding of ethics dealing with alternative values, purposes, and priorities shaping the policies of governments and corporations. There are able leaders of important societal organizations, therefore, who think that it is not only possible but necessary to separate ethical and moral considerations from the exercise of power and the shaping of policy.

On the other hand, there are a considerable number of self-appointed "moral leaders" who think of themselves as the keepers of the conscience of society and believe that they can lecture governmental and corporate policymakers about ethics as though they were a group of recalcitrant teenagers. The mistake made by such moralists, whether of a conservative or liberal bent, is to identify ethics with their own moral convictions, uninformed by the perspectives and expertise of those in policy-making positions. In response to this moralism, some policymakers maintain the view that the introduction of morality in any form undermines the ability of leaders to exercise power in a pluralistic society. Those who take this position may be expert and experienced in their own areas of operation, but their view of ethics is not well informed, deriving perhaps from a sophomore course in philosophy or from moral preachments of current media evangelists. Ethical reflection and moral judgment pervade the process of making decisions and developing policy — even though they may not be recognized. The issue is the quality of the ethics used.

Dean Acheson, former secretary of state, distinguished *moralism*, the attempt to impose one's own or one's own nation's moral judgments on others, from *morality*, the acting out of one's own history, tradition, values, and purposes with clear-eyed recognition of the traditions and values of both friend and foe. In this perspective, ethics is reflection on the moral significance of action, whether undertaken by an individual, an organization, or a nation.[4]

Nonrecognition of Ethics

A fourth problem with ethics concerns the failure to recognize the setting of priorities among alternative goals, the trade-offs among values and purposes, and the evaluation of results that are integral to the policy-making process as ethical decisions. No individual can operate in a social context without engaging in the appraisal of conflicting or uneven moral directives and the development of criteria for action. In the same way no group of leaders can guide the affairs of an organization without ethical reflection.

To have ethics or not is never a possible alternative for policymakers. Instead, the issue is the quality of ethical reflection informing policy formation and implementation in a corporation. Are there ways to enhance that reflection? Are there resources that will improve the processes of evaluation? The management of values is always taking place and never unimportant because upon it depends in considerable measure the performance of the corporation.

Need for Adequate Terminology to Discuss Ethics

A fifth problem concerns a general lack of adequate language and terminology for examining ethics overtly and the resulting tendency to leave ethics within the tacit, undiscussed elements of the policy process. Corporate executives, both by educational training and by experience, have learned the terminology of various sectors of finance and commercial operation. Whatever in these areas was not acquired in school was rapidly picked up on the job. Neither in school, in management training courses by corporations, nor in the day-to-day experience of the executive — until recently — has much been done to help managers raise ethical reflection from the inarticulate level to the articulate level where the discussion of values and purposes is as routine and precise as the discussion on financial data. It is expected somehow that moral sensitivity and the capacity for ethical judgment will have been acquired from the social atmosphere and will be exhibited in a person's character. But the means for bringing ethics articulately and expertly to bear within the corporate policy process have seldom been developed. In projects with organizational policymakers, we have found that almost every person, through background and community involvements, is deeply concerned about ethics and has intense moral commitments informing his or her life. But it was unusual to find persons able to articulate these well enough to feel comfortable discussing ethics explicitly in policy situations. And we found few corporate contexts where provision had been made for careful attention to the processes of value judgment in which everyone is engaged.

When we examine the ethical dimensions of what business executives are actually doing, what do we find? People who manage corporations are part of a process in which decisions are made, policy shaped, and action taken for implementation. Results are then evaluated and revised decisions, policies, and implementation hammered out. In this process, choices are made about what is valuable and desirable, what purposes are more important, what goals are to be pursued in the short run and in the long run, and what constituencies are to be served. *Reflecting on the choices to be made and developing criteria for ordering priorities among values and goals is what we mean by ethics in corporate policy.* It involves neither esoteric terms nor irrelevant moralism. Instead, ethics is already operative in business organizations. It goes on in the daily round of evaluation and choice underlying the formation and implementation of policy.

When Bill, in the conversation that began the chapter, sets the policy of his loan company against financing casinos, he is basing his action on a specific pattern of ethical reflection. Though his colleagues may learn about it later, Bill has shaped the ethics and policy of the corporation decisively in regard to one issue.

Ethical consideration and action are always taking place covertly or explicitly. The issue is whether corporate leadership will improve its skills in managing values by becoming more aware of the corporate culture and value commitments that shape policy. Increased attention to the ethical dimensions of policy can lead to a more comprehensive style of management and to higher levels of corporate performance.

RECOGNIZING ETHICS — INDIVIDUAL AND CORPORATE

How are we to understand the meaning of ethics, not only for individuals but also for corporate policy? By drawing on the experience of business executives and the ways they perceive ethics, we have made a beginning. Let us continue by exploring moral directives, evaluation of alternatives, and ethical judgments as we encounter them in the ordinary fabric of human living. Then we shall see how these same experiences occur in organizational settings. We shall discover that corporations, though run by individuals, have a corporate character and a culture that shape the way individuals think and act as agents of the corporation. Corporations are moral agents, operating in environments of value outside, in the surrounding society, and also inside, among the varied groups making up the corporation. Effective management of corporations requires precise information and insight regarding values no less than accurate legal and economic knowledge and guidance. Corporate performance and even corporate survival may depend on how well the business executive today learns to manage ethical concerns in a world of changing social values.

What Is Ethics?

Understood in its most comprehensive dimensions, *ethics is reflection on the moral significance of human action.* The word *ethics* derives from the Greek term *ethika,* and *moral* from the Latin *mos, moris.* In either language the terms mean customs, conduct, and character that are valued. In the Western tradition *morals* has remained closer to its ancient meaning, while *ethics* has come to mean reflection on values and morality in relation to human action.

Every society has its customs, its approved conduct, and its conception of good character, that is, its morality. Certain actions and goals are valued, others not. A society has comprehensive beliefs and cultural values that provide legitimation for particular purposes and ways of living. There are also sanctions to reinforce these social judgments and to discourage goals and life-styles regarded as less desirable. Ethics is the continuing reflection on the moral significance of action by means of which communities and individuals relate customs and conduct to values and beliefs.

Though every society has its morality and engages in ethical reflection about its moral life, what is regarded as good and right varies from one society to another. These differences come about in part because the context and challenges of societies vary and in part because there are different traditions of religious faith shaping their morality and ethics. The understanding of ethics as reflection on the moral significance of human action is sufficiently comprehensive to apply to different societies with varied moral norms.

Darrell Reeck shares this understanding of ethics and adds this explanation:

> *Action,* an important term in this definition, has a broad scope. It includes what individuals and groups do to each other, to others, and to their environment. An adequate ethical understanding of action likewise requires a knowledge of the circumstances, including the motives and values, that give rise to them.
>
> Another important concept is the notion of *moral.* A great share of human action has moral significance. This becomes apparent when one raises standards for action, such as the justice or injustice of a judge's decision, the truth or falsity of a physician's prognosis, or the good or bad consequences of a corporate business policy. To do ethics, then, is to apply one's intelligence to human action using standards of moral evaluation.[5]

Societal customs and morals provide the context of ethical reflection. Humans emerge as selves in a social location permeated by moral directives. From womb to tomb, every human exists within a fabric of moral relations. Moral awareness and response are as natural for human living as air and breathing. Beginning in infancy, humans are subjected to a barrage of moral directives from parents, peers, and community. As children develop within social locations, they begin to internalize these directives, to make them their own. So long as there is no conflict or tension among these directives, our growing moral life remains coherent and relatively simple. As we become aware of divergences in the moral directives given us, we begin to develop criteria and principles for deciding among alternatives, trying to lessen the tension among the directives to which we are subject. This is the beginning of ethical reflection, and it is in this way that ethics emerges from the context of moral directives. Humans use ethical reflection to evaluate alternative courses of action in moral terms and to guide their behavior through the maze of moral directives. All of us will recall contending with different pressures to behave in one way or another and recognize our own development of ethical consideration and judgment.

Organizations, social groups, and nations, indeed all human collectivities, exist in the social context of moral directives. Within these social relationships a corporation — no less than other organizations and individuals — must consider the meaning of its policies and actions in terms of the moral directives impinging upon it both internally and externally. *Discussion, reflection, decision,* and *implementation* are the familiar terms for the processes of developing ethics in organizations. Corporate ethics or business ethics makes sense in the same way that individual ethics and political ethics make sense. Ethics is necessary for individuals and for collectivities because moral choice is an element in every social context. An organization must give careful attention to its environment of moral directives and guide itself through the varied expectations of the social groups upon which it depends.

"Business ethics," according to Clarence Walton, "extends the range of criteria whereby human actions are judged to include such things as societal expectations, fair competition, the aesthetics of advertising and the use of public relations, the meaning of social responsibilities, reconciling corporate behavior at home with behavior abroad, the extent of consumer sovereignty, the relevance of corporate size, the handling of communications, and the like."[6]

Ethics cannot be expected to offer a single, absolute way of behavior. Reflecting ethically is akin to navigating a ship through currents and shoals or learning to play chess. There is, however, an important difference: Humans cannot escape moral involvement and ethical reflection, whereas we may decide for or against sailing and playing chess. Throughout their careers, as individuals and as managers of organizations corporate executives are engaged in ethical reflection within a context of moral directives and choices. It is possible to improve the skills of ethical reflection, but there are no final answers for every situation and every culture. What is the ethical action? is not a question with a single rule valid for all circumstances, rather, it is more like asking, What is the right course for the ship? or What is the right move in chess? Ethics is the way individuals and social collectivities evaluate and guide their actions in terms of the values, ideals, and purposes acquired from the family, from society, and from religious communities.

Reason plays a part in ethical reflection — but only as it functions to integrate experience, information, and criteria. As with navigating a ship, careful use of sextant and charts is essential but only within the context of watchful, experienced steering of an actual vessel in a real body of water. Navigational theory is not navigation. Ethical theory is not ethics. Theory has a contribution to make only as it is shaped by the needs of practice.

In this perspective ethics is a central and unavoidable dimension of organizational policy-making. Organizational ethics is a policy science and, as such, should be included at the core of management education.

Choice and Responsibility

Though the saying goes that only death and taxes are certain, we must not forget that making choices and being responsible for the results are no less inevitable in human life and come around even more often than death and taxes. Choice and responsibility are as real and urgent for corporate management as for families or individuals. The realization of this fact adds excitement, zest, and problems to participation in upper management. Making decisions that involve choices among alternative courses of action and taking responsibility for the results are at the center of moral awareness and ethical reflection for corporate executives.

While choice is at the core of ethical consciousness, ethics cannot be reduced to choosing among alternatives when an issue arises. This is *dilemma ethics*. Because choices are a crucial element in ethics, dilemma ethics is inadequate rather than completely wrong. Ethics involves much more than seeing an issue and making a choice. First, there is the background against which a dilemma or an issue is perceived. Only a few years ago, affirmative action was not an issue for many businesses. Over the past century the climate of public opinion has turned monopolies and trusts, child labor, and a living wage into issues requiring response. Ethical issues or dilemmas arise only within a changing social context of moral values. Second, ethics includes not only the climate of moral opinion that produces dilemmas and issues but also attention to the traditions and environments of value that provide resources for developing standards of action to meet new situations as they emerge.

Choice and the necessity of making decisions provide the focus for ethical reflection. Around that center, other elements of ethical reflection take on meaning and usefulness:

1. Identifying the issue;
2. Exploring the moral background, both internal to the moral agent and external in the surrounding society, that makes it an issue for this person or group;
3. Using this analysis in combination with knowledge of policy possibilities to develop realistic alternatives for action;
4. Projecting the probable results of various policies;
5. Shaping specific policy in line with value priorities and purposes desired;
6. Taking action to implement the policies chosen; and
7. Evaluating policy, implementation, and results for improved performance.

Though the sense of responsibility for actions taken gives moral weight to ethical reflection, it is important not to focus so exclusively on responsibility as to turn ethics into perfectionism. For perfectionists and idealists nothing less than the perfect merits the name *ethics*. Such a notion eliminates all standards by which to measure what is better by admitting only the criterion of the best. Achieving instant and total victory becomes the only valid goal. No intermediate measures to guide along the way are possible or significant. Perfectionism becomes the enemy that destroys ethics. In addition, such a view obscures the actual human situation of competition among many good things needing to be done and the necessity to order priorities among goals, all of which we want to achieve. Ethics helps human moral agents in real situations develop standards for action in a world where difficult choices have to be made and not all the goals we value can be achieved simultaneously.

It might be simple to begin and end instruction in the game of golf by telling a person to go immediately and win the British Open, the U.S. Open, and the Masters' Tournament — simple, even valid in some remote way, but not of much help in learning the game. It is necessary to teach and to learn how to hold the clubs and swing them, what are the rules to be followed, what short-range and long-range goals the players pursue, and how to get the experience and evaluation that enable them to become proficient under different conditions of play. Hopes of winning the Masters' or even the local duffers' tournament can inspire beginners, intermediates, and experts, but such visions must not obscure the need for developing basic knowledge and skill. The same is true of ethics. Whether particular executives are beginners or experts at dealing with ethics in corporate policy, the point is to improve insights and skills, not to aim at instant perfection.

Though ethics cannot be reduced either to making choices or to taking responsibility, these elements of the human moral situation provide the cutting edge that makes us aware of the dimensions of human living that inescapably involve ethical reflection. Background and training often make choices so clear-cut that we are hardly conscious of making a decision. The traditions, character, and culture of a corporation can operate in the same way, so that giving a falsely optimistic report of earnings to the directors and shareholders may never become a serious issue requiring overt choice within a corporation where the accepted value commitments place strong emphasis on accuracy and honesty. When new problems emerge, patterns of action instilled by organizational character and habit may not provide easy answers as to what course of action to pursue. It is during the times when choices are not clear-cut that ethical reflection becomes especially necessary, important, and difficult.

If the corporate culture is not strong and integrated, or if that culture has not emphasized the development of criteria for corporate action, then more and more choices will slip by with inadequate attention to alternative values, and dilemmas that are recognized will require excessive agonizing. A corporate culture that raises ethical consideration to a conscious, articulate level and provides strong value commitments to support its managers and employees will be better equipped at all levels for the management of values.

Choice and responsibility also point to another crucial aspect of ethical reflection. Those who have responsibility have a perspective and awareness different from that of observers with an external, detached location. Those inside usually have the experience and the information to perceive possibilities and limitations with greater precision than those who have a more distant view. The insiders will probably have a more realistic view of the choices and policy alternatives available. Outside resources have much to contribute to policymakers. They may bring new viewpoints and material that executives have not had time to explore. The interaction of outside and inside perspectives can lead to mutual learning that will open up alternatives neither has seen before. It is also possible that insiders have become locked into limiting "groupthink" horizons, which outsiders can help to expand. In the end, however, those with the responsibility are usually those with the power to set policy; it is they, together with those who are the recipients of policy, for whom corporate ethics has the most meaning.

Interrelation of Individual and Corporate Ethics

In a perceptive article in the *Harvard Business Review* entitled "The Parable of the Sadhu," a managing director of Morgan Stanley & Co., New York, tells of an experience he had while on a hike in the Himalayan Mountains of Nepal as he and a companion were attempting to get through an 18,000-foot pass. As they were nearing the summit, they were confronted with an almost naked Indian holy man, a sadhu, who was near death. The way he and the other persons in the vicinity attempted to deal with the situation becomes a parable through which the author examines the symbiotic relation between individual and group ethics and suggests how the incident in the high Himalayas throws light on the highest levels of corporate life in the United States.

"Because corporations and their members are interdependent," he suggests, "for the corporation to be strong the members need to share a preconceived notion of what is correct behavior, a 'business ethic,' and think of it as a positive force, not a constraint." He concludes: "That is the lesson of the sadhu. In a complex corporate situation, the individual requires and deserves the support of the group. If people cannot find such support from their organization, they don't know how to act. If such support is forthcoming, a person has a stake in the success of the group, and can add much to the process of establishing and maintaining a corporate culture."[7]

Individual and corporate ethics are not to be contrasted and separated. They go together and interpenetrate one another. We are all shaped by our social and organizational environments, and we also help, in turn, to shape those surroundings. We are responsible as individuals and as members of groups, and other individuals and the groups to which we belong are responsible to us. Corporate ethics cannot be separated from individual ethics. Just as individuals must be aware of societal values, so a corporation can be adequately reflective about ethics only if it takes account of the individual values operative inside the organization as well as values on the societal and global levels.

Another way to put this is to emphasize the importance of the environment of values for corporate ethics, both the environment that is internal to the company and the environment that surrounds it. The internal environment involves the values of individuals, the values of significant groups within the corporation, and the traditions of character and culture inherited from the company's history. The external environment includes other corporations, important social groups related to the company, governmental entities at various levels, the national society with its history and culture, and the global society as it impinges on corporate activities. These environments of value are not static; they are in the process of continual change. The effective management of values in the contemporary world requires having the means to monitor the changes taking place in the relevant context of corporate activity. The management of change and the management of values are coordinate enterprises for policymakers in today's corporations.

SUGGESTIONS FOR GROUP STUDY

1. Review the conversation at the beginning of the chapter. Based on the value judgments expressed in this dialogue, reflect on the relationships between individual ethics and corporate ethics as described in the chapter. Have part of the group take the position that all ethics in corporations is individual; have the others defend the corporate nature of ethics in business. After the discussion, try to develop a group consensus on the issue.
2. Read the article in Appendix D by Bowen H. McCoy, "The Parable of the Sadhu," *Harvard Business Review*, September-October 1983. Discuss the moral dilemmas posed by this parable. Work through the rationale for applying the lessons from this article to the ethics of business organizations. Give particular attention to the application of the parable to the conversation with loan company executives on the criteria for lending to casinos.

3. Read recent editions of the *Wall Street Journal, Business Week,* or other publications and identify articles that provide evidence of the growing interest in business ethics. Bring several of these articles to the group for discussion. You will find it valuable to continue this review of publications to find illustrations of the real nature of ethical concerns in the business world, whether or not identified as "ethical."
4. Have each member of your group examine his or her own views of right and wrong in business practices. What is the background in the person's life for these ethical sensitivities? As you share the insights on your own background, pay special attention to the form and language with which you express your ethical convictions. One way of approaching this is to have each member of the group describe and analyze his or her social location — family background, education, religious training, work experiences, marriage and family situation, and so on. Each of these elements contains clues as to the social perceptions and ethical sensitivities that the person now has. Observe the ease or difficulty your group has in discussing ethics in relation to business. Do you run into the same problems of communication that are reported in this chapter as common among corporate executives?

Three

CORPORATE CULTURE AND MORAL AGENCY

Stan was eagerly looking forward to taking over as senior vice-president for marketing in the corporation where he had worked during the past 12 years. He had performed superbly in sales and had innovative ideas for improving the entire marketing operation. The new job would give him an opportunity to demonstrate the leadership skills he knew he had as well as provide needed additional income just when his oldest child was beginning college.

It was a good time in his life. He and his wife were leaders in the community where they lived, and recently they had both joined the group of top lay officials in their thriving local church. Their home was a good one. Their children did well in school and were happy.

As Stan suspected, the Marketing Division had problems. What he had not known before but soon discovered was that price-fixing arrangements had been going on for years, and no one among the senior management regarded these agreements as anything more than business as usual. Though not a lawyer, Stan felt sure that there was illegality involved. In addition, it went against the grain of all he had learned from parents, church, and community as he had grown up.

"We ought to reconsider all this immediately and, if there's any doubt, get an opinion from our legal counsel," he told the president. "If we ever get caught, there's probably going to be hell to pay."

"We've been doing it for years. Nothing has happened. And it pays off. Just do your job," was the gist of the president's reply.

It became clear to Stan that price-fixing had become an accepted part of policy and that if he pushed the issue, it would only hurt his future in the company. His only alternative was to leave. Stan agonized over the matter for two weeks and decided to accept things as they were and stay. Gradually, he settled into his job but with many uncomfortable feelings.

Almost a year later, the Feds showed up. They took the company to court. The agreements were indeed very illegal; and as the executive in charge of marketing, Stan was sent to prison. With time off for good behavior, he was out in 18 months. While there, he helped reorganize the educational program and improve the purchasing procedures of the prison.

Through his difficulties his wife and family were very supportive. The corporation, however, was not much help while Stan was doing time or after he was released. He was the symbol of a big embarrassment everyone wanted to forget. Even though he was retained in the company, the position to which he was assigned had no real authority and was almost invisible. His church carefully kept at a distance from his problems. Neither he nor his wife were asked to resign from their positions in the congregation, and no one — not the pastor nor any of the members — ever mentioned his legal difficulties or visited him in prison. So far as the church community was concerned, it was as though nothing had occurred.

For Stan, as for many at every level of management, two cultures existed side by side within him. In this case they had crashed into one another. Without strong faith, the support of his wife and children, and a surprisingly productive existence in prison, Stan might have come apart. Instead, he survived and emerged hurt but much stronger and wiser.

In organizational settings, individual and corporate ethics are inseparable but not identical. Ethics is never exactly the same for individual behavior and for corporate policy. What individuals in an organization regard as good has impact on the operational values that shape corporate policy and action. The more powerful the positions that persons occupy in the corporation, the more their individual value commitments can mold the corporate culture and determine the ethics of the corporation. At times the culture and values of a company become the extended vision of a powerful leader. Individual managers will be caught up in that vision, and their actions as part of a management team will represent the corporate ethos. Differences will remain, however, between the ethics shaping corporate policy and the varied ethics shaping individual behavior. The values even of charismatic leaders and powerful corporate cultures will be modified as policies from top management are interpreted and implemented by employees of diverse religious and social backgrounds.

In the illustration given above, Stan's ethical convictions differed sharply from the convictions of those who had set the price-fixing policies of the company's Marketing Division. Some candidates for the job would have found no conflict between their individual values and those governing corporate policy. Others might have resigned once the practice of price-fixing was discovered and the corporation refused to modify its practices. In any case, corporate ethics is closely related to the ethics of individual executives but is different from, and more inclusive than, the ethics of any one person.

Because individuals are from birth to death members of social groups, and because they are shaped in outlook and behavior by those groups, individual managers tend to become agents of the corporate ethics while on the job. But the same individual will think and act differently when in a family group or recreational setting. In each different context persons take on the values, behavior patterns, and responsibilities belonging to them as members and/or policymakers in those social and organizational relations.

Writing of President Harry Truman's decision to drop atomic bombs on Japanese cities in the closing days of World War II, Robert Batchelder comments on the power of organizational process: "Social institutions appear to take on an independence and a power of their own which defy the attempts of individual humans to control them. General Groves has said of President Truman's decision to use the bomb: 'Truman did not so much say yes as not say no. It would indeed have taken a lot of nerve to say no at that time.' "[1] If we are to deal with the realities of contemporary society, we must remember what Kurt Lewin emphasizes: "It is as a member of a group that the individual is most pliable." The culture and ethos of an organization tend to absorb individuals, so that they act not so much by their own moral perceptions as by the norms and values composing the ethics of the organization.

There is no reason to regard this social fact of life as somehow demonic, as do William H. Whyte and Jacques Ellul in varying ways. Nor is it necessary to complain, as does Robert Nisbet, that "what has in fact happened during the past half century is that the bulk of power in our society, as it affects our intellectual, economic, social and cultural existences, has become largely invisible, a function of the vast infra-government composed of bureaucracy's commissions, agencies, and departments in a myriad of areas."[2] What will be more helpful is to discard the illusion that ethics and values relate only to individuals and to recover instead the perspective familiar to Plato, Aristotle, the biblical writers, and most thinkers of the Western tradition until recently — namely, that ethics is as applicable to social collectivities such as governments and corporations as to individuals. Individuals are social beings by nature, and social groups are made up of individuals.

This perception of individuals and social groups as symbiotically related emerges clearly in the recent studies of corporate culture. The culture of a corporation permeates and shapes the outlook and actions of individuals within it. Corporate culture involves values and value commitments and relates closely to corporate performance. It is, therefore, through an examination of corporate culture and moral agency that we shall better understand the relation of corporate ethics and performance.

In this chapter we shall examine: (1) the importance of organizations for our society, (2) the meaning of corporate culture, and (3) what it means to speak of corporations as moral agents. In the process we shall further illumine the nature of corporate ethics and its relation to corporate performance.

OUR ORGANIZED SOCIETY

The recession of the early 1980s brought hardship to millions and underscored how human life is interrelated within nations and around the globe through the political, economic, and cultural organizations providing the fabric of society. The closing of a steel mill or an automobile plant has immediate impact on workers, families, and the cities. But the shutdowns are the product of declining demand over a much broader area, and the consequences of the closing will cause shock waves in government at every level and in the national and world economies. In the same way, the opening of new businesses or the reopening of plants brings jobs, improves conditions for families and municipalities, and infuses renewed activity through the organizational channels of the economy. Organizations in general and corporations in particular exert their impact on the well-being of an increasingly interdependent global society.

The Importance of Corporations

Virtually every person on the planet has a vital stake in the performance of corporations and the way values are managed in economic organizations. The reason for this is clear for people and communities closely connected to nearby corporations. The interests are equally plain but less dramatic in relation to the wider network of commerce upon which all people in varying measures depend. Add the effects near and far together and the larger picture emerges. Collectively, the business corporations of the industrialized world exercise tremendous power in shaping the present and the future of global society.

Business is only one major sector of the landscape of social organizations. Other sectors include governments, labor unions, the media, the legal and health professions, educational institutions, churches and other religious communities, charitable enterprises, and cultural groups. All are interrelated; all affect one another; and all, in combination, exert a decisive influence on what happens in every area of society — human rights, the natural environment, issues of war and peace, the sources and uses of energy, and the development and deployment of new technology.

We live in a highly organized society, with increasing interdependence throughout the world. In recent centuries Western society has undergone massive technological and organizational development consisting, as Kenneth Boulding puts it, "in a great rise in the number, size, and power of organizations of many diverse kinds, and especially of economic organizations."[3] Significant results of this revolution are the shift in control of these organizations away from those who own them toward those who manage them, the development of vast and intricate networks of communication, and the greater availability of powerful technological instruments.

These changes have brought a host of problems with them. For example, the renewal of business activity after a recession no longer necessarily means the re-employment of the people out of work. Many of their jobs have been taken over by machines and computers. This increasing loss of jobs through technological innovation appears to be permanent.

The development of the organized society that characterizes the contemporary world has brought sweeping changes in human living. Many of these are highly desirable; others range from less desirable to questionable to dangerous. The importance of corporations looms large — partly as problem, partly as solution — in modern society.

Contributions of Organizations to Society

Many of the advantages and benefits enjoyed by people in Europe and North America have been made possible in part because natural resources have been available but also in large measure because Western inventiveness has brought about the development of large organizations, the means of mass production and distribution of goods and services, and the complex technology to support and extend these innovations. Throughout the spectrum of benefits constituting a high standard of living — from monetary resources and industrial production to health services and social reforms — the quality of human living has been vastly improved for most people in the industrialized nations by means of the organizational patterns — economic, political, voluntary — that characterize our societies.

In these societies the level of human existence has, over the past five centuries, undergone remarkable improvement. Measured by such criteria as lengthened life span, better health and physical well-being, decline in infant mortality, elimination of slavery, curtailed child labor, improved conditions and shorter hours for workers, rising income and economic resources, better housing and food, increased availability of education and cultural opportunities, greater political power and participation, and more control over one's own life situation, the standards and quality of living have risen dramatically in the industrialized nations. From a feudal social pattern in which a small elite group controlled most of the wealth and social power, the North Atlantic community of nations has changed into a varied group of middle-class democracies, with a high proportion of the populace participating in economic and political control and sharing in societal benefits.

The middle-class revolution of the Western nations has produced wave after wave of rising expectations and political change around the world as other people have sought the social improvements they have witnessed in the industrialized democracies. Forms of state capitalism in the Communist bloc, different forms of socialism elsewhere, and varied attempts at political-economic development in the Third World have resulted. Only Japan has gone far in reproducing the social progress exemplified in the North Atlantic nations.

Ambiguities and Difficulties

Many problems remain. Old ones are still only partly solved. New problems not previously perceived have emerged over the horizon. Though many injustices and inequities hang on tenaciously in Western societies, few suggest a return to the "good old days" when living conditions were so terrible for most of our ancestors. In the majority of non-Western societies, improvements in the quality of life have spread slowly and unevenly. Exploitation from elite groups within the developing nations as well as from the economic powers of the developed world (both Communist and non-Communist) impedes the rise in standard of living. The Western nations resist sharing their gains with others. The Soviet bloc suffers under continuing Russian colonialism. And within the Third World, old feudal powers or new military dictatorships limit or prevent the extension of the benefits of modernization to the majority of their populations.

Furthermore, the organized world of Western society has created problems in addition to its contributions to the improvement of human life. As organizations have increased in size and complexity, it has become clear that the same patterns that produce plenty and provide benefits also create difficulties, even dangers, for human existence. Industrial capitalism, for example, as it expanded rapidly in western Europe and North America in the nineteenth century, threatened to develop monopolies, destroy competition, and turn into an economic tyranny as perilous for the majority of the people as were the kings and nobility of the old feudal societies. Over the past century, control through various checks and balances has limited this danger. The tendencies toward laissez-faire capitalism have turned into varied types of mixed economies in the industrialized nations. In Western Europe the tendency has been toward democratic socialism. In the United States and Canada, private enterprise and the market system have continued to be central in the political economy. In the Communist bloc, where unrestrained state capitalism has threatened to become almost as repressive as the feudal systems it displaced, it has become necessary to reinstitute elements of private enterprise, on both covert and overt levels, in order to maintain a measure of economic health and growth.

Other ambiguities of our organized world have surfaced. Private enterprise works better for fueling economic production than for ensuring equitable and just distribution of resources. Regulation of business by government is intended to address problems of corporate power but creates increasing bureaucratic difficulties. The exploitation of nature, once considered essential for industrial productivity, has led to a deterioration of the natural environment that could endanger the quality of life and even life itself. Education, often regarded as a cure for all social ills, has not fulfilled the hopes invested in it. While the benefits of extending educational opportunities and the scope of research have been massive, the democratization and mass methods of education have endangered its quality and threatened to limit the contributions it can make to human welfare in the future.

In parallel fashion governments intended to increase participation and control by the people have — through sophisticated organization — threatened freedom by too much regulation, endangered privacy by means of information collection and storage, and developed new means of oppression via control of social welfare benefits. Even the media of communication cannot be regarded as wholly benign. Though the media have, with the aid of technological developments, done much to free humanity from ignorance and insularity, the control of information can become a threat to freedom.

The list of ambiguous elements in our organized society could be extended. Clearly, organizations are a mixed blessing. Even though organizational power has opened up new possibilities for humanity, it also presents genuine perils. At the same time, there appears to be no alternative to continuing and extending organizational structures.

Given this situation, it becomes an imperative of our time to give careful attention to the ethics of our organizations. Organizations in any social sector are not necessarily good in themselves. Their "goodness" depends on the purposes for which they are operated and on the way values are managed by those charged with the responsibility for making and implementing policy. The culture and values of a corporation, or any other organization, become crucial in determining whether the results of its policies will be beneficial or dangerous to the human community. In our organized society, therefore, corporations are too important for us to ignore them, to fail to do all we can to improve the management of values in them, or to neglect doing everything possible to ensure that ethics makes a difference in the way they are run.

DIMENSIONS OF CORPORATE CULTURE

Every organization has its distinctive ethos, culture, and value commitments. From the experiences of our Berkeley group with specific corporations, we wrote: A corporation has "its own history and traditions, its own rules and ways of operating derived from its constituting character and its customs, its own patterns of informal understandings, its own purposes and goals, its own particular network of influence and factions within it, its own relations to other organizations, its own particular place in a nexus of social and cultural functions."[4] With this in mind, we shall explore the dimensions of corporate culture in terms of its history and background, its structure as a community of persons and groups, and its overall character. By examining the corporation in this way, we shall better understand the meaning of corporate ethics.

The Corporation in Historical Perspective

The modern corporation must be viewed, first, as a specific kind of social entity that has developed over the course of Western history; and second, as a particular organization, existing today, with its own history that shapes its patterns of operation in the present and its projections with reference to the future.

The Corporation in History. Though diverse corporate entities are well known in human history, business corporations as they exist today are late arrivals on the social scene. In ancient and medieval times religious groups or trade guilds or even towns might have had corporate status — but not a group organized for commerce and profit. The notion of providing a public service is deeply rooted in the history of the corporation, and this element has never been completely lost. The rise of the modern corporation begins with the organization of trading companies in the sixteenth and seventeenth centuries and coincides with the emergence of the middle class as a political and economic power and the expansion of trade around the globe. Because individuals lacked the funds to finance and risk the losses of the commerce developing with Asia, Africa, and the Americas, early business corporations were designed to bring together enough capital for large-scale trading operations. Examples are the East India Company, the Company of Adventurers of London Trading into Africa, the Hudson Bay Company, and the joint stock companies that settled the Virginia, Plymouth, and Massachusetts Bay colonies. Chartered by governments, they were kept under tight control in regard to spheres of operations and their sharing profits with the king and the nobility. Only in the nineteenth century does the older system of controlled chartering, with its inevitable favoritism, disappear and the present practice emerge of open chartering for any group seeking to establish a corporation with purposes fitting within broad social norms.

As it exists today, the business corporation shares with similar entities of the past and present that characteristic of being an institution that "can endure beyond the natural lives of the members of the association" at any given time.[5] It is also a means for concentrating capital and management resources beyond the abilities of individual entrepreneurs. It can sue and be sued, act as a unit, and provide its incorporators with the advantage of dispersed and limited liability. Most important for the modern world, it has been the major vehicle for building highly developed and industrialized societies. In this role it has far outgrown Chief Justice John Marshall's oft-quoted definition of the corporation as "an artificial being, invisible, intangible, and existing only in the contemplation of the law."[6] As Clarence Walton observes, "George Washington would have been more at home with the entrepreneurs of Aristotle's day than he would have been with either John D. Rockefeller or Henry Ford."[7]

Now it is relatively easy in the industrialized nations, as contrasted with three centuries ago, to secure a charter of incorporation for a commercial corporation. Though the process of chartering is more open, this does not mean the absence of supervision and control by government and by society. First, the purposes of the proposed corporation must fit into accepted categories. Considerable latitude of purpose is permitted but only within implicit limits set by what can be called, following Hobbes and Locke, the *societal covenant*. Second, the tax laws assure continuing scrutiny and careful checking to ensure that corporations operate according to the purposes established in their charters. And third, the close governmental control in the chartering process that had in the late eighteenth and early nineteenth centuries gradually been relaxed was reaffirmed in the late nineteenth century through governmental actions aimed at regulating the establishment and impact of business corporations.

Laissez-faire capitalism never existed except as an economic theory. As the older constraints of the mercantile economy were being thrown off, new constraints of antitrust legislation and regulatory commissions were being instituted. It is accurate to say:

> Any attempt to develop a new social consensus must recognize the clear lessons of history: a laissez faire system of self-regulating markets is a utopian dream existing only in the minds of economists. The reality is that all peoples have always embedded the economy into the total social system. The market economy is no exception. Since its inception, every group in society — business, labor, farmers, consumers — has struggled to abort the workings of the market. Any realistic policy must accept this fact and design a policy which utilizes and subordinates markets to the attainment of individual's and society's moral values and goals.[8]

Business corporations are powerful and generally accepted institutions in most societies today. This is especially so in the industrialized nations. It is inaccurate, however, to say that these corporations operate in free enterprise, capitalist economies. Private enterprise constitutes an important component in all the industrialized nations, though, for example, it is more important in the United States than in Sweden. All these nations actually have *mixed* political economies — not ones that can be characterized precisely as *capitalist* or *free enterprise*. The term *capitalism* tends to be used only by free enterprise idealists who favor less governmental and societal control of the economy or by Marxists who oppose the mixed systems of the

First World and seek, by caricaturing them, to undermine their support.

Paradoxically, one of the "purer" forms of the market mechanism operates today in the underground economy of the Soviet Union, a nation in which the official political economy is state capitalism. The covert private enterprise sector of the Soviet economy is so large and powerful as to make it clear that the Soviet Union also has a mixed political economy, though the mix is quite different from that in Western Europe and North America.

Within the industrialized nations the struggle continues over how much freedom for business corporations is essential for economic growth and societal well-being and how much regulation is necessary to ensure that corporations operate within the evolving covenant of social values. Corporations are here to stay. Management cannot forget, however, that corporate policy and action must take account of the environment of laws, values, moral climate, and customs within which the corporation operates and upon which it depends for its existence and its legitimacy.[9]

A view of the corporation in history discloses that its development has taken place within the larger culture and value commitments of society and that the culture of any particular corporation is inevitably shaped by that social environment of values. Awareness of this history provides one clear dimension of the close relation between ethics and performance for the modern business corporation.

The History of a Corporation. Corporate culture derives not only from the surrounding cultural environment but also from the history of a particular company. A corporation is founded at a particular time, has purposes that are written into its charter, and is given direction by the original leaders and by subsequent ones. There is success and growth, or failure and demise. There are crises requiring effective response if the corporation is to be maintained in good health. Patterns for making policy and implementing it develop and evolve over time. Certain value commitments are made, emphasized, and come to permeate the corporation. All these go to make up the internal culture of a corporation.

Viewed in one way, the history of a corporation is shaped by crucial events and strong leaders. But only as events and leaders are embodied in the enduring values of company tradition do they enter the real history that continues to be influential. History is not what happens but rather what is remembered. It is the past that continues to be important and valent in the ongoing present.

The past is remembered in the present through organizational habit patterns. One medium-sized business I know of changes the locks every year on its warehouse and offices. When I asked one of the executives, a woman of Oriental background, why this was done, she replied with an enigmatic smile, "It's an old Chinese custom." Then she gave a thoroughly California smile and added, "It's been part of the standard operating procedure since the place was founded, and every president thinks it one of the main reasons we have almost no theft." Whether or not the belief was correct, the pattern had become institutionalized — an organizational habit.

The past is also remembered through the stories that are told. Peters and Waterman report: "All the companies we interviewed, from Boeing to McDonald's, were quite simply rich tapestries of anecdote, myth, and fairy tale. . . . The vast majority of people who tell stories today about T. J. Watson of IBM have never met the man or had direct experience of the original more mundane reality. Two HP engineers in their mid-twenties recently regaled us with an hour's worth of 'Bill and Dave' (Hewlett and Packard) stories. We were subsequently astonished to find that neither had seen, let alone talked to, the founders. . . . Nevertheless, in an organizational sense, these stories, myths, and legends appear to be very important, because they convey the organization's shared values, or culture."[10]

This history is the continuing impact of the past upon the present and future. As such, it is a crucial dimension of corporate culture.

The Corporation as Community

In addition to the remembered past that continues to have power, corporate culture is a community of persons and groups in the present. This community, though in continuity with its history, is the corporation at any given moment. And it is this community that bears the responsibility for making decisions and taking action to meet the challenges of the present, reshaping the corporation for changing conditions, and passing it on to the future. The top executives and directors have more power and more responsibility within the community that is the corporation, but all the persons and groups making up the community influence what the corporation is today and what it becomes.

In his book *Making America Work*, James O'Toole sees the economic difficulties of the United States in the early 1980s as caused by changing culture and values within the nation and around the globe. Alterations in economic policies will not be sufficient to make the United States "work" again. What is needed is a new understanding of corporate organization and management that can mobilize the community and culture that makes up the corporation so that it can respond effectively to the challenges of the changing environment of values in society. One primary way to achieve this new philosophy of management, O'Toole suggests, is by supplementing individualistic, psychological approaches to managerial problems with an understanding of the corporation provided by the insights from anthropology. The corporation, in this perspective, is a community with a culture and value commitments. As a community it is an organizational context of persons and groups; a system of customs, expectations, values, and purposes; and a system of action and interaction.[11]

Persons and Groups. Most obviously, the corporate community is made up of particular persons and groups related through the patterns and purposes of the organization. Within the organization every person and group is assigned a role, a status, and functions. These define the pattern of relations among the varied parties making up the community, though it is necessary to take the informal as well as the formal organizational structures into account. These persons are not merely organizational functionaries, they also have relations in the larger community. They belong to families, they are citizens of cities and states, they participate in political and voluntary community groups, and they are members of religious organizations. On the one hand, these wider relations mean that loyalty to the corporate community will always exist within a context of varied and more inclusive loyalties. This does not make company loyalty less real, but it provides its context and meaning. On the other hand, these diverse relations can be seen as an important way that the corporation is involved with the social environment and as a crucial resource for responding to shifts in social values. It is through these relations that the corporate culture can be creatively linked to the societal environment of culture and values upon which the corporation depends for its continuing health.

Within the corporate community the top management and directors form a group especially important for policy-making and, therefore, for the direction of the entire corporation. As the corporate community is set within the larger society, so the policy-making group is a smaller community within the corporation. As the most powerful group in the corporation, the top executives have more responsibility for corporate performance than do other persons. So it is of highest priority that they be aware not only of the technical and financial aspects of the corporation but also of the corporate culture. In this way they develop and extend their competence in the management of values.

Customs, Values, and Purposes. As a community a corporation is not only an organizational context of persons and groups in relation; the corporate community is also made up of customs, values, and purposes. Customs are those relations and actions that have been approved over a sufficient period of time to make them social habits within a community. Values represent those goals and standards used for judging relations and actions as better or worse. Values, therefore, provide criteria of evaluation, which over time shape and reshape the customs of a society. Purposes express values in terms of goals to be attained in the future and thus introduce the basis of change into the organizational context of a community.

As customs, values, and purposes come to be shared by the persons and groups within the corporation, they form the fabric of community, providing expectations that are mutually understood and accepted. Communication becomes easier and more effective. Communal relations become closer and more supportive. When groups have internal cohesion, members feel a sense of identity with one another.

Even as we prize community and seek to overcome the fragmentation that disperses energies, we need to remember another lesson: Too much sameness tends toward a static community characterized by groupthink, which can dampen creativity.

Taken together, customs, values, and purposes are cohesive elements binding persons and groups into a community. They provide a network of commitments informing action. In one way such a network makes communal action possible. In another way the network of commitments ensures stability in situations of change. In still another way the network provides a framework for absorbing innovative notions. To the extent that the persons and groups within the corporation represent the diversity of customs, values, and purposes of the wider community, they can serve the purpose of relating the corporate community to the society and enriching the corporate context with diverse perspectives that can enhance creativity.

Action and Interaction. Communities are also made up of agents, that is, persons and groups who are acting and interacting with each other. As O'Toole points out, these actions and interactions as systems of action are central elements constituting the culture of a community. Such systems may be viewed as ritual, as relation, as power, and as policy.

On one level the pattern of interaction in any society has a formal, repetitive character that can be regarded as *ritual*. Persons coming to the office greet one another with the same gestures and words morning after morning. Not to speak constitutes a breech of etiquette, a variation in the pattern of expected action requiring explanation. The routines of coffee breaks, lunchtimes, and closing are distinctive. So also are the more important events of corporate life — divisional conferences, sales meetings, budget planning sessions. A board of directors meeting has its special patterns surrounding it and transpiring within it. Communal ritual serves as oil to make human interaction smoother. The giving and receiving of "strokes" provides a way to express inner feelings appropriately. On a more important level, ritual conveys a tacit level of important meanings in a community and is a way to remind members of those meanings and to reinforce them through acting them out.

On a second level social interaction embodies *relations* among persons and groups in a community and offers channels for maintaining the relations. Evaluation sessions are a context for discussions that build realistic relations and give helpful feedback. The regular use of task forces can build creativity and the constant anticipation of innovation into the corporate community. Channels of communication serve the purpose of getting information around but also define patterns of accountability.

On a third level systems of action and interaction in a corporate community convey *power* and delineate the patterns of power. Organizational charts and documents containing ideas can obscure the primacy of agency and power in human life. An organizational chart means little unless it represents the lines of power that are actually acted out in a given context. Ideas and the words written or spoken are not to be ignored or regarded as meaningless. Their significance, however, is not in their existence but in the extent to which they inform and become embodied in action. Ideas and words do have power — as they are caught up in and shape human action. Only as this important element of community is recognized can ethics be properly understood as reflection on the moral significance of human action and the possibility of making power more responsible to humane values be realized.

Building on these three levels, a fourth emerges into view. Systems of action and interaction within community, as these are shaped by ethical reflection and become intentional expressions of communal values and purposes, are transformed into *policy*. A corporate culture cannot be understood apart from its directionality toward the future, its impulse to assemble and shape its energies toward goals, and the intentional character that underlies this action. As a community with a culture, the corporation is involved continually in reflecting on values and purposes, on how these may be embodied in action, and on ways to evaluate and improve the goals and the action. This policy level of corporate community inevitably involves ethical reflection and exhibits the character of a corporation.

The Corporation as Character

"Large social systems," writes C. West Churchman, "seem to take on a character of their own. Since character is closely tied into morality, the conclusion is that large social systems develop an ethics that is independent of the wishes and morality of the individual."[12]

The history of an institution appears to be a given, something passive and simply "there." When we understand the corporation in terms of its character, however, it becomes clear tht we are speaking of a dimension of corporate culture that is inescapably dynamic, committed to values, and future oriented in the sense of shaping the present reality of the corporation toward a reality that it may become. Character emphasizes the intentional element of corporate culture.

In his seminal work *Leadership in Administration,* Philip Selznick makes use of the psychological analogy of character formation in order to illumine the concept of organizational character. For Selznick, organizational character is historical, integrated, functional, and dynamic.

Selznick applies these attributes of character drawn from psychology to organizations:

1. The technical, rational, impersonal, task-oriented formal system (the "organization") is conditioned by the responsive interaction of persons and groups.
2. In the course of time, this responsive interaction is patterned. A social structure is created. This patterning is *historical,* in that it reflects the specific experiences of the particular organization; it is *functional* in that it aids the organization to adapt itself to its internal and external social environment; and it is *dynamic,* in that it generates new and active forces, especially internal interest-groups made up of persons committed to particular jobs or policies.
3. Organizations become institutions as they are *infused with value,* that is, prized not as tools alone but as sources of direct personal gratification and vehicles of group integrity. This infusion produces a distinct identity for the organization. Where institutionalization is well advanced, distinctive outlooks, habits, and other commitments are unified, coloring all aspects of organizational life and lending it a *social integration* that goes well beyond formal co-ordination and command.[13]

For our purposes here, I have used corporate culture as the encompassing notion. The historical dimension refers to the past of that culture, providing it with its founding charter and the way of organizational life that has brought it to the present. The communal dimension refers to that integrated, functioning entity that is the corporation in the present. Corporate character is that pervasive pattern of valuing and future orientation that defines the way in which the corporation is dynamic and specifies the particular configuration of values and purposes shaping the movement into the future.

Character is not something easily defined with reference to individuals, but most people accept it as real and make appraisals on a daily basis. Corporate character is no easier to delineate with simple precision. But it is there as a dimension of corporate culture, and the evaluation of corporate character goes on routinely in the business world.

THE CORPORATION AS MORAL AGENT[14]

The idea of organizations as moral agents is an old notion that has been obscured in recent centuries by attempts to wrest individuals out of their social relations and define them as separate and autonomous. For Plato and Aristotle, for Amos and Isaiah, it was a commonplace that humans are social beings by nature and that societal collectivities — nations, peoples, tribes, and so on — are moral agents responsible for their actions.

In Plato's *Republic,* for example, the understanding of justice that emerges in the course of the discussion is decisively social. Justice, it is said, cannot be achieved in society as a whole until individual souls become harmonious and filled with justice. But justice in the human soul cannot be achieved until the society becomes just. Collective moral agency and individual moral agency are real and symbiotically related, that is, mutually interdependent. The Hebrew prophets affirm collective moral agency in the most dramatic terms possible. They declare the judgment of God upon entire kingdoms and peoples and call all nations, including Israel and Judah, to become responsible to the justice, peace, love, and faithfulness commanded by God's covenant. The view taken by the Greeks and explicated in the Bible is continued in Augustine, in Thomas Aquinas, in Martin Luther, in the Reformed tradition, and in virtually all theological, philosophical, and political thought until individualism came to prominence in the late eighteenth and early nineteenth centuries. Now the longer perspective is being recovered. As individualism has proved unsatisfactory, humanity is learning again to apply moral criteria and expectations to the performance of governments, corporations, and other societal organizations.

In an article on ethics and business, Kirk Hanson of the Stanford Graduate School of Business suggests three levels of ethical concern: individual, institutional, and systemic.[15] Individual ethical concerns arise, he says, between one individual and another. Institutional ethics concerns organizational actions and relations. Systemic ethics deals with the norms for guiding the national and international economic systems of which we are a part. Perhaps another level needs to be inserted between the institutional and the systemic levels for dealing with sectors of society such as, for example, professions, health care, churches, and education. In any event it is helpful to see ethics as applicable to different levels of society so long as we recognize that though they are distinguishable, they are inseparable and interrelated.

Three contemporary perspectives illumine the nature of corporate moral agency. These are the legal, the social scientific, and the ethical.

Legal Responsibility

The most obvious way that corporations are viewed as moral agents today is in the legal tradition and usage. The corporation before the law and in the courts is a fictional person. As such it is regarded as a moral agent. The corporation can be taken to court as a legal entity, it is regarded as responsible for its actions, it can be held accountable in judicial proceedings, and it can be punished if found guilty. While it is true, as a judge once complained, that a corporation has "no pants to kick or soul to damn," it has sufficient existence to sue and be sued, to act and be acted upon, and to judge and be judged for what it does.

Corporations are included as persons quite specifically under a variety of statutes such as the Federal Food, Drug, and Cosmetic Act and environmental protection legislation. Corporations have also been "regarded as bearers of natural rights: (1) they are included among the persons referred to in the Fourteenth Amendment to the U.S. Constitution who are not to be deprived of 'life, liberty, or property, without due process of law'; and (2) in 1978 the Supreme Court of the United States upheld the right of corporations to free speech, including the right to promote political ideals through paid advertisements on television and in newspapers."[16]

In legal discourse, corporations are described in terms that clearly ascribe moral agency to them. Corporation A has wrongly claimed certain tax exemptions. Corporation B has deceived the government by shifting domestic profits to a foreign subsidiary. Company C has engaged in wrongful environmental practices, is responsible for damage done, and is liable for payments to correct the situation. Or Company X acted in a socially responsible manner in its affirmative action program. Company Y made the right decision in withdrawing from South Africa. Corporation Z is innocent of willful disobedience of fair employment practices laws.

The moral agency of corporations is taken for granted by the courts. While this agency cannot be equated with the moral agency of individuals and the expectations of the former are not exactly identical with the expectations of the latter, there is sufficient similarity to justify use of the term *moral agency* in both cases.

In Social Scientific Perspective

A second point of view helpful in understanding the corporation as moral agent comes from the social sciences and management sciences. I have already referred to the work of Philip Selznick in which he gives attention to the distinctive pattern of making decisions and acting that can be called *organizational character*. Developing character and exercising character involve choices with reference to value. "The formation of an institution," he writes, "is marked by the making of value commitments, that is, choices which fix the assumptions of policymakers as to the nature of the enterprise — its distinctive aims, methods, and role in the community."[17]

The evolution of the management sciences also gives support to the view of corporations as moral agents. Frederick Taylor contributed the notion that management must take account of the interaction of all elements in the organization. Unhappily, he thought that these elements were rational and that management could become an exact science. Elton Mayo widened this perspective to include such nonrational factors as attention to and concern for the employees. Chester Barnard added the crucial insight that a corporation must be understood as a social organization, human in its wholeness. Values and purposes are central for this perspective, and, in Barnard's view, the task of corporate leadership is, above all, to shape and guide organizational values. Fascination with developing technology and management techniques obscured for a time in the 1960s and 1970s the lessons that could be learned from Taylor, Mayo, Barnard, and, we would add, Selznick. The problems with technique and technical expertise have led to a recovery of those insights from the past in the current attention to corporate culture and values.

The work of Edwin M. Epstein illustrates well this new direction in management science. He points out that much of the difficulty with the notion of corporate social responsibility derives from viewing it only as a *product* rather than understanding it also as *process*. In explaining what this means, he writes:

> Corporate social responsibility can be usefully thought of as a *Process:* a system of decision making whereby corporate managers try to anticipate and consider the *total* consequences of business policies and operations before they act. What managers consider to be relevant to formulating and implementing corporate policy encompasses not only economic factors but also the social, political, environmental, and cultural consequences of corporate action. This broader decision-making transforms social responsibility from a Product to an institutionalized Process. . . . It requires that the firm build into and utilize in key aspects of its normal operating business practices (particularly areas unregulated by government) structures that require it to consider in its decisions criteria once thought "exogenous" or irrelevant. Within the last few years, for example, a number of corporate lenders have begun to review both their loan portfolios and individual loan decisions on the basis of the social consequences of their loan policies.[18]

Terrence Deal and Allan Kennedy in *Corporate Cultures*[19] confirm and extend the conclusions of Peters and Waterman, referred to earlier, that excellence in corporate performance comes about when leaders are able to infuse values into the corporate structures so that a strong culture permeates the entire operation. The emphasis that O'Toole gives to the mutually supporting systems of belief and action in the organizational context of the corporation also sharply illumines the notion of corporate agency and the ethical, moral quality of that agency. Though not dealing with all aspects of the corporation as moral agent, the understanding of corporate culture with its elements of collective values and action that is emerging in the management sciences tends to confirm such a view as a profitable direction of inquiry.

A further development in the social sciences helpful in understanding corporate moral agency is the shift from focus on individual decisions and individual decision makers to emphasis on the corporate policy process and the communal, interactive nature of decision making. Decision making, once treated as though made up of discrete choices by separate individuals, is now seen as the interaction of various units of reflection and decision brought together and integrated in the policy process of an organization. By means of this process, an organization sets priorities, shapes policy, carries out policy through varied forms of implementation, and evaluates the results for purposes of revised or new policies.

Important components of the policy process in a particular corporation may be manufacturing, marketing, personnel, legal, and strategic planning groups, and so on. These groups are related in the formal and informal patterns of management and are governed in their interrelations by explicit rules and tacitly accepted understandings. Top management oversees and relates to all these groups, integrates the information and recommendations coming from them, shapes policy in consultation with those or other persons, and sends out directives for implementation. Corporate policy processes may range from highly centralized or integrated ones to those that appear to be a loose alliance of independent units. By understanding the policy process and the reflection on values that it embodies, we can grasp additional aspects of the corporation as moral agent.

In the Perspective of Ethics

When ethics is understood not as a rigid set of rules to be obeyed but rather as the continuing reflection on the moral significance of action, it becomes clear that persons and organizations are constantly involved in such reflection. Actions are considered, issues are discussed, and alternatives are evaluated.

Corporate moral agency does not consist of adherence to a list of ideal norms. Instead, corporate moral agency refers to that process of choosing certain goals rather than others, selecting means for attaining them, setting standards of performance, guiding implementation, and evaluating results.

To the extent that the diverse elements in the action of a corporation fit together, the organization will have greater moral integrity. When intentions, goals, and performance reinforce, rather than conflict with, one another, a corporation or an organization will function better and with integral wholeness.

Insofar as possible, therefore, the disagreements between the ethics of the corporation and the ethics of the individuals who are a part of it ought to be examined and overcome. Probably all unevenness of fit between individuals and the organization cannot be eliminated. Nevertheless, the reconciliation of individual and corporate ethics will enhance the integrity of employees as well as of the company itself.

In projects the Berkeley group has conducted with executives of corporations and other kinds of organizations, there is often an initial reluctance to discuss ethics because they think it involves applying unrealistic rules from outside business to the policies and choices of the corporate world. Once this roadblock is removed, we discover that each individual brings many ethical convictions to his or her job and that ethical reflection is also going on in the organization — sometimes on an explicit level but more often as a tacit dimension of the policy process.

At the Berkeley Center there is what is called an Executive-in-Residence program. Under this program a corporate executive spends a period of time in Berkeley participating in seminars and projects, speaking to and attending classes in the business schools and in the theological schools, and engaging in reading and discussion about business ethics. The faculty and students involved in the program learn a great deal from these executives, and the experience is apparently instructive for them.

Recently, a top executive from an investment banking firm in New York spent three months, partly at the Berkeley Center and partly at Stanford Business School. In one of the discussions shortly after he arrived, he made it clear that he believed ethics and character applied only to individuals, not to corporations or other groups. Several weeks later, in a seminar session, someone asked him whether in appraising corporations whose stock issues his company might handle he and his colleagues looked only at the ethics and character of the individual executives in the company or also at the corporate ethics and character of the entire company. He thought a moment and replied that, of course, they looked at the total company, not only at the individuals running it. Then he gave an engaging grin and added, "I suppose I've thought in terms of corporate ethics and character all along and have just discovered it." From that point on he was able to provide us with better insights into corporations and their moral agency than we as outsiders could hope to attain on our own. One looks at the corporation's past, at the way it relates to other firms, at its record in affirmative action, at the integrity of its accounting methods and auditing procedures, at the way persons inside the company are treated, and at its awareness of and responsiveness to the changing environment of values in society.

In these ways we can see that the corporation is not only an agent but also a moral agent. In subsequent chapters we shall be exploring more carefully what this means and the impact that ethical reflection as an integral part of corporate moral agency can have on performance.

SUGGESTIONS FOR GROUP STUDY

1. Reread the story about Stan at the beginning of this chapter as an illustration of the clash between personal ethics and the corporate culture. Assign parts to members of your group to play the roles of Stan, the president of the company, the legal counsel for the corporation, the trial judge that sentenced Stan, the warden of the prison where Stan was "rehabilitated," the pastor, and members of Stan's church. See how each of these players interprets the personal ethics of Stan and the corporate culture within which Stan operated. What alternatives were open to each of these persons/groups that would reflect different interpretations of the nature of personal and corporate responsibility in this case?
2. Read *The Champion Way* (Appendix E). It contains a statement of Champion International Corporation about its corporate culture. There is a description of the company's goals in terms of the character of organization it wants to become and how it is working to achieve this goal. Divide into subgroups, each group choosing a company that the members know well. Using the Champion statement as a guide, have each group prepare a profile of the

Suggestions for Group Study / 75

corporate character of that company. Share these profiles in the group and discuss ways of arriving at an understanding of the corporate character. Identify the customs, values, and purposes that exist in the organization and, to the extent possible, the counterparts in the larger society.

3. Read Appendix F, the article by Kirk O. Hanson, "Ethics and Business: A Progress Report." See if you can identify within the profiles of corporate character you have prepared the elements of the three levels of ethical concern that are identified in the Hanson article. In a group session discuss how this form of analysis can be used to build an understanding of the ethical concerns of a corporation you know.

4. Identify the ways in which our society regards, explicitly or implicitly, the role of corporations as moral agents. One way you can approach this is to examine the U.S. government's moves to establish agencies and enact laws designed to control the actions of corporations. Antitrust laws and the Environmental Protection Agency would be among the logical choices. Obtain information from current sources on how these laws and regulatory agencies work to protect various groups from the actions of corporations. Some of your group might want to examine the role of one or several protest groups, such as those that have developed around interest in environmental protection. Discuss the assumptions concerning the nature of the modern corporation underlying these laws, the governmental regulatory agencies, and the actions of protest groups.

Four

FROM SOCIAL RESPONSE TO CORPORATE ETHICS

In spite of the air-conditioning the bright sunlight made the office a little warm. Jim, Ted, and I were trying to decide on a case study for use at the next meeting of the seminar on ethics and corporate policy. The primary participants were 12 top executives and 3 outside directors of a fast-growing multinational company. Jim and I were the outside resource people leading the discussion. Ted was the member of the group who served as our contact person for planning and for communications inside the company.

"What we need," Jim was saying, "is a case study that reflects a moderately hot policy issue that this group is actually facing or has faced recently. And it ought to be near the core of company operations, not peripheral."

"We picked up a few ideas when we talked to each person in the group individually," I added, "but you may have just the right thing on the tip of your mind, Ted."

"I've been giving it some thought since our last discussion. The group is clearly feeling comfortable enough talking among ourselves about ethics and policy decisions to tackle something a little more controversial," Ted replied thoughtfully.

"That's certainly my impression," I said.

"One good possibility is the flap last year with the EPA," Ted suggested.

Jim and I glanced at each other.

"Several people mentioned that in the interviews," Jim observed. "As I recall, you almost got hauled into court about pollution of the river near the Alston plant."

The Crisis of Ethics and Policy / 77

"Well, it's pretty complicated, but you are exactly right about the point where the cookie almost crumbled," Ted said with a slight grimace. "You see, everyone here thought we were complying. We have always tried to do what we've been told to do about the environment. Our public-spirited CEO is chair of CUE — that's Citizens United for the Environment. And I'm sure he means it."

"What happened?" I asked.

"We were complying with information that was out of date. The order went down from on high," Ted explained, nodding across the beautifully carpeted outer office toward the president's inner sanctum, "that we are good environmentalists and that the plant manager should act accordingly. The manager thought he was doing just that, but he's no expert on EPA regulations and followed the wrong guidelines."

"That sounds perfect," Jim said and paused, "unless it's too hot."

"Last year, it was tense around here, but we got through okay. It would still be touchy if that plant manager were going to be in on the discussion, or if we were trying to blame someone here. But we've been doing some soul-searching and know that we need more than well-intentioned general orders." Ted seemed lost in thought for a moment. "I think there are several people with some ideas about what ought to be done."

"If that's so, then it will be exactly right," I replied. "It gets at the matter of whether a corporation wants to be responsible by reacting when some outside group applies pressure or wants to be sufficiently well prepared to stay ahead of the game."

"That's what we'd prefer," Ted affirmed. "We want to be proactive, planning how to shape events rather than reacting to them passively. To do that, we need better capability for looking ahead and preparing people here at headquarters and in all our plants for doing what you call 'managing values.'"

"Let me have the basic information," Jim said, "and I'll draft a case study. Then we'll run it by you, Ted, and anybody else you say to make sure it's got the facts right and raises the issues sharply."

In his recent best-seller, John Naisbitt says we are moving from an "industrial society" to an "information society."[1] The conversation reported above provides a vivid illustration of Naisbitt's point. It also offers a glimpse of a condition that is becoming increasingly prevalent, a challenge that is confronting corporate management today, and a shift that is occurring in companies that want to perform well in times that are fast moving. The case under discussion makes clear not only what Naisbitt calls the *"knowledge theory of value"*[2] — that is, that information is valuable — but also that effective management today requires *information about values* and the *ability to deal with values*.

The leadership of this corporation was aware of the social issue, in favor of protecting the environment, and willing to comply with external pressures to clean up the pollution caused by the company's plant. But there had not been sufficient preparation at the main office or at the plant to carry out the compliance with precision. No provision had been made for assembling well-researched information about the environmental protection laws and the specific ruling with reference to this plant and getting it to the plant manager or for training plant personnel for compliance with environmental regulations. The good intentions of the CEO were not enough. The managers at the level of implementation had not been included in the planning or prepared adequately for responsible action. Intentions at the top must be supplemented with planning, information, communication, and training that are built into the policy process with reference to social issues and with reference to the value dimensions for all policy and implementation.

Because there is increased awareness of the importance of corporate culture and value commitments within a company, the tendency is diminishing to interpret social responsibility as responding to pressures when they occur. The movement is under way toward the development of a corporate ethic. In this chapter we shall explore the reasons for the movement beyond social response toward a corporate ethic that involves a comprehensive proactive position appropriate for management today.

THE CRISIS OF ETHICS AND POLICY

Corporate executives have been discovering that the world is a different and, in crucial respects, a far less simple place for the management of organizations than was the case a few centuries ago or even a few decades ago. The increase of difficulties arises from two fundamental changes that have occurred: the escalation of human problems and the increasing power and complexity of organizations. Each of these changes has contributed to the crisis of ethics and policy felt around the world.

The Escalation of Human Problems

Though the quality of life as compared with the past is greatly improved for many sectors of humanity, modern society faces social problems more numerous and of greater magnitude than ever before. There are the problems of environmental devastation and its threat to human survival; hunger, poverty, and population explosion on a global scale; the emerging shortage of energy and natural resources; inflation and economic instability; political revolution and oppression; competition among nation-states and the threat of nuclear catastrophe; and corruption and mismanagement in those centers of societal power that we might have expected to provide solutions for our mounting problems. It is not so much the case that such problems did not exist earlier as that we are now more vividly aware of them. The information society knows more about problems than it does about solutions. Awareness of difficulties has escalated faster than ways to cope with them.

An additional dimension of the escalation of human problems is the paradox of capability and expectation. Our growing competence in solving problems has produced rising expectations that all problems can and will be solved. Only a few centuries ago, oppressed and deprived peoples accepted their situation as fate. This is no longer the case. Humanity has developed the ability to hope. And this hope not only opens up new possibilities but itself becomes an additional difficulty because it leads humans in all sectors of society to want and anticipate that all our proliferating problems can be solved simultaneously, immediately, and completely. So we face the paradox of increasing hope and mounting despair as our growing ability to solve problems creates a situation of greatly increased expectations that cannot be met. The pressure of the paradox adds intensity to human problems and frustrations.

Regardless of how the current increase of problems may be explained or envisioned as capable of being resolved, there is emerging consensus on these points: first, we are undergoing a great shift in the conditions of human existence and history, a shift with possibilities and perils; second, within a few years we shall all see the world and the organizations in it very differently because our world is becoming characterized by information systems and the values shaping them; third, the challenge to every sector of society has ethical as well as technical dimensions, requires innovative insight, and involves creating a global society with more humane values than exists in any society today; and fourth, underlying the escalation of human problems is the basic question of how to relate ethics and policy in this organized world.

Organizational Power and Complexity

A generation ago Kenneth Boulding described "the organizational revolution" that has taken place in Western society over the past three centuries. This revolution means (1) that the major organizations of modern society exercise great power over the conditions of human living and (2) that these organizations have grown tremendously in numbers and complexity. Boulding points out that many corporations today are larger and have greater impact on more people than do most of the world's nations.[3]

Writing in the same decade as Boulding, Adolph Berle confirmed the view that corporations have great power and asserted that a small group of very large corporations represent well over half of the economy of the United States and that a comparatively tiny number of executives control the policies of these companies. More recently on corporate power, Edwin M. Epstein, with less of the Reform era animus than Berle exhibited, still sees tremendous concentration of power in the hands of corporate management — power that is exercised in all sectors of society: "Given the vital role which corporations currently play and, in the foreseeable future, will continue to play in American society, it is imperative that experts, activists, and citizens alike comprehend realistically the multi-faceted and complex nature of corporate power. Such realistic comprehension is essential to the preservation and advancement of social democracy in the United States."[4]

With this power has come an intricacy of corporate organization that makes control by any particular group uncertain and delineation of responsibility for corporate actions exceedingly difficult. The attempts of the founders of the U.S. republic to develop partial separation among economic, political, and religious forms of power has proved to be a stabilizing element in our U.S. society. The organizational revolution has diminished the distance between these centers of power and created growing problems.

It is not surprising, therefore, to discover that — as a consequence of such change — U.S. society and all the societies of the Western industrial world are currently in the midst of a crisis of values. This crisis has intensely personal dimensions, manifest in confusion over individual identities and in family relationships. On a national and global scale, the crisis finds expression in the urgent quest for greater control over the decisions that shape the social environment and for more adequate resources in improving the quality of life. At stake in the view of many competent observers is the very survival of humanity.

On an organizational level this crisis of values emerges most clearly as a crisis of ethics and policy. We live in a world in which complex organizations exercise massive power. Though the insight and ethical sensitivity of individuals remain important, no solutions can be effective that do not take account of and shape the policies of the major political and economic organizations of national and international society.

The organizational facts of contemporary life mean that even partial solutions are difficult to come by or to put into effect. The complexities of institutional structures in every sector of society obscure the lines of accountability, render almost invisible any social vision related to the whole of humanity and the future, and drastically restrict the alternatives available for action. In home and community and around the globe, we are dependent upon social organizations, but it is increasingly difficult to infuse organizational policy with humane values.

This crisis of ethics and policy, therefore, involves at once a crisis of *responsibility*, with the processes by which policy is shaped often not available to the public forums of accountability; a crisis of *vision*, with very different views of the good society and of social priorities hidden by conflict; and a crisis of *inadequate alternatives*, which appears to bind the future to the limitations of the past.

Responsibility. The crisis of ethics and policy cannot be dealt with apart from confronting the issue of responsibility squarely. In the first place, this means working with those who have the power and therefore the responsibility for shaping the policies of major organizations. In the context of the present discussion, these policymakers constitute the management of corporations. Second, the issue of responsibility refers to the complexity of large organizations and the resulting difficulty of having strong lines of accountability for policy. And third, the issue of responsibility points to the necessity that those who make policy take account of the views of the recipients of organizational policy and listen carefully to protests against the results of corporate policy and action.

Any meaningful discussion of responsibility and of corporate ethics must take place primarily among those people directly charged with shaping policy. The responsibility is theirs in the most immediate way because they are the ones accountable for the results, because they are in a position to know the most about the realities of policy, and because it is the policymakers who have the power to change corporate action.

In organizational situations, it is true, caution, prudence, and groupthink may triumph over innovation and humane sensitivity. So it is important that outsiders through pressure and protest raise ethical issues overlooked by insiders. Revision and enhancement of corporate ethics, however, must ultimately take place within the organization itself, among the community of policymakers, and through changes in the corporate policy process.

Dealing with responsibility for ethics and policy in a realistic manner, therefore, must confront the complexity of modern organizations. Though accountability to humane values has never been a simple matter with reference to the major institutions of society, the problems are compounded today. Because of the intricate structure of large corporations, which are the ones with the most power over the conditions of human living, policy decisions often emerge without any clear locus of responsibility. If the bureaucratic structures necessary to operate complex organizations are added, the issue of accountability becomes even more elusive. It is at this point especially that modern management skills capable of consolidating control over and integrating complex elements of an organization are essential for corporate ethics. Then it becomes possible for management to infuse value commitments throughout a corporation, to build a strong ethos and corporate culture, and to carry out the management of values effectively.[5]

Responsibility on the part of policymakers also requires responsiveness and sensitivity to those outside the policy process who can provide help in evaluating the impact of policy and its implementation. Nothing can undermine the relation of ethics and policy more decisively than a top management that cuts itself off from criticism. Those on the receiving end of policy can offer useful information about policy and its impact. Personnel have an important perspective on personnel policies. Contact with ordinary people and diverse levels of society can broaden executive awareness. Policymakers in business or government who travel only in elitist circles of affluence will be unable to understand the problems of the middle class, much less those of the poor and disadvantaged.

In one company that prides itself on excellent personnel practices and good relations among various layers of management, the CEO had close enough touch with middle management and was a good enough listener to discover a major problem. The policies promulgated by the CEO for evaluation of middle and lower management were completely contradicted by the evaluation procedures actually in use. Rather than reacting defensively, this CEO employed a consultant to investigate and make recommendations. Within a month steps had been taken to ensure that the implementation followed company policy.

Listening can make a company responsive and responsible. Customers have a great deal to teach corporate management about improving marketing policies. When management stops learning from those it intends to serve, it runs the risk of walking away from its base of support. Complaints from ethnic groups, demands from senior citizens, pressure from women for equal treatment — all may assist an alert management to discern problems needing attention. Dealing with protests about business with South Africa or Chile, stockholder resolutions about the environment, or visitations from persons concerned about peace may take time, but they can be helpful indications of problems needing attention, of a shifting climate of values, and of information important for an inclusive corporate ethic. The effective management of values requires wandering enough to get outside the circle of executive groupthink and to widen the horizons of awareness, information, and responsiveness.

Vision. The crisis of ethics and policy is also a crisis of vision. Tunnel vision is no less a problem than complexity and groupthink. As institutions grow, develop wider relationships, and affect increasing numbers of persons and groups with their actions, policymakers may limit attention to their own organization and have difficulty gaining the perspective to see it in relation to other organizations and sectors of society. Short-term values eclipse the longer view; narrow interest crowds out broader concerns; and immediate forums of accountability can obscure a vision of the larger community that will be the ultimate determiner of performance and survival.

Handling baggage at Christmas may not provide new and startling information to Delta executives, but it probably plays a crucial role in preventing their vision from narrowing down to the boardroom. The open offices and peripatetic habits of executives at Hewlett-Packard and Champion International may serve to keep them looking at the larger picture as well as relating them to the wider community inside and outside the corporation. Without inclusive goals and vision of the social whole, it is impossible for policymakers to make short-range decisions that are sound or to appraise adequately the values informing their policies in the midst of a context of conflicting views about the good society and of the right social priorities.

Alternatives. The crisis of ethics and policy is a crisis of limited alternatives, as well. The situation of inadequate alternatives may derive from a sense of being bound to the past, choked by the present, or blind to the future.

First, alternatives may be limited by the conviction that the past and tradition determine what is possible now. Henry Ford was so successful at developing the assembly line and the methods of mass production that he became locked into his own brilliant past. Letting what had been done so well for so long block out new alternatives proved costly for Ford when at last the company was compelled to shut down and engage in massive planning and retooling for a new model. Corporations that constantly consider a much wider range of alternatives than those provided in the past are the ones ready for new demands, new technology, and new values and consequently more likely to perform well under changing conditions.

Second, the limitation of alternatives may come from a constricted view of the present. The demands that are immediate, that are here now in all their complexity, often appear to be so urgent and immense that they close off factors that may be exerting less pressure at the moment but will be of primary importance for performance over the long haul. This overwhelming preoccupation with the present to the exclusion of next week is especially apparent in governmental contexts where political considerations are paramount. Policy in governmental agencies and legislative committees is turned out all too frequently under conditions that consider only the pressures of today and seem to assume there are no tomorrows. But the same politicized atmosphere can be found in corporations and, when present, can serve to obscure creative alternatives and distort the policy process. Policies formulated under such conditions are not only insufficient for the future; they are also inadequate for the present because they fail to consider a spectrum of alternatives that includes preparation today for transition into the future.

Third, limited alternatives may derive from an inadequate view of the future. In any corporation strategic planning and personnel development are central for making policy today. Emerging technology and values are no less important than careful attention to the present environment and to traditions from the past for shaping policy. Making policy is like aiming at a moving target: effective policy requires estimating where the target will be, not where it is now.

This is probably why overbureaucratized corporations have reflexes too slow to perform well and why corporations that make good use of fast-moving ad hoc groups respond most effectively to changing conditions. Because values are changing as rapidly as any other factor in our world, ethical reflection within the corporate policy process can be a primary element in shaping policy toward the future and reminding executives that policy must be aimed at tomorrow. The apparent dilemmas of social responsibility today may disappear as new conceptions of humane values emerge in the future. Conversely, practices and policies that seem acceptable now may be out of step with the values emerging on the horizon of the next decade. A vivid sense of alternative futures and an active imagination can open up new choices and assist in overcoming the limitations that impede and shackle policy-making.

Viewed in these ways, it becomes clear once again that ethics and policy are inseparable. The making of policy always involves evaluation, ethical reflection, and moral choice as well as accurate information and technical expertise. Ethical reflection and evaluation as a constitutive element of the corporate policy process interprets information, sets priorities, and identifies those policies and actions that fit the vision of a good society and a humane future shared by the corporate leadership. The management of values is seen as essential and central, not peripheral, to policy and performance.

CHALLENGE TO INNOVATE

As the crisis of ethics and policy has become apparent in recent decades, it has provided a challenge to leaders in all social organizations to find ways to ensure that these organizations will find new and effective ways through their policies to become more responsible citizens of the human community. Nowhere has the response to this challenge to innovate been more apparent than among leaders in business.

Development of Economic Ethics and Concern for Social Responsibility

Throughout this century, among corporations and corporate leaders there has been a growing sense of responsibility to society and a developing realization that the interests of any group, corporate or consumer, are interwoven with the interests of all. The "robber baron" was real and rampant in the nineteenth century but rare in the twentieth. Even in that age of nearly unbridled capitalism, corporate giants such as John D. Rockefeller, Andrew Carnegie, and Cornelius Vanderbilt did not lack all sense of ethics, as R. H. Tawney has mistakenly charged.[6] Instead, they thought they were pursuing the ethics enjoined by their religious communities. Indeed they were. This ethic, as formulated by John Wesley, the influential founder of Methodism, was: "Gain all you can, save all you can, give all you can."[7] The robber barons were devout church members. They followed the ethics they learned religiously. Unhappily, an ethic that had been appropriate when preached to lower socioeconomic groups in the eighteenth century became destructive when practiced by wealthy industrialists in the nineteenth century. Great principles of love and justice are not meaninglessly relativistic. But they will be irrelevant to reality unless elaborated through criteria and values related to actual conditions of human oppression and need in the present.

In this century there has been a gradual rejection of the ethics of laissez-faire capitalism within the business community itself and a developing sensitivity to issues of economic justice and the rights of labor and minorities. One impressive wave of this concern was manifested in a 15-year project conducted by the National Council of Churches on Ethics and Economic Life. Business leaders, social scientists, and theologians participated in this project that resulted in a series of interesting and distinguished publications, among them Kenneth Boulding's *The Organizational Revolution,* Howard Bowen's *Social Responsibilities of the Businessman,* Marquis Childs and Douglass Cater's *Ethics in a Business Society,* and Victor Obenhaus's *Ethics for an Industrial Age.*

Over the past two decades this growing awareness has been evidenced in the increased number of "corporate responsibility" committees and "vice-presidents for social policy" and in the development of such instruments as the social audit and human resources accounting. While some of this corporate activity derives from outside pressures, much of it also arises from within corporations, partly from persons with deep commitments to social goals and partly from realists who recognize that corporate survival depends on the continuing acceptance of business as legitimate by the general public and on a healthy social environment in the local community, in the nation, and around the globe.

The "social responsibility" movement must be commended for wrestling with such problems as minority hiring and affirmative action, but the concerns associated with social responsibility have most often been those related to the corporation in its daily functions as employer or to the corporation as good citizen.

More and more, however, the challenge to innovate has drawn attention to areas of policy at the core of the operation of the corporation. Here social pressures or intuitive feelings are not enough. Careful development of criteria that can serve for setting priorities, making projections, planning, developing policy, implementing, and evaluating is necessary. The support of extensive information systems is essential. The challenge to innovate involves creating a corporate ethic that permeates the policy process and the entire corporate culture.

Toward Corporate Ethics

The crisis of ethics and policy as represented in the escalation of human problems and in the developing power and complexity of corporations delineates the situation that takes us beyond social response toward corporate ethics. Meeting this challenge requires learning to integrate ethical reflection into the entire corporate policy process and to recognize the ethical dimensions of every step in the making and implementation of corporate policy. The movement is from social response to social responsibility; then from social responsibility to corporate ethics. Attaining a consciously and carefully crafted corporate ethic, however, does not mean leaving social responsiveness and responsibility behind but rather including them in a more encompassing perspective. Let's take a closer look at this movement.

First, there is the pattern of *response* to social values and ethical concerns. A corporation may not deal with the value dimensions of policy on a conscious level because it lets the value judgments take place without consideration, discussion, and deliberate choice. Social issues and values are not avoided in this way. Instead, they impinge on corporate purposes, priorities, policies, and implementation as pressures from the internal or external environment. Management can ignore these pressures when they are weak, but it must respond to them when they are strong. With this pattern, management is dealing with values by reacting when they become powerful.

Second, there is the pattern of *social responsibility*. As different social issues appear and disappear, as pressures from outside and from within the corporation ebb and flow, management may come to realize that it is neither in line with the character of the corporation nor with its interests to continue to ignore the environment of values in which the company and all its employees exist. From a reactive stance, management moves to a position of recognizing issues and values in society and leading the corporate community in taking responsibility for the quality of life in the world around. The corporation self-consciously seeks to become a good citizen and to encourage good citizenship on the part of its members. Corporate social responsibility means contributing time and money to worthwhile community activities. It means taking a stand and, often, action on issues of discrimination in clubs and civic activities. It will require taking action on equal employment opportunity and environmental cleanup ahead of protest pressures and laws. With this pattern the corporation has moved beyond response to responsibility.

Third, there is the pattern of *corporate ethics*. The movement on the part of corporate management from a policy that is primarily reactive to social values toward social responsibility has long been emerging. Now a further movement is under way representing the view that management must be proactive, rather than reactive, in relation to values. No longer, in this view, can corporations afford to let groups external to management take complete charge of setting the agenda of values. Management must take the initiative in developing criteria for ordering priorities and lifting up issues for attention and action. Rather than merely responding to pressure or taking responsibility in community affairs, management develops a corporate ethic that controls corporate policy and participates in shaping societal values. Once this pattern is adopted, it becomes apparent that corporate ethics is applicable to the entire range of policy and implementation in the company and not only to issues on the edges of the firm's central operations. Whereas social responsibility tends to deal with issues and to use mechanisms that are on the periphery of the corporate structure, corporate ethics begins with the top management, deals with the central apparatus of the policy process, and concerns the entire range of corporate action from the center outward to the edges and from the boardroom to the factory floor.

From response to responsibility to ethics is a movement requiring attention to corporate culture on the part of executive leadership and to control exercised through value commitments. Corporate ethics requires increased initiative on the part of management in dealing with the value dimensions of corporate policy and performance. To develop a corporate ethics does not neglect what is going on in society. On the contrary, a corporate ethic carefully and consciously scans the external and internal environments of values. Nor does the movement to corporate ethics imply any diminution of social responsibility. Instead, it means that the task of managing values is taken no less seriously with reference to the core activities and operations of the company than with reference to the issues on the periphery of the corporate policy process. In subsequent chapters we shall explore the ways in which corporate ethics includes responsiveness and responsibility, while at the same time dealing with the value judgments and criteria related to the totality of policy and its implementation.

A Triad of Resources

In order to develop corporate ethics effectively, it is necessary to utilize diverse resources. Some of these resources are to be found among academics and from specialized disciplines. Other resources must come from the experience of persons actually working in societal, organizational contexts.

The ethical reflection involved in social policy and the policy processes of complex organizations is the concern of a wide range of people, all of whom can contribute to the development of corporate ethics:

1. In a fundamental and primary sense, policymakers and the persons affected most directly by policy and its implementation;
2. Scholars in social ethics and policy ethics, especially those with interest in and experience related to large organizations; and
3. Social scientists in studies related to corporations and their operation — management scientists, economists, organizational behavioral specialists.

The development of corporate ethics depends on having this spectrum of persons not only present but also committed to the project and involved with one another. Each person and group has a crucial part of the whole — but still only a part. For these parts to interact fruitfully, there must be mutual learning and mutually interrelated inquiry. The method for this enterprise, therefore, can be called a *triadic methodology,* involving at its heart the mutual learning and inquiry among ethicists, social scientists, and persons directly a part of the policy arena.

Another way to express the triad is by speaking of the need to combine *commitment, expertise,* and *power* in order to overcome the crisis of ethics and policy and to move toward the development of effective corporate ethics. Commitment may belong to any or all of those in the three groups. Each sector has its own particular expertise to contribute. And though policymakers are in a special position to exercise power in the arena of policy and its implementation, it is also clear that each group possesses important elements of power, as the recognition of the power of knowledge and know-how underscores. Moral imagination is always a quality in demand when the ethical dimensions of policy are at stake. Technical expertise, as well as careful analysis, is always needed. The same can be said for information and the value judgments by which data are gathered and refined for information systems. And none of these is effective without the continuing commitment to responsible action.

The need for interaction in this triadic methodology may seem obvious, but it also needs emphasis. Ethical reflection that takes place at a distance from the realities of social process can make little contribution to policy. Social scientific inquiry about public issues and processes will have little relation to or effect upon policy if isolated from the locations where policy is shaped and from the ethical reflection that can inform its values and its purposes, placing the collection and analysis of information by the social scientists within the context of personal knowing. At the same time, the making of policy is at best inadequate and at worst destructive if not informed by good technical information, by precise understanding of social processes, and by an inclusive moral vision. Thus the triadic approach requires the *fusion* of the varied perspectives and power represented in this multiple approach. Nothing less is demanded by the crisis of ethics and policy and the need today for corporate ethics.

Even though the need for this triad of resources may be apparent, it must not be assumed that it can be assembled and utilized easily. Academic specialists are isolated from one another. The jargon of their disciplines makes it difficult for them to work closely or even converse with other specialists with reference to inclusive human problems. The difficulty is compounded by the separation created by living and working in differentiated sectors of society, so that the corporate executive has difficulty understanding the perspective of academics, and they are usually too involved in their disciplinary theories to listen closely to practitioners.

Because these diverse resources are crucial for corporate ethics, it is worth the time, patience, and effort to gather them together and enable them to interact productively with one another. First, there must be an interest on the part of those from each sector in working together. Second, there must then be a willingness to listen to one another and learn from one another. And third, there must be the hard work of developing a common language and integrated perspectives. When these are accomplished, it becomes possible to develop the criteria, the policy research, and the realistic insight necessary for policy ethics adequate for contemporary corporations.

DEALING WITH THE WEB OF SOCIAL VALUES

Several years ago, the president of a forest products company told me that his corporation wanted to be more responsible for the environment but could not afford to do so if competing companies were not. What was required, he said, were laws that would apply to all companies, and his company was taking the initiative to get such laws enacted. This corporation was shifting from the practice of responding to external forces, while privately deploring damage to the environment, toward the development of a corporate ethic that would guide it in taking action to reshape the world around. This president was learning to manage values.

When we speak of the *management of values,* we are not talking about attempting to manipulate values. Manipulating values is probably impossible, though advertising may create the temporary illusion that it can be done. Instead, we are talking about management that is *aware* of the environment of values in which it operates, develops its own *criteria for action* rather than merely responding to pressures, builds *institutional support* for its corporate ethics, and takes responsibility for continuing *evaluation of performance* in order to improve its policies and their implementation. There is a great difference between leadership that simply responds to societal pressures as they occur and leadership that develops a corporate ethic. The difference is made possible through learning to manage values.

As we speak of values in relation to the development of corporate ethics, we must remember that values are not static entities. Values must be understood as an integral dimension of the shifting terrain of contemporary human life. Change, rapid change, is occurring today on every level of society and in every part of the world. The most obvious area where change is occurring at an incredible rate is technology. An adult today has witnessed more technological change than had occurred in all previous human history. Underlying changes in technology and all other forms of change, however, are the dramatic shifts taking place in social values.

The world will not be the same next week. Vast changes will continue to occur over the next years and decades. Policies based only on the urgencies of today will certainly be outdated in the near future. The rapidity and global scope of change can overwhelm leadership and lead to serious crises. Getting on top of the situation, not only with reference to technology and techniques but also with reference to changing values, is a central issue for corporate leadership today. Sound organizational policy requires anticipation of change, especially in the area of human values.

In the chapters that follow, we shall be examining in more detail various aspects of the management of values in relation to social change. Let us look briefly at the central elements.

Awareness

"Managers today," writes Archie Carroll, "are at the center of a complex web of values. These values come from such external sources as religion, philosophy, culture, the law, and the professions. In addition, internal forces in an organization affect the manager's values and actions. These forces include the authority structure, loyalty, conformity, and pressure for results." In spite of the complexity, Carroll believes that the problem of improving ethics in business can be addressed — that "business ethics can be influenced, shaped, and, in fact, managed."[8]

The first and basic element in the management of values is recognizing and taking careful account of the environments of values within which the corporation operates, both internal and external. No business could begin or continue for long if those in charge had no awareness of the context of wants, interests, and concerns in the surrounding society. Selling air conditioners in the Yukon may be a good test of sales skills, but it exhibits deplorable knowledge of the territory — the physical climate as well as the climate of values. Evaluation of the reliability of clients is an elementary part of this awareness. The environment of values as represented in laws is also fundamental. So also are the mores and customs of the community.

Beyond those in the society around, there are other contexts of values needing attention. Internally, companies can learn to be sensitive to the feelings and interests of minority groups. The values of employees have taken on increasing importance in a time when labor has become active and powerful. On a global basis, if a corporation plans to operate in other cultures, it must take pains to understand the environment of values embodied in what may be an unfamiliar culture and to integrate that understanding into policy. Across national lines, in different sections of a country as large as the United States, and even within a corporation itself where diverse groups are employed, there are the problems of plural values and how to shape policy in the light of these differences. Learning to manage values demands a high level of awareness.

Criteria for Action

The situation of changing values makes effective management difficult, especially given the plurality of values confronting policymakers and the consequent diverse directives and crosscurrents of pressure to which corporations are subjected.

Does management simply play a passive role and respond to the varied pressures from government and activist groups? Or does it take on a more active role? Becoming proactive requires developing criteria and clear objectives. It means shifting from social response to corporate ethics. Instead of adjusting to the crosscurrents of social directives, becoming proactive requires learning the management of values.

After taking account of the environment of values in some depth, ethical reflection must relate the surrounding values to the purposes and interests of the corporation and develop criteria and guidelines to be used in making and implementing policy. Undoubtedly, such reflection is going on in the management of every business and must go on for it to survive. The question is one of improving this ethical reflection by recognizing it, expanding the resources and information on which it draws, and giving increasing attention to the formation of criteria for action and applying them in the corporate policy process.

Institutionalization

If the management of values is to be developed beyond a corporate ethic operative in the thinking and discussion of top executives, it must become institutionalized and develop institutional support. In one way *institutional support* refers to the information systems by which management extends its knowledge of the external and internal environments of values and enlarges its capabilities to examine the results of its policies upon various sectors of society. In another way *institutional support* refers to the patterns for communicating values and drawing diverse constituencies into the processes of value management and corporate ethics. Building a strong corporate ethos and culture is crucial. So also is bringing various levels within the corporation into the information systems and making them aware of the criteria on which policy and action are based. Not only will policy be understood and implemented better, but there will also be opportunity for additional input that can substantially improve policy and performance.

In a sense the development of institutional support moves in the direction of participative management and a certain amount of decentralization. It does not, however, imply massive decentralization of the place where final decisions are made within the policy process. Rather, it is (1) a movement toward greater coherence and integrity in the processes by which policy is made and implemented and (2) improvement of those processes by means of an increased flow of information, up and down, that represents more input from appropriate levels.

Evaluation of Performance

The final component in the management of values involves careful, continuing evaluation of the quality and results of policy and its implementation. On the one hand, this means getting feedback in order to see whether what was intended actually happened. On the other hand, it is developing information on the basis of which the criteria used in making policy can be reevaluated and revised. Different results may occur from those anticipated; there may be good or bad effects in unexpected directions; or the consequences wanted may indeed happen but not look as good once they actually appear as were the hopes when the policy was planned. Internal response and performance as well as external results need evaluation. Though no one wants a major crisis to occur, the Tylenol poisoning tested the strength of Johnson & Johnson's corporate culture and provided a superb opportunity for evaluating the company's performance in all its dimensions.

In addition, performance and the policies shaping corporate action must be formulated and evaluated within the context of the global as well as the national economy. Few corporations, even those that are not transnational in organization, can say that they are not influenced by the global economy or that they have no impact upon the international scene. So evaluation of performance must take into account the network of relationships extending into the surrounding society and beyond into the worldwide environment.

In all these ways effective leadership in the corporation, rather than being pushed around by changing contexts, must develop ways to perceive the internal and external environment of values clearly, to take initiative in shaping these environments, to utilize ethical reflection in the making and evaluation of policy, and thus to enhance performance through the management of values.

SUGGESTIONS FOR GROUP STUDY

1. Using the conversation at the beginning of this chapter as a base, prepare a recommendation to the management of that corporation on the policy it should adopt in relating its environmental decisions to the realities of the outside world. Identify the relationship of this policy to existing governmental regulations and to the responsibilities of the corporation to communities where its plants are located. How do you perceive the "environment of values" that must be recognized in formulating this policy? Use the results as a basis for group discussion.
2. Assume that you have been retained to advise the president of a corporation with which you are familiar on how he or she might better keep in touch with the value shifts in the groups of importance to the corporation. How would you help this president to identify the groups involved? By what means can contact with these groups be best maintained? What are the ways of identifying the changes in values of these groups? How should the corporation organize to respond most effectively to the shifts that affect its policies and performance? How should the CEO monitor progress? Develop your recommendations to be used as a basis for group discussion of the ideas contained in this chapter.
3. Read the minicase in Appendix G on Aetna Life and Casualty Company's sponsorship of community redevelopment in Chicago. In discussing this case, consider the difference between response to pressure and the "management of values" at Aetna as they apply to this situation. Would a comprehensive ethic have helped Aetna in its decisions? Given the current situation, what should Aetna do now to put its good intentions into practice?

Five

A COMPREHENSIVE ETHIC FOR CORPORATE POLICY

Jason was an outside member of the board of directors of a large manufacturing corporation. Dick and I had been talking with him primarily about his relation to its management policy and what he thought were the major ethical issues needing discussion in the company. Toward the end of the interview, the conversation turned toward his own position as CEO of a major utility.

"You're making me realize that we do a lot more ethical reflection at my own shop than I thought," he was saying.

"In what way?" I asked.

"I suppose I've considered ethics as limited to clear-cut moral issues like bribery or price-fixing," Jason responded slowly. "But I'm beginning to see that value judgments and choices are going on all the time, and they involve ethics, too."

"Give us an illustration of what you mean," Dick said.

"I could give quite a few. The most important one that occurs to me immediately is all the thought and investigation and wrestling with alternatives that go into our choices about sources of electrical power."

"Do you mean whether or not to build nuclear plants?" I queried.

"Oh, it's much more complicated than that. You and many other people may disagree, but I'd build them again. We haven't had any trouble with ours."

He paused for a moment in thought and then continued, "Coal is the cheapest source now, and that's what we were using not too long ago. But we began to be worried about the pollution of the atmosphere long before the environmental people became vocal. We had already been shifting to oil. Then the information came along about acid rain, and we stopped using coal completely."

"But there have been problems with oil, too, haven't there?" I asked.

"That's putting it mildly," Jason replied. "The cost of oil went sky-high, and there were times when we weren't sure we could get enough. We can, of course, pass the cost on to the consumer, but we don't want to cause hardship for low-income people. The shortage really alarmed us. Fortunately, we were ready with a nuclear energy plant and then another one not long after. So we were able to keep the cost down, have a reliable source, and avoid pollution."

"Aren't nuclear reactors dangerous?" I persisted. "Why not use solar energy?"

"Solar energy is out of sight at present so far as cost is concerned," he responded. "The public wouldn't accept it. Maybe it will be a better solution further down the road. From the perspective of balancing all the different values and disvalues, the dangers of nuclear power do not seem high."

"I hope you're right," I said.

"Apart from specific issues on which we may or may not agree, you helped me see that managing involves weighing alternative values against one another. It's impossible to have every good thing simultaneously. Cheap, plentiful, nonpolluting energy sources that are completely safe — they don't exist in that ideal combination. At every level of management, we are constantly balancing one value against another, one cost against another, and trying to discover what set of trade-offs preserves most of the values we want. It's not a world where we can satisfy everyone, especially the single-issue groups that want their *particular* value utilized and forget the others."

"Yes, judgments that demand balancing values and making difficult trade-offs require careful attention by management," I added.

"I agree," Jason replied. "That kind of evaluation is going on all the time in companies. It needs to be recognized and accepted as an integral part of making policy. When that is done, I suppose it could be called a corporate ethic."

As the Berkeley group conducted projects with different types of organizations and learned from the executives in these organizations the value judgments operative in making and implementing policy, the components of a comprehensive ethics for corporate policy began to emerge. Not all of these elements are utilized by every policymaker in all of the corporations with which we have worked. Some of the elements emerged easily and with clarity. Others had to be extracted through careful listening with an ear capable of transferring what was said into the language of ethics.

Whether discovered effortlessly or with painstaking care, it became clear that value judgments permeate the policy process of all organizations at every level of management. Ethical consideration takes place in various ways. What may come as a surprise to many outsiders is the depth of concern we found present in most cases about human well-being, even when the methods for integrating this concern carefully and critically into the policy process were not well developed.

One of the strangest anomalies to be observed on the social scene in the United States is the contrast between the conviction of social activists that corporate executives have no operative ethics and are interested only in financial profit and the firm belief of most corporate leadership that they are carefully ethical and responsible. Our investigations disclosed that both are partly right.

Corporate leaders in Western societies have been shaped by the same religious communities and context of social values as have the activists. Executives and activists have similar value commitments but interpret them from within different institutional locations. Activists correctly perceive that corporate leaders do not have the same priorities, purposes, and perception of results as do they. The differences are likely to be less significant with reference to overall principles than in regard to the best ways for realizing them.

The activists are often self-righteous and ethnocentric in their understanding of ethics. Persons committed to social causes are sometimes of the firm, if unreflective, conviction that ethics requires thinking about right and wrong, good and evil, in exactly the way they do. Persons who have other ideas are "unethical." The insight that Muslims and Buddhists are not irreligious and unbelieving because their religious believing differs from our own has not penetrated deeply into the thinking of many people about ethics. When Socrates asks Euthyphro what it means to act with piety, Euthyphro responds with naive certainty that it is doing what he is doing. The ethical sophistication of some of the most committed social activists has not advanced significantly beyond that point.

Corporate executives, as a result, frequently find themselves cast in the role of villain. One executive, an active and devout Christian, an elder in his local Presbyterian church, tells of representing the corporate perspective at a regional church meeting called to discuss the marketing of baby formula in the underdeveloped sectors of the world. Though in sympathy with much of the criticism leveled at Nestlé this executive wanted to view the issues in terms of realistic business policy. Before he opened his mouth, however, he found himself regarded as evil. Business was looked upon by many attending the meeting as unethical. Like this executive, other business leaders who have ethical sensitivities often find themselves excluded by definition before the discussion of social issues begins. Further, corporate managers have a different terminology for talking about policy and are unaccustomed to using terms familiar to the social activists. Even when both want to bring ethics more overtly into the policy process of corporations, they may lack a common language to discuss the values and goals they share.

On the other hand, the pressure that activists bring to bear upon corporations as well as other institutions is often helpful in bringing issues to the attention of the public and awakening the sensitivities of policymakers. Executives are sometimes as hasty in condemning activists as irresponsible, as activists are in regarding policymakers as amoral or immoral.

Bribery, fraud, price-fixing, and kickbacks do occur, and the public needs to know about them. They are frequently covered by the press and "make news" — perhaps because such stories sell newspapers and increase TV ratings. We need the reporting of such things by a free press, but we ought not to be blind to the ambiguous aspects of private enterprise in the media as well as in industry. We must remember that the misdeeds of persons in our society become interesting and "newsworthy" only against the background of a majority who go faithfully about their jobs. The more impressive part of the business story, therefore, is that goods are produced, things needed for a decent standard of living find their way onto supermarket shelves and into homes, persons are provided with work to do and a livelihood so they can live with some dignity, and most managers go about their tasks with reasonable efficiency and uninteresting honesty.

This chapter reports — in the form of a comprehensive ethics for corporate policy — what corporate managers say about the criteria they use in making policy. In subsequent chapters, we shall explore how such an ethics becomes operative and can have a major impact on effective performance.

CRITERIA FOR CORPORATE ACTION

Kenneth Boulding says that in the light of the organizational revolution that has taken place in Western society, "the basic question is by what standards do we appraise institutions" and their policies?[1] This is a crucial problem for our entire world. It is critical for those who seek to manage large organizations, manage them well, and ensure their continuing responsibility and legitimacy. We turn now, therefore, to criteria applicable in the policy processes of corporations.

Ethical reflection and criteria have important roles in the moral life and decisions of individuals. It is equally true that ethical reflection and the development of criteria for action are central for corporations as moral agents. An organization is not an individual human being. But organizations confront ethical issues, must choose among alternative courses of action, develop criteria for setting purposes and priorities, make policy, and implement it at various levels of management. The contexts, problems, and policy processes of an organization are different from the comparable components of moral agency for an individual, but both are moral agents.

The ethical perceptions and convictions of key persons in a corporation exercise a more powerful role in the reflection and action than do the views of junior levels of management or peripheral constituencies. The CEO will probably have the strongest influence on the criteria for corporate action at any given moment, far more than a foreman in a plant or a secretary in the personnel office. The directors will exercise great influence over a period of time and, if they do not approve of the values of the CEO, can replace that person.

While those with the top positions exercise the greatest influence on overall policy, persons at every level have impact and often can alter or frustrate the intentions of senior policymakers. In a graduate institution of higher education with which I was at the time associated, it was discovered that a person in the admissions office had been routinely classifying as "rejected" the applications of fat people, regardless of their academic qualifications. When the practice was discovered, the person said that fat people were obviously undisciplined and therefore unsuitable for advanced academic study. Needless to say, this unintended policy was changed but not before it had been operative for several years.

No one person alone defines the operative ethics of an organization. Especially powerful personalities that have put their imprint upon a corporation in the past continue to shape its culture and its value commitments in the present. Those in charge of planning and the persons responsible for personnel selection and development have great valence in shaping purposes and priorities. All these people and factors, some with greater power than others, interfacing together create the range of influences, pressures, constraints, and possibilities making up the corporate policy process. With its components of reflection on values and its development of criteria for action, the policy process is governed by a corporate ethic.

The present challenge is to understand better the concepts and methods of ethical reflection applicable to organizations and the ways an ethic permeates a community of policymakers. The following criteria for action are those we have found to be actually operative in the planning, development, and implementation of corporate policy. It is unlikely that these criteria will be discussed overtly or extensively. They have emerged as top executives have interacted with ethicists, social scientists, and other executives about the valuing that underlie policy.

THE ETHICS OF CORPORATE SELF-INTEREST

One of the most basic and pervasive ethical perspectives shaping corporate policy is the self-interest of the corporation as an organization. Most often self-interest is expressed in terms of the priority of profits, productivity, and survival. Economists such as Milton Friedman, and his disciples, hold that this is the only valid purpose of the corporation. He writes:

> The view has been gaining widespread acceptance that corporate officials and labor leaders have a "social responsibility" that goes beyond serving the interest of their stockholders or their members. This view shows a fundamental misconception of the character and nature of a free economy. In such an economy, there is one and only one social responsibility of busi-

> ness — to use its resources and engage in activities designed to increase its profits so long as it stays within the rules of the game.... It is the responsibility of the rest of us to establish a framework of law such that an individual in pursuing his own interest is, to quote Adam Smith again, "led by an invisible hand to promote an end which was no part of his intention.... By pursuing his own interest, he frequently promotes that of the society more effectually than when he really intends to promote it."...
>
> Few trends could so thoroughly undermine the very foundations of our free society as the acceptance by corporate officials of a social responsibility other than to make as much money for their stockholders as possible.[2]

This view, which may be called the position of *classical liberalism* or *laissez-faire capitalism,* holds that the pursuit of self-interest is not only a desirable endeavor but also an ethical imperative. The rules of the game that Friedman mentions with the self-assured innocence of an academic specialist loom larger in our past than he seems to suppose. Adam Smith was a professor not of economics but of moral philosophy who placed self-interested humanity in a social, moral, and theological context as well as an economic one. His views are distorted and rendered incomprehensible when reduced to laissez-faire economic dogma. Still further, though self-interest played a prominent role in shaping the capitalist economic system, it has never been permitted to operate in the marketplace or in any sector of society apart from laws, customs, and moral norms. These controls mean that a laissez-faire economic system has never existed in the industrial nations. Even so, the times have changed. The mixed political economies of the contemporary world are even more highly regulated than they were in the days of Andrew Carnegie and John D. Rockefeller, Sr. Neither in the past nor today is an ethic of self-interest to be identified with a laissez-faire economy.

To understand what it means now to speak of self-interest as a component of corporate ethics, we must be clear (1) that self-interest is a valid element in most ethical traditions, (2) that the mixed political economies of today have environments of values far different from those of the nineteenth century, and (3) that the corporate self and its interests need not be interpreted in the most crass and narrow sense. Once the inadequacy of views like Friedman's are clarified, it becomes possible to understand self-interest as an important and valid element in a corporate ethic.

The Western Tradition of Ethics and Self-Interest

There is an ethical theory that regards self-interest as inherently unethical. The ethics of Immanuel Kant holds that only a good will is good and that anything pertaining to interest or consequences must be excluded from ethics. This theory has given rise to a line of philosophical ethics that would reject not only self-interest but also any kind of ethics relying, like utilitarianism, on results.

This attempt to exclude self-interest rests upon a rational authoritarianism with little basis in the longer traditions of ethics in West or East, religious, theological, or philosophical. Prudence, or practical wisdom, as a virtue permeated by caution, self-interest, and reliance on consequences is a prominent theme in the ethics of Plato and Aristotle, in the wisdom stream of ethics in the Jewish and Christian scriptures, and in Roman ethics. It is a strong motif in Hindu and Buddhist ethics. And, though not regarding it as the highest good, Jesus includes self-interest in the ethics he teaches when he enjoins humans to love God and to love their neighbors as themselves. In the Middle Ages and in the modern period, Christian ethics has, except where it has come under the rationalistic influence of Kant, continued to include prudence and self-interest within the scope of ethics.

The Emergence of Mixed Political Economies

Adam Smith, who taught moral philosophy or ethics, formulated the best-known version of the ethic of self-interest. In opposition to the view that the government ought to control economic activity, a view known as *mercantilism,* Smith put forward the position that the wealth of societies will develop more rapidly if individuals are permitted and urged to pursue their own self-interest in the marketplace. Smith was also convinced, as the quote from Smith given above by Friedman indicates, that individual pursuit of self-interest in commerce is more likely to produce good for the entire community than if merchants set out to improve society.

Smith's economic teachings must be related to his moral philosophy, which understands humans as subject to sin yet having moral sentiments built into their nature, and to his theology, which views the natural order and history under the governance of God. His economic analysis helped the emerging bourgeois merchant class break the control of mercantilism and develop a strong industrial order. On this economic basis, corporations as legal individuals proliferated, grew in size and power, and greatly enlarged the wealth of the North Atlantic nations, just as Smith had predicted. The expanded access to commercial enterprise that was opened to large sectors of society excluded by federalism and mercantilism, together with the productivity of the factories, raised the standard of living enormously for a significant portion of the population in Western nations. The economic power accompanied and reinforced the democratizing drive toward republican government. At the same time, through the religious awakenings of the eighteenth and nineteenth centuries, the emerging middle class became active participants in religious communities, imbued with a deepening social conscience. Reform movements were organized to help the poor and oppressed. Slavery was abolished. Action to protect the laboring classes was undertaken, with special attention to women and children, who in laws and customs held over from feudal society had no legal rights. Economically, politically, and socially, the nineteenth century was a time of change and of emerging liberation consciousness in the nations of western Europe and North America. As a leader in this movement, the United States was looked to as the land of freedom and a new power that had — through the Monroe Doctrine — contributed directly to the political liberation of Latin America and the beginning of its movement out of the oppressive feudal structures imposed by European conquerors. The nineteenth century was bright with human hope, and liberal capitalism was an important element fueling the liberation movement.

The economic developments in the nineteenth century, however, as shaped by governmental, societal, and religious norms, produced results that were unanticipated and, for many, unwanted. First, the factory system delivered thousands of families from rural poverty but enslaved them in oppressive working and living conditions in the growing slums of the industrial cities. Second, the thriving economies of western Europe needed raw materials for their factories, and the race for colonial possessions became increasingly obsessive and oppressive. Third, the growth of business enterprises, a major achievement of liberal economics, threatened to destroy itself through monopoly control by corporate leviathans and to undermine the movements struggling for economic and political liberation. The incredible energies released and shaped by economic self-interest became overheated and dangerous.

As a result, in the late nineteenth century new limitations and modifications of economic operations were added to those already existing; the movement continued and escalated in the twentieth century. Antitrust, antimonopoly laws were enacted. Regulatory agencies began to proliferate. Social legislation was passed defining the rights of various groups and setting limits on corporate activities. The rights of children, women, labor, and ethnic groups were gradually established and supported by laws and voluntary societal groups. In Europe, socialist political movements modified the emergent capitalism and produced the mixed political economies existing today in every industrialized country. Private enterprise remained a central element in every First World economy, more important in the United States than in most other nations, but in various forms it was the mixed system that prevailed.

Laissez-faire perspectives remain as a never-realized ideal of classical economists. Most corporate executives, even those who prefer greater emphasis on private enterprise, still accept the mixed political economies that have developed over the past century. Most share in considerable measure the view that human rights are to be protected and corporations should contribute in their operation to the well-being of the entire society. The views of Milton Friedman are not held by many business leaders, though some may think he serves as a corrective to excessive governmental control of the economy, and corporations do not operate according to his notion that the only valid purpose is increased profits. The government does not let them operate that way. Social pressure compels corporations to have mixed goals. And corporate leaders, as family members and citizens, make sure that diverse purposes inform corporate policy.

Once all this is said, it remains true that self-interest is a valid element in human ethics and, viewed in relation to other ethical perspectives and purposes, is a crucial component of a comprehensive corporate ethic. It is essential that corporate leadership define clearly and explicitly what the interests of the corporation are and how these are to be carried out in corporate policy and action. So these questions remain: What is the corporate self that has interests? And what precisely are its real and appropriate interests?

The Corporate Self and Its Interests

When we understand the corporation as a moral agent with a history, with a present culture and character, and with policies and purposes that are projecting it into the future, the shape of a corporate self emerges. As with an individual, the selfhood of an organization derives from many factors in the past and present. Yet these elements, inseparably combined in an agent and its action, add up to a character that interprets, plans, and acts in fairly dependable ways. Every organization has its distinctive sense of who it is, and the persons who staff that organization, especially its leaders, are aware of serving that collective identity and, in the process, modifying it.

Corporations with "strong" cultures, as noted by many observers, have the ability to impress upon those working within them their own distinctive value commitments and to render these commitments clearly visible through corporate actions and overall performance. Wells Fargo Bank exemplifies a corporation with a powerful sense of identity that influences those who manage the organization. The sense of corporate selfhood is exhibited in the policies of the bank and maintained as a proud and worthwhile heritage. There is a Wells Fargo character that typifies the way its leaders think and act as members of this corporate community. Part of this selfhood has been shaped by leaders of the recent past like Richard Cooley and Ernest Arbuckle. But the corporate character of Wells Fargo was already embodied in a tradition that they inherited and that those who have succeeded them continue in changing form.

The interests of a corporation will be interpreted and implemented in accord with this selfhood and its character. "Quality, Service, Cleanliness, and Value" are part of the self-interest of McDonald's, along with making a profit, because founder Ray Kroc built them into the selfhood and character of the organization. The "HP Way" at Hewlett-Packard, the impact of the Haas Family on Levi Strauss, and the "Champion Way" at Champion International represent in different ways what those corporations are, what they are becoming, and thus what their interests are. The tampon "shock-syndrome" crisis at Procter & Gamble and the Tylenol "arsenic-poisoning" crisis at Johnson & Johnson revealed strong corporate characters that defined their interests *with* the public interest, willing to confront the situation as honestly as possible and prepared to take major losses in order to discover what was wrong and to ensure safety.

Practically speaking, self-interest and concern for the public interest go together in corporate operation. No one would buy the products of a company that had lost credibility. A business that does not interpret its interests in relation to those of its customers and potential customers is probably headed for trouble.

In one of the corporate ethics projects conducted by the Berkeley Center, Arjay Miller, former president of Ford Motor Company and then dean of Stanford Graduate School of Business, was an enthusiastic participant. Self-interest, in the view that he defended vigorously, is the basic and the only component of a corporate ethic. But the interests of the self, he maintained, can be interpreted in a narrow sense or in a larger and more enlightened sense. Only a thoroughly enlightened understanding of self-interest that includes the interests of customers and various publics as well as the interests of shareholders and management, in Miller's view, is adequate and realistic for the modern corporation.

Even in these dimensions, self-interest does not seem able to encompass all the crucial components of a corporate ethic. But Miller's view does underscore that interests can be crass or enlightened and will be interpreted in terms of the selfhood and character that shape the management and the policy-making process of the company.

In summary, we will do well to recall these words from the 1950s:

> Corporate business must still consider profits, and it has an obligation to do as well by its equity investors as it reasonably can. But when economic theorists describe business as "maximizing profits," they are indulging in an impossible and unrealistic degree of precision. The farther a firm's policies extend into the future, the less certain can it be just what policy

> will precisely "maximize profits." The company is more likely to be consciously concerned with reasonably assured survival as a paramount aim, and beyond this, to formulate its governing policies in terms of some such concept as "sound business," usually contributory to healthy growth. . . .
>
> Where there is this margin of uncertainty as to precisely what policy would "maximize profits," there is room for management to give the benefit of the doubt to policies that represent good economic citizenship. And it seems that an increasing number of managements are giving increasing weight to this kind of consideration.[3]

To the extent that the corporate self is understood as existing within and dependent upon the society around it, its interests will be interpreted in terms of the responsibility of the company to varied groups, inside and outside the organization. We come then to a second major component of corporate ethics.

THE ETHICS OF MULTIPLE RESPONSIBILITY

In recent years corporations have increasingly, in their policy processes and actions, acknowledged and recognized their responsibilities to diverse groups involved with or affected by the actions of the company. Legislation and governmental policy have been among the most visible and powerful instruments in shaping the nature and extent of these corporate responsibilities. Behind, and often in addition to, government action, there have been public pressure groups lobbying lawmakers and bringing issues to the attention of corporate officials. Underlying the pressure groups, however, has been the shift in the social environment of values that gives rise to movements of change. It must be remembered that governmental officials and corporate managers exist within this social environment, just as do those who organize pressure groups focused on particular issues. Awareness and concern about emerging issues such as ecology, pollution, and human rights are present within governmental and business organizations as well as represented in public interest groups. It is this combination of internal and external responsibility that usually leads to action.

In many instances corporate management has moved only in response to action by government or to pressure from outside groups. But the change will seldom occur unaccompanied by similar concerns among persons within the corporate policy process. In some cases persons related to corporations or corporations themselves may participate in securing legislation in order to ensure that all companies of a particular class will have to comply in taking certain socially desirable actions. Then no one company will be in an unfair competitive position by taking the action on its own. This may be an effective way to discharge responsibility to shareholders and employees as well as to society and the natural order. "Many aspects of corporate impact on the environment and on society," write Henry Manne and Henry Wallich, "can indeed best be handled by legislation. Corporate management would be well-advised to give support to well-designed legislation.... Appropriate support would be one form of discharging its responsibility."[4]

The relationships between a corporation and the many groups affected by its actions involve value judgments and ethical reflection. A corporation that actively considers the needs and claims of those who in some way receive the impact of its policies or to whom there is some form of accountability is pursuing the ethics of multiple responsibility. One way to formulate multiple responsibility is through the concept of *stakeholders*. In a book focused upon the importance of this notion for management, R. Edward Freeman writes: "Simply put, a stakeholder is any group or individual who can affect, or is affected by, the achievement of a corporation's purpose. Stakeholders include employees, customers, suppliers, stockholders, banks, environmentalists, government and other groups who can help or hurt the corporation. The stakeholder concept provides a new way of thinking about strategic management."[5]

As Arjay Miller wanted to resolve corporate ethics into a widened conception of self-interest, so Freeman would organize strategic management around the notion of the stakeholder. His treatment, in terms of the perspective represented in this chapter, is a helpful expansion of the theme of "multiple responsibility" in management. It remains important, however, to keep in mind the points of view suggested by "self-interest" and "social vision" as elaborated in the previous section and in the section that follows below.

Recognition

The first task of the ethics of multiple responsibility is to identify the various groups who are recognized as having a stake in corporate policy and action. This is not a task that can be carried out and completed once and for all. As changes occur in social relations and in the environment of values within society, new groups will appear within the circle needing recognition and other groups will recede. In recent centuries emperors, kings, and nobility have faded in importance but have not completely disappeared, whereas minority groups, women, senior citizens, and the environment have moved nearer to the center of attention.

Several years ago, while the Berkeley Center was working with Wells Fargo, Richard Cooley, the president and CEO, developed an address entitled "The Prism of Responsibility." In it he noted the need for recognizing groups not previously regarded as within the circle of corporate responsibility and ways found to carry out that responsibility. The ability to recognize the groups to whom the company is accountable and responsible, its stakeholders in Freeman's terms, is a basic element of the ethical awareness and reflection of management.

Stockholders, directors, employees, and customers are groups to which the management of corporations has long acknowledged responsibility — and also accountability in the sense that these groups are able to exert pressure for response and responsibility. The accountability of the corporation to government cannot be ignored. Corporate responsibility to ethnic groups, women, the elderly, the young, and the handicapped has been recognized more recently and the element of accountability increased. Corporations vary a great deal in the extent to which they feel a responsibility to the arts, to groups providing social services, and to educational and charitable institutions. The circle of responsibility can be expanded beyond the immediate community — to the nation and to the global community — and is more likely to be enlarged if the corporation has branches or subsidiaries in distant locations.

Understanding

Beyond recognizing those to whom the corporation is responsible, there is also the task of grasping clearly who makes up the group, what their needs are and how the corporation affects them, and what is appropriate for the corporation to do in relation to this group. A bank is unlikely to have significant responsibility for health delivery to the elderly but has major responsibility with reference to loan policies for senior citizens. Action by the Gray Panthers led banks to discover that older borrowers are more likely to repay debts, resulting in a reappraisal of their responsibilities to that group. Research proving that home care is more effective and less costly for many types of patients brought changes in health insurance coverage important for the development of the hospice movement.

Understanding requires communication and listening. While it is important for a corporation to gather information about groups to which it is responsible, it is crucial to hear from the groups themselves, learn their own perspective on their needs and hopes, and develop responsible action on the basis of mutual rather than one-way understanding. For example, many institutions use committees of disabled people, some in wheelchairs, to advise on how to make their facilities accessible. With membership like that the insights provided are based on the experience of experts.

Responsibility to varied groups is an important element in a corporate ethic; but in addition ethical issues arise and are shaped by the circumstance that groups affected by policy may not be represented in policy-making contexts or their views taken into account. Ethics that will be most adequate for corporations or other organizations must have the means to include the perspectives of those who will be the recipients of policy. The criterion of multiple responsibility offers a way to ensure that policy and its implementation include diverse, and often divergent, interests, goals, and convictions.

Balancing Conflicting Demands and Values

It takes no great amount of experience or imagination to know that the scope of responsibility can easily grow beyond the abilities of one corporation or even of society to carry out completely and effectively, especially if the hopes and purposes of everyone are taken seriously. Demands multiply and responsibilities inevitably come into conflict.

To carry out an ethic of multiple responsibility, it is necessary to have a corporate ethic that can develop criteria for action capable of setting priorities among responsibilities. Conflicting claims must be evaluated and, when possible, reconciled. It is also necessary to have sufficient strength to operate in situations where all demands cannot be satisfied.

With the increasing interdependence of persons and groups in our world, there is an ever-widening circle of those to whom some measure of relation and responsibility must be acknowledged. The older, limited circles defined by immediate connection and primary communities are no longer sufficient. Communication, travel, and weaponry have intensified our mutual accountability around the globe. But limits must be set to the scope and character of responsible action. Acknowledging the necessity for and the expanding quality of multiple responsibility and yet having the insight and strength to know how and when to draw the line provide the most rigorous test of a corporate ethic.

THE ETHICS OF SOCIAL VISION

A third perspective from which to understand the ethics of corporate action concerns the ways in which plans are projected, results are evaluated, and the future of society is envisioned. The ethic of social vision in these ways is present in corporations and represents within management acceptance of the obligation to adopt a long-range perspective on society (local, national, and global) that identifies specific social problems, and plans changes that will move us from where we are now toward a more humane world.

Although it is important to be wary of trying to impose particular solutions to problems or specific political directives, the criteria by which management develops policy are the product of ethical reflection with implications for the future. Social vision is present and provides the basis for distant purposes and for the appraisal of immediate consequences. It is not so much a question as to whether social vision will be present in corporate policy but rather the extent to which such vision is self-consciously developed, deliberately discussed, and critically integrated into the policy process.

The ethic of social vision must encompass both economic and political factors. Attempts to isolate economic components from the social whole are artificial and academic though ordinarily doing no great harm in a society like the United States in which democratic processes ensure that varied viewpoints and interests have the power to maintain themselves. When transnational companies enter societies that are underdeveloped or have a feudal political economy, consideration of economic factors in isolation from the impact of corporate actions on the total society may lead to the reinforcement of oppressive political patterns, even though management at corporate headquarters intended the opposite. Private enterprise has had good overall results in the industrialized nations, not because it alone led to the improved quality of life but because it was one crucial element in a mix of other equally important social components that interacted and influenced one another. Thus republican politics forced the change from mercantilism to the mixed political economies in which private, not free, enterprise remains central. At the same time, the strong Judeo-Christian impulses of Western society produced continuing criticism of social oppression and has led to many voluntary movements working for continuing and increasing liberation of diverse groups. Where different cultural conditions exist, as in developing countries, the dynamism of private enterprise may serve neither to lift the quality of life nor to liberate humans from oppression. Instead, the presence of First World corporations may only increase the chasm between the rich and the poor and add to the power of political oppressors.

Social vision, to be a part of an effective corporate ethic, must be responsive to broad social trends and tendencies. Such vision must be informed by precise knowledge of societal processes and an understanding of the mutual influence of interacting parts. The areas where the corporation has power or influence are those where the social vision embodied in policy is most likely to be effective. In areas where corporate influence is caught up in the larger forces of a total society, the intentions shaping its actions are much more likely to be submerged and even distorted.

Methodology needs to be developed more carefully for defining corporate social vision and discovering how best to integrate it into the processes of policy-making and implementation. At the same time, social information systems must be created by which to appraise the consequences of corporate policy and to learn what changes are needed for more effective results.

Each corporation must take the initiative to search out and define a social vision appropriate for its own character and purposes. Only then can it be useful in its policy-making processes. This vision should take into account the goals of other organizations and social groups, other sectors of society, and diverse views of what a humane society will be.

Such basic principles as justice, equality, and freedom, central to many streams of ethics in the Western tradition, can provide guidance in shaping the social vision component of a corporate ethic. It must be remembered, however, that not all who believe in *justice* attach the same meaning to the term. The same is true also for *equality* and *freedom*. Sufficient agreement exists in the society of the United States to provide the basis for coalitions and covenants working for greater justice, but as one moves into other societies, the meanings become more varied and the basis for common action becomes more difficult to find.

Justice, as well as other social values, is not a concept that can be defined by reason without reference to location and perspective. Justice is understood differently by the Greeks and by the Hebrews and still differently in a closed society such as Switzerland as compared with a dynamic society such as that in the United States. And even a similar understanding of justice must be applied differently in diverse situations of oppression and possibility. John Rawls, for example, in his book *A Theory of Justice*,[6] relies heavily on an implicit covenant of middle-class, rational humanity. The views Rawls presents are intelligible within the enclave of U.S. academic society to which he belongs, in which he was trained for particular functions, and of which he is an accepted member. His theory of justice will be neither rational nor convincing to those outside his limited social location. Even so, Rawls has a schizoid view of human nature that will undermine his persuasiveness even among those who adhere to the same community of interpretation as does he. Economic humanity, in Rawls's view, acts only out of narrow self-interest, whereas political humanity acts on the basis of a vision of the common good. I doubt that human agents lend themselves to bifurcation in this manner; even the authoritarian methods of academic specialists cannot remake actuality by definition.[7]

Not only is it important to understand the social locations of various interpretations of justice; it is also crucial to remember that justice may mean little in a society with few goods and services to share. For justice to have real significance, attention to economic development is necessary. John Bennett writes:

> No degree of justice in the organization of economic

life can compensate for failure to be efficiently productive, for on this depends the capacity to provide adequately the food, the clothing, the shelter, and other goods which are required by the community. Those who represent Christian theology and ethics are tempted to underestimate the significance of this test of effectiveness in their concern to apply ethical tests, just as economists have often shown an opposite kind of one-sidedness and have declared the independence of economics from ethics.[8]

Along with other ethical concepts such as *equality* and *freedom* and *productivity, justice* takes on meaning through specific interpretations in particular locations and relations. Rather than assuming that any of these notions have single, universal meanings that can be dealt with by rational analysis apart from historical context, it is necessary to remember that persons and societies are shaped by communities of family, faith, and worship from which emerge their perspectives, their fundamental convictions, and their sources of interpretation. Only to the extent that these communities are similar is it possible to develop adequate bases of consensus and covenant for agreement and common action.

COMPREHENSIVENESS AND THE CONTEXT OF POLICY

In a comprehensive approach to corporate ethics, one of these three approaches is not to be adopted and the others excluded. Inclusiveness of all three and balance among them are crucial. Such breadth is essential for ethical reflection applicable to policies of organizations set within diverse and changing contexts. I am proposing a complex corporate ethic. But nothing less can satisfy the demands for the management of values in this complex and interdependent world. The context of policy must be comprehensive (1) in the integral wholeness of theory and practice that action implies, (2) in the enrichment of meaning and the expansion of policy alternatives that takes place when the different components are placed in interaction with one another, and (3) in its provision for setting priorities and making trade-offs essential for effective policy.

Wholeness of Agency

Policy and action are not separable; rather, they are elements present in the wholeness of corporate agency. Action is constant, and reflection takes place in the midst of action. There is no split between theory and practice to be overcome in this view because activity includes both in integral wholeness.

So ethics is not a way of rational theorizing that one learns in academic settings and applies in practical situations. Ethics, as part of the human wholeness in which we are always located, is that reflection on the moral significance of action planned, in process, and retrospectively evaluated. Such reflection may be about my actions as an individual or about the actions of some social collectivity or organization. In either case ethics pertains to wholeness of agency.

Interaction and Expanded Meaning

A comprehensive ethic for corporate policy combines and reconciles the three components and criteria outlined above — the ethic of self-interest, the ethic of multiple responsibility, and the ethic of social vision. Each one supplements the others, serves as a check against the excesses and dangers of the others, and balances out their inadequacies. Each element of a corporate ethic takes on wider dimensions of meaning when related to other elements.

For example, self-interest in this context becomes broadened beyond narrow selfishness and shifted toward an enlightened understanding that views corporate interests as bound up with the long-range well-being of the human community and the world. This perspective on corporate self-interest contributes to the policy-making process by identifying a wider range of alternatives for action. A larger arena of policy emerges into view, with expanded criteria for planning and evaluation.

A comprehensive corporate ethics involves the acceptance of self-interest as a consideration integral to all human decisions. But it also recognizes that narrow self-interest does not serve best the longer, enlightened interests of a corporation in this interdependent world.

In a similar way the problems and limitations of an ethics of multiple responsibility are overcome once responsibility is seen not in isolation but rather within the interacting context of a comprehensive corporate ethic. In this setting, responsibility extends beyond those groups having the power to compel accountability. The scope of responsibility is opened up to the total society and may be perceived as including apparently powerless groups or organizations whose interests and purposes seem on the surface to be alien to those of the corporation. The Bank of America became the largest bank in the United States by taking banking services out of the narrow enclaves of the financially secure into the neighborhoods where ethnics and immigrants were striving to make a better life for themselves and their children. By extending its arena of responsibility, the Bank of America discovered a wider community of interest than had bankers who stayed safely enclosed in downtown Greek temples of high finance.

With the additional perspective of social vision, the scope of responsibility is enlarged to include wider geographical areas and a time line that reaches into the future. The interest and well-being of groups related directly to a corporation are understood as interwoven with the welfare of regional, national, and global communities. Policy considerations include not only present realities but anticipated changes in society and what effect these changes will have as the implementation of policy unfolds in a shifting context. Cybernetics was originally developed to make it possible to aim guns at moving targets on the sea or in the air from a platform that was rolling and pitching at the bidding of the ocean. Social vision discloses the horizon of moving targets and the shifting internal environment of the organization that provides the meaning of multiple responsibility. A comprehensive policy ethic for corporations discloses the cybernetic, steering dimensions of policy-making in the most inclusive way.

The perspective of self-interest provides helpful curbs on multiple responsibility. When policymakers seek to become responsible to groups distant in space or social location, with less power to make their views known, it can remind them that these groups have distinct interests that need to be understood with sensitivity and without paternalism. In a comprehensive context of ethics, there must be the continuing attempt to understand constituencies and other groups through their own self-understanding, through their own interests, hopes, and aspirations, rather than responding to them only from the perspective of corporate interests and purposes.

Although useful and necessary within a comprehensive corporate ethic, the visionary component has disadvantages. It can lead to founding policy on ideals rather than realities. It can rely too heavily on consequences projected on the basis of current conditions. And it can shift too much attention away from existing interests and present responsibilities toward future possibilities. By keeping social vision in continuous interaction with self-interest and multiple responsibilities, many disadvantages of an ethic of social vision can be mitigated. Specifically, social vision can be anchored in real possibilities that are defined by the interests and responsibilities of the corporation as it is operating in the present.

Corporate or individual action is always in a real and present world. Remembering the past provides a firm sense of identity and infuses ethical reflection with the realism of experience. Carefully surveying the resources and relationships of the present keeps policy attuned to actual possibilities. And social vision, if it does not become isolated from past and present, can expand the horizons of policy alternatives and empower action with informed boldness. Inclusiveness and comprehensiveness are central for an effective corporate ethic.

Priorities and Trade-Offs

An ethical framework sufficiently comprehensive to include the three components of self-interest, multiple responsibility, and social vision and to integrate them into policy formulation will open up a wider range of alternatives for consideration, provide criteria for setting priorities among alternatives, and enable the trade-offs among values to be made in an ordered way. There is no substitute for decisive action by management. Excessive analysis and referral to task forces is a perilous method of management in any kind of organization, with the dangers increasing in proportion to the speed and pervasiveness of change. The demand to do something must, however, never be understood as a call for uninformed and unevaluated action.

120 / A Comprehensive Ethic for Corporate Policy

The alternative to endless study, on the one hand, and uninformed haste, on the other, is the development of a comprehensive ethic for corporate policy that becomes an integral part of the culture and policy process of the organization. In this way the evaluation that is essential to the ordering of priorities and the inevitable making of trade-offs becomes a carefully reflective dimension of policy at every stage of planning, shaping, implementation, and reappraisal. Further suggestions for how this can be accomplished will be explored in subsequent chapters.

SUGGESTIONS FOR GROUP STUDY

1. Reread the conversation at the beginning of this chapter. Develop group discussion around the evidence of ethical reflection revealed in this interchange. Organize a debate on the question of the response of that corporate management to the changing environment, social and technological, that seems to be shaping its policies. Identify the ways a corporation can be socially responsible in such a changing world.
2. As a second exercise, use the opening conversation as a basis for identifying the elements of self-interest, multiple responsibility, and social vision that underlie corporate reflection and action about energy as reported by Jason. Try to identify the various groups that the corporation recognizes, explicitly or implicitly, in framing its policy. Define the apparent social vision that underlies the actions of the company. How are these various perspectives integrated to form a comprehensive ethic that simultaneously recognizes and reconciles this diversity?
3. Ask a member of your group, or an invited corporate executive, to meet and discuss with a representative of an environmental group the subject of the responsibility of contemporary corporate management for protection of the environment. Follow this up with a group discussion of the differences in perception of environmental problems and their solutions represented by both parties. Are there real differences in perspective and are these irreconcilable? How can an accommodation be arranged?
4. Read in Appendix H the book brief on *The Silent Revolution* by Ronald Inglehart. Assign to members of your group the task of finding evidence in current periodicals of the types of social

change referred to by Inglehart. Is there any evidence of a new swing in values that is superseding his observations from survey data in the late 1960s and early 1970s? Reflecting on your own "social location," can you find evidence in your own life of values that would support Inglehart's thesis?

Part Three

MANAGING VALUES FOR PERFORMANCE

Six

POLICY PROCESS AND CORPORATE PERFORMANCE

"If at all possible, I'd rather it not even be discussed. It's embarrassing that it even happened, and I think everyone would rather forget about it." Les was CEO of the corporation where we were conducting a corporate ethics seminar with the senior management.

This particular "it" had emerged at one of the sessions where the topic was the meaning of participative management. Jim and I had picked up on it immediately and thought it worth discussing with Les as a possible case study in the seminars. The company had a well-deserved reputation for responsiveness to social issues as well as regularly increased profits. In this instance a policy on affirmative action quotas for each division of the corporation had been adopted by the directors and announced to division heads without any advance consultation with them. The opinion of the senior managers was that checking the proposed policy with those responsible for its implementation prior to its enactment would have vastly improved the probabilities of good affirmative action performance with continuing profitability.

"There has already been some mention of it, and I suspect that means it is being talked about. If we use it for a case study, then it will bring feelings out into the open and provide guidance for the future," Jim said.

Les grimaced and remained silent.

"And," I added, "you may get some good ideas for improving what may become a difficult situation."

"I'd rather leave bad enough alone," Les responded, but there was a thoughtful look on his face. "There have been some sounds of anguish from several division heads who say that there's no way they can meet the profit plan set and also the affirmative hiring quota."

"How did it happen?" Jim asked.

Les came out of his reverie and glanced sharply at Jim. "We didn't give it a thought at the time. We were preoccupied with a crisis over . . . well, you'll hear about that too — a crisis over inventory control. The sales forecasts and the production and overhead budgets had been discussed several weeks earlier. They had been taken down several levels, gone over, and brought back up with revisions. The directors reviewed the changes and passed a final version. Then I sent the results to all divisions."

"Is that the usual pattern for establishing the goals for sales, production, and profit?" Jim asked.

"That's the way we've done it for the past five years," Les said. "We're convinced that consultation up and down has proved to be effective."

"But you did not use that procedure for the affirmative action directive?" Jim continued.

A shadow of discomfort crossed Les's countenance. "Well, no," he answered. "The affirmative hiring issue came from the committee on corporate responsibility of the directors. We all were in agreement that we wanted to endorse affirmative action and maybe be a little ahead of the pack. So it was passed, with quotas for every division. I didn't even get around to sending out a directive on it until the next week, after the inventory flap had settled down. At the time I signed the memo, it occurred to me that it might seem abrupt to those who hadn't heard about it before. Then I began getting some real flack about which did we want — profits or a clean nose."

"Would you do it the same again?" Jim asked.

"Hell, no," Les answered emphatically. "But there's no doubt the principle is right and that's where we want to move. We'll have to do it eventually. I'm not sure what we could have done differently about a clear-cut moral issue that we've agreed needs action."

"That is exactly where airing it and having this group of top management look at it carefully might help with involving both upper and middle management more effectively in such matters," I said. "They may have suggestions for getting out of the immediate situation as well as for avoiding a repeat in the future."

Les rubbed his jaw carefully as though it were sore. "Okay, that would clearly be a good thing to do at this point," he replied finally. "But let's make sure we do it at a meeting of the group when I cannot be there," he added, pursing his lips ruefully.

Action: Decision Making as Policy Process / 127

The management of values can be carried out effectively only to the extent that ethical reflection and judgment permeate organizational procedures as well as individual behavior. That means that ethics as reflection on the purposes and impact of corporate action must be integrated into the processes by which policy is formulated and implemented. In this chapter we begin to explore ways to accomplish such integration and to understand more clearly how managing values effectively relates to performance.

As reported in the first chapter, the views of practicing business executives reveal that profit, or "the bottom line," is only one of the values guiding corporate policy. Weighing various alternatives in policy formulation, making trade-offs among competing values, and setting the criteria for evaluating performance are components in managing values that are central in the decision making that takes place daily in corporations. The second chapter presented an understanding of ethics and value judgment based on the insights of executives into what actually takes place in the policy processes of business organizations. The third chapter discussed the importance of corporate culture and character for ethical reflection related to policy and performance, emphasizing how the environment of values within an organization shapes the thinking of corporate executives and all employees. In the fourth chapter a distinction was drawn between corporate policy based only on response to the external environment of values and corporate policy based upon ordered and reflective management of values, that is, management with a self-conscious corporate ethic. The focus of attention in the fifth chapter was an examination of the major elements composing a comprehensive ethic useful in corporate policy-making.

In the chapters that follow, we explore how to relate these perspectives on values and policy in the first five chapters to the policy processes and performance of a corporation. We examine how the corporate ethics outlined above operates in policy formulation and the kind of information, pattern of institutionalization, and style of management essential for the enhancement of performance.

The conversation with Les reported above illustrates corporate ethics at work in a particular corporation and problems that can arise when value commitments are not coordinated with one another or dealt with carefully at different management levels. Policies promulgated by the directors and CEO exhibit different values. In one instance the values of productivity and profit represent the criterion of self-interest at work in making policy. In the other instance the values of human rights and affirmative action represent the criterion of multiple responsibility shaping corporate policy and, also to a certain extent, the criterion of social vision. So far, so good. But the two policies were not handled in the same way, and the dealing with alternative values in the policy process, from formulation to implementation at all levels of management, is as important as using sound criteria.

The policy involving the sales forecasts and the production and overhead budgets embodying the values of productivity and profit was discussed at different levels of management before it was given final form and sent out for implementation. Care was devoted to involving lower and middle management as well as top management. Managing these values was done well.

The policy regarding affirmative action quotas embodying the values of human rights and social justice was promulgated from the top without discussion at various levels because the policy was obviously "good" and "ethical." As there was no doubt what "right" was, there was no reason for careful discussion before sending it out to be done. But both policies involved value judgments and ethical reflection. Even more important, the two policies represented alternative values that would at various points of implementation come into conflict. The effective management of values requires recognition of the moral significance of actions to be taken as a result of both policies. It is necessary to weigh the alternative values and make trade-offs. It may not be possible to meet high goals of productivity and profit and high quotas for affirmative hiring at the same time. Integrating this ethical reflection into the policy process requires consulting levels of management involved in reconciling these alternative values in order to determine what is realistic and how both profit and affirmative hiring can be actualized at the highest levels.

Failure to deal with the policy on affirmative hiring in a way similar to the policy on profitability suggests at least two things. First, the ethical intentions of management were better than their patterns for managing values. Second, whether or not intended, what was done could send a signal to those outside top management that the really important value was profit, whereas the policy on affirmative hiring was promulgated more for public relations and corporate image than because of a deep commitment to human rights. The delay of a week in sending out the directive while the inventory crisis was handled could strengthen that impression. As CEO Les believed that he and the directors were as committed to affirmative action as they were to profit. But their corporate ethic needed more careful integration into the policy process and the performance patterns of the company than had been done up to that point.

When we discussed the problem with the managers in the corporate ethics seminar, they agreed that affirmative action policies ought to be reviewed up and down the levels of management at least as carefully as profit goals. Further, they came up with the proposal that a strong affirmative action training program was crucial in order to decrease the conflict between the value of profit and the value of social justice in hiring practices.

"There's many a slip 'twixt cup and lip" is one familiar way of putting the problem presented in the conversation with Les, but the matter is clearly more complicated than that. We have already suggested that ethics useful in corporate settings must emerge primarily from the human interaction within and around corporate communities rather than from academic disciplines and scholarly theories. Ethics — theological, philosophical, and social — can contribute much to the development of corporate ethics. But it must be remembered that corporate ethics arises among corporate policymakers and operates within the corporate community.

Now we shall examine a dimension of corporate ethics that is equally important: *corporate ethics must be institutionalized throughout the structures, patterns, and operations of the entire corporation in order to be effective.* The management sciences can contribute substantially to such an undertaking. The intentions and commitment of top management are crucial. Staff resources and committees on corporate ethics and policy can be helpful. None of these is sufficient, however, unless reflection on the value dimensions of corporate action is built into the total process by which the corporate community shapes the interaction of persons, formulates policy, and carries it out. It is to this comprehensive and difficult task that we now turn.

The first part of this task is to understand and examine the patterns by which decisions are made and implemented, that is, the corporate policy process. We shall do this by looking at the wholeness of policy process (1) as *action*, (2) as *politics*, and (3) as *evaluation*. With this perspective we can then explore what is needed to integrate, or institutionalize, ethics into the corporate policy process for the increased effectiveness of the management of values.

ACTION: DECISION MAKING AS POLICY PROCESS

" 'Decision-making,' " writes Philip Selznick, "is one of those fashionable phrases that may well obscure more than it illuminates."[1] Speaking of decisions as though they are isolated events affecting what comes after but isolated from what precedes them can distort as well as obscure their background, context, and significance. This is as true for individual as for organizational decisions, but it is the latter that is of special interest here.

The making of decisions in an organization takes place by what can best be called the *policy process*. Although there are specific points where it is possible to say that decisions have been made and choices have been ratified, these points are no more isolated than drops of water in a flowing river or moments in a golfer's swing. A drop of water is real and so is the moment when club meets ball, but each has its reality and meaning only within the process of which it forms a significant part. To understand decisions it is necessary to grasp the larger pattern, the process, within which they have their reality and meaning.

In his book *Where the Law Ends*, Christopher Stone observes that there are important differences between *setting rules* for making decisions and *specifying how* policies are to be developed. In considering governmental controls on business, Stone urges a move away from rule setting about decisions and toward specifying more generally the process by which corporations go about policy-making. He points out, for example, that a regulation mandating how high in the management structure a policy must be considered as it is being shaped can have a more important controlling effect on the quality of policy than mandating a particular decision.[2]

This insight that policy in organizations can be understood more accurately as a process of action and interaction than as rules needs to be extended and emphasized. Policy formulation, as we describe it here, is a continuing process, emerging from the past of corporate character and culture, taking place in the present from formulation to implementation through the interaction of many groups and factors, and always being shaped with an eye on the future, anticipated and unanticipated. This perspective illumines the wholeness of policy and makes clear how the management of values is central in the entire process.

In the vignette at the beginning of this chapter, we saw how careful use of the policy process led to effective management of values in relation to goals for sales, production, and profit. Because that same awareness was not present in setting quotas for affirmative action, that policy and its implementation were in trouble. Managing values through the institutional structures of the corporation is as important in one area of action as the other.

In previous chapters we have already begun to glimpse the primary elements making up the corporate policy process. Now they need to be seen as a whole in constituting the pattern of decision making. We shall examine this totality as context, as valence, and as results.

Context

Policy evolves, decisions are made, and action takes place within a particular situation or context. Each situation has a past, present, and future, and it has external and internal environments. Both time line and environment are crucial components of corporate policy process.

The founding of an organization and the course of its development, with its leaders and decisive events, is its past. Out of this past as it is carried into each succeeding present, there is a sense of the corporate history and identity. As this past flows into the present and is remembered by the community now making up the company, this history becomes the corporate culture and character shaping the policy process as it operates now. Out of the decisions and actions made in the present emerges the future of the organization.

The external environment of a corporation changes over time and influences the people making policy and the possibilities of policy in every successive situation. The context of the corporate policy process is to be found in the social environment within which the company is founded and develops. The people who make up the cast of characters in the corporation are shaped by the institutions and values of this environment before they enter the corporate community, and they continue to be influenced by the larger society throughout their lives. In considerable measure this social context determines the agenda for the policy process — products and services wanted as well as acceptable ways of operating. As one analyst of policy puts it, "Social learning or indoctrination creates a climate of opinion that keeps many issues, especially issues challenging the fundamentals of the political-economic system itself, off the agenda."[3] It places other items on the agenda, keeps them there for a time, and then removes them.

Context also involves the internal environment of an organization. Policy develops within the corporation as memorable events and strong personalities create a history. Through stories and heroes the past shapes the culture of the corporation with its distinctive internal environment and value commitments, with its accepted rites and ceremonies, and with its networks of relationship. The culture impels its participants to tell the stories, and the telling confirms teller and listener as members of this community. Organization provides the patterns of interaction and defines the sectors to which members belong in the community's internal environment.

If culture expresses the passive aspect of this corporate wholeness, the active aspect is conveyed by speaking of a corporate character. To the extent that the present community is both shaped by the past and in the process of reshaping its heritage, it has a dynamic element, a character that envisions a future and moves toward it through plans, projects, and policy.

"Poorer-performing companies often have strong cultures, too," Thomas Peters and Robert Waterman remind us, "but dysfunctional ones."[4] However, corporate leadership that recognizes elements in the culture that do not contribute to strong performance can take steps to change the culture toward a form that contributes to effective performance as well as to strength. Every corporation has a culture. It takes character to recognize and maintain a good culture and even stronger character to recognize dysfunctional elements and deliberately reshape the culture.

Champion International exemplifies a corporation having a strong character. The present corporation was formed over the past two decades through the combination of two companies, later a third, and more recently a fourth company, each with a strong heritage and distinctive culture. At one point the company made a start at becoming a conglomerate and increasing its diversity. That direction was quickly abandoned because it led toward even more diffuseness in corporate culture. Under new and energetic leadership, the company divested itself of peripheral businesses and went back to what the original companies had done well — forest products and paper. The diverse cultures persisted. Though the corporation performed well, it was gradually recognized that the remaining differences in style were in part dysfunctional. In 1980 a bold move was made to create a strong, unified culture. The "Champion Way" is the name given to this culture that is in part already actualized in corporate action and in part represents the company Champion intends to become.[5] Champion's top leadership has exhibited vision by embarking on such a program and character by carrying it through successfully.

Whether inherited in a form that makes for effective performance or reshaped in that direction, the context of the policy process deeply affects the horizons, shape, and possibilities for all decisions. No attempt to manage values effectively can afford to overlook the importance of culture and character in the corporation.

Valence

In addition to context a second way to look at the wholeness of the corporate policy process is through power. Too often, however, power is understood simply as force. When power is reduced to force, it cannot account for times in history when a protagonist with less force emerged victorious over those with greater force. Power derives as much from the strength of commitment and valuing by those who use force as from the force itself. *Valence* is intended to capture the combination of power as sheer force and power as the valuing that mobilizes human energies. Human agents use various forms of force to actualize what they value. The history of nations and of corporations provides countless examples of when the element of disciplined value commitments outweighed the element of force in determining the valence and the outcome of conflicts. To speak of valence rather than of power also reminds us that conflicts at their core are conflicts among alternative values held by persons and social groups committed to them.

When Philip Selznick says that "the general problem of leadership is *control* of core-formation, whether to build one congenial to desired policy or to restrain one that creates unwanted rigidities in organization and policy,"[6] he suggests how context and valence are closely related in organizational policy process. Control is not achieved through force but by means of a context permeated with value commitments, that is, a culture, that provides a field of valence shaping reflection, planning, and policy for all the participants.

Valence includes that empowering quality of values that is characteristic of companies that perform well. No code can compel this phenomenon where it does not exist nor contain it where it does exist.

Valence also involves those who are empowered, the people who are participants in the policy process. These participants are individuals, but, as members of groups, individuals become "team members" integrated into the action of the group. Within an organization it is important to understand persons not only in terms of their roles as individuals but also in terms of the roles they play and the groups to which they belong within the policy process. Persons and groups, with their particular positions and authority within the organization, interact with one another and with the surrounding social environment. Out of this interaction, policy emerges.

The policy process, in business corporations as well as in other social organizations, is neither so tidy as the rationalists assume nor so unpredictable as the exponents of clashing interests suggest. The valence of interacting values and interests develops the agenda of policy and also the form it takes in responding to specific problems and in carrying out particular purposes. The demand for equal opportunity for women in employment and pay could not have been predicted with precision far in advance. But managements were able to perceive the issue emerging and to develop effective response in the degree to which they were alert to the changing social environment and had cultivated value commitments to human rights. The varied elements making up the policy process cannot be totally "controlled," but they can be recognized and "managed."

Another aspect of valence in the policy process appears as values come into conflict. To the extent that resources are limited, it is impossible to realize all the values or to achieve all the goals of the diverse groups with a stake in policy. Unless increased productivity and profits make more money available, higher pay for employees means a lower dividend for stockholders. Support of an arts program or the Olympics may, in the absence of better earnings, trim both raises and dividends. We should not assume a sum-zero situation. It is often possible to enlarge the pie before dividing it. Whether it is product quality in relation to pricing or the appraisal of the best ways to do effective marketing, policy-making requires trade-offs among values and interests, difficult choices among competing goods and purposes. A solution for one group may well become a problem for others. The policy process takes cognizance of the varied stakeholders and their interests, assigns priority among conflicting goals, and attempts to include as many values as possible in the actions chosen to pursue. Valence determines the weighing of values that must take place constantly among those responsible for managing organizational policy.

The movement of the policy process from formation through implementation takes place in accord with the field of valence established. Policy is shaped both by the possibility of implementation and in the light of projected results of particular programs of implementation. As policies are carried out, another crucial phase of the process emerges into view: the results.

Consequences

Although some would prefer to conclude the policy process with implementation, this is not possible. Policies have results — impact — upon various groups. All recipients of policy actions have an interest, a stake, in the corporate policy process. The consequences for all, as well as their responses, must be included. In this way the ongoing aspect of policy is underscored. A decision is not thrown like a stone into a void and forgotten. Policy-making is always a matter of truth *and* consequences. Policy actions are like boomerangs that return again and again with credit or blame, depending on their impact on constituencies.

Many outcomes can be predicted and plans made for dealing with these results. It is unanticipated consequences that cause the greatest turmoil. In the conversation at the beginning of the chapter, the CEO was facing the unanticipated consequences of a policy shaped by the best of intentions. The clash between profit as the value shaping the policy on production and sales projections and social justice as the value underlying the policy on affirmative action was not perceived in advance. Nor had appropriate trade-offs been carefully explored or alternatives that could have encompassed both values developed. What had not been dealt with at one point in the policy process showed up as an even more difficult problem at another point. The pattern of decision making has a wholeness and a continuing, interactive flow about it that permits the identification of context, valence, and consequences as distinguishable but inseparable elements in the corporate policy process.

THE POLITICS OF CORPORATE POLICY FORMULATION

So usual is it to associate politics with governmental processes and economics with business that it is easy to forget that every social setting is political. Schools are political and economic in their functioning as well as educational. Churches are certainly highly political in their operations and cannot be regarded simply as "religious." In the same way, corporations are political in their internal relationships as well as in their interaction with other institutions in society. Only the illusion that reality is divided into separate sectors because the isolated disciplines of the university attempt to define it in that segmented way could make us forget how political the corporate community is.

Not only does the political perspective provide another way to view the wholeness of the policy process, it also places the ethical dimensions of that process in sharp relief. The political dimensions of a community disclose it as an arena where divergent interests and conflicting values are represented in persons and groups. Only as the problems are seen in personal terms rather than as impersonal forces is it possible to work toward solutions. Viewed in one way, interests and values are political; viewed another way, they are ethical. Each viewpoint throws light on the other. In the conversation at the beginning of the chapter, Les saw clearly the political dimension of developing quotas for production and profit. He was learning that setting quotas in relation to ethical concerns is equally political.

The politics of corporate policy process can be grasped most clearly under five headings: the participants and the issues; the identities and loyalties represented; the power and resources available to each group; the negotiation and reconciliation necessary for the formulation of coherent policy; and the leadership essential for guiding these groups and processes and bringing something productive out of the mix.

Participants and Issues

In any political context the first element to consider involves the primary actors, the issues and interests they represent, and the context in which the issues emerge and are defined. For corporate management as it seeks to deal with values, the primary actors are both outside and inside the company. There are external groups pushing particular issues and interests as well as internal groups with their own agendas of concern. Managers themselves make up one crucial group in this spectrum of stakeholders, as R. Edward Freeman calls them in his *Strategic Management: A Stakeholder Approach,* to which reference was made in the previous chapter. Managers, however, also make up the group charged with the task of mediating among these stakeholders on behalf of the corporation and developing policy that includes and reconciles as many interests as possible. A basic function of management, as it seeks to manage values, is in this way inevitably political.

Identities and Loyalties

The actors and stakeholders important for corporate policy are not inert entities or impersonal vectors but rather human agents. As humans they are committed to the goals of the groups in which they participate and to the groups themselves. Their identities are tied up with the issues and interests of these groups. And, to greater and lesser degrees, the loyalties of these human agents are given to the various groups to which they belong. Politics cannot be viewed in adequate dimensions if seen only in terms of power understood as force. Politics is an intensely personal and human enterprise.

Put a different way, we may say that the ethics of personal identity and loyalty as operative in organizations discloses the stakes in political interaction. The personal investments are high. And no solutions will have a chance of working if this aspect is not recognized. So political solutions must always seek to preserve the dignity and the interests of the participating individuals and groups, rather than being aimed primarily at winning victories.

Programs must represent encompassing positions that include the diverse interests — and be able to command the loyalties and represent the identities — of those who might have regarded themselves previously as opponents. Politics above all, therefore, requires ethical sensitivities and insights. In this way politics provides the human element linking participants and issues to policy.

Power and Resources

In addition to the participants and issues and the identities and loyalties these human agents have invested in the situation, the politics of the corporate policy process must also take account of the power and resources available to the persons and factions who are the primary actors in the policy-making context. Some will be virtually excluded from a significant role in shaping policy, even though they have a real stake in what is adopted, because they lack the power and resources to make their influence felt. Others may be able to exercise considerable control over policy — not because their interest in the outcome is deeper but because they occupy a position of power. Power and its use are central to politics, although it must not be forgotten that power exists only as human agents have interests and values that call forth their commitment and energies. Power and resources take on political meaning not in themselves but in relation to all the elements of the policy process.

Negotiation and Reconciliation

Now it becomes possible to focus on the crucial stage on negotiation and reconciliation of interests and values. Compromise among competing purposes and coalitions among diverse factions are essential if policy is to be developed with sufficiently broad support to make it likely to become operative. The first step is to bring the major groups and interests into interaction for the purpose of negotiation.

Next is the process of getting values, purposes, and interests to the surface and exploring their meaning on the level of identity and loyalty as well as intellectual significance. Then it becomes possible for participants to make appraisals with reference to the extent of divergences, to reduce conflict, and to develop coalitions. Along the way, there will be opportunity to try out alternatives and to develop new formulations. Through negotiation of differences and discovery of alternatives that represent reconciliation of apparently opposing interests, it becomes possible, if not to resolve all conflicts, at least to find ways to combine the diverse perspectives into policy.

Leadership

An understanding of political process is not complete without including the function of leadership. It is the role of leadership to carry out negotiation and reconciliation or to provide a context in which others may work toward joint solutions. Leadership must reach out, relate to diverse perspectives, and take the trouble to touch the various groups, to reinterpret interests, and to redirect loyalties. Leadership requires moral imagination as well as patience. And it demands a commitment, not just to a single solution but to the process of finding one that is broadly acceptable.

Only through political process understood in some fashion similar to that described above can responsible policy be formulated that encompasses and combines diverse interests and values. Authoritarian situations only appear to require less political process. Authoritarianism simply buries the process beneath the surface. More democratic forms of leadership ensure, in spite of messiness, a stable openness.[7]

EVALUATION: ETHICS IN POLICY FORMULATION

As suggested above, ethics is always incorporated into management patterns of decision making, at least on an individual, intuitive level. I have also reported specific criteria operative in the decision making of organizational executives as my colleagues and I discovered them in corporate ethics projects with management groups. Now we shall explore what it means to utilize ethical perspectives in the actual processes by which corporate policy is formulated.

This discussion is intended to be a point of beginning rather than of conclusion. There is too much yet to be learned about the ways ethical reflection and criteria function in policy-making to regard any position as more than preliminary. Having ethical concerns and sensitivities is clearly what is needed as a basis. Corporate executives usually bring such awareness with them from their participation in one or another religious community and in the social movements of our society. With that foundation assumed, it is possible to investigate what it means to utilize the criteria for policy ethics previously set forth.

We have identified and described the ethics of self-interest, the ethics of multiple responsibility, and the ethics of social vision. These ethical perspectives have been found to be operative, implicitly or explicitly, in the patterns of decision making in organizations today. In corporations, however, the prevailing policy processes strongly emphasize self-interest. This is not always by intention so much as by default. For example, present information systems are much more likely to provide executives with precise and current data relating to sales, market share, production levels, financial position, and profit. Although there probably is significant recognition of multiple corporate responsibilities and a genuine desire to carry out these responsibilities well, there are little current and reliable data to provide executives with an information base to support policy using this ethical criterion effectively. For the same reason, the ethics of social vision tends to be developed on an individual basis rather than within the policy process, with little emphasis on systematic attention to overall social goals in discussions of policy formulation and implementation or on the assembly of data that would support such attention. The management of values and the use of corporate ethics will be greatly enhanced when information systems with social and ethical data relevant to policy are available to business executives.

Books by Daniel Bell, Neil Chamberlain, George Cabot Lodge, Prakash Sethi, Lee Preston and James E. Post, Edwin Epstein and Dow Votaw, R. Edward Freeman, John D. Aram,[8] and others are useful for different aspects of managing values in relation to social trends and factors in the social environment. In the absence of better information systems, the kind of overall perspective they provide on social change is very helpful. The availability of such material ought not to obscure the need for information about social conditions and values that is as detailed and precisely tailored for use in formulating policy as are data on financial matters.

In order to visualize the potential functioning of a comprehensive ethic within the corporate policy process, it is important to see what it would add over and above the more narrow ethical base usually operative. First, a policy process capable of placing greater emphasis on multiple responsibility and social vision will have a wider range of policy alternatives available. This can provide substantially increased flexibility for corporate action without abandoning or impairing the criterion of self-interest. Indeed, it might clarify the interests of the corporation and strengthen policies designed to carry out those interests. Second, because a comprehensive ethic emphasizes the future and the changing environment, the criterion of social vision will identify courses of action that may create greater opportunities for the company as social values shift. Third, such an ethic will provide greater personal satisfaction and mutual benefits for individuals and groups within the company and strengthen the relation of the corporation to various constituencies outside the company. In these ways and more, a comprehensive ethic will improve corporate performance.

To see more clearly how ethics understood comprehensively through the criteria of self-interest, multiple responsibility, and social vision can operate in policy formulation, we shall use the example of a bank's loan policy. Lending is central to the business of a bank and forms a significant part of a bank's corporate power. Because it affects the lives and interests of many persons and groups, loan policy must be at the center of the operation of a bank's corporate ethic. The following paragraphs also suggest the importance of executive leadership in the management of values in a corporation.

Social Vision in the Corporate Policy Process

Social vision refers to an ethical perspective concerned with a better future for society and for those in it. This vision may refer to the long-range future; but it must also include the impact of corporate action in the middle and short-range distance. This element of a corporate ethic focuses on what the consequences of alternative policies will probably be and evaluates them partly in the light of anticipated impact.

For this ethical perspective to be useful and effective in policy formulation, at least three things must be done. First, management must arrive at a substantial consensus on corporate purpose and identify social goals that contribute to shaping a more humane future. One corporate executive protested that he and his colleagues have no right to play God about the future. This is not the issue. No corporation alone has sufficient power to determine the future. But every corporation does have impact on particular sectors of society and participates in shaping the course of the entire society. The important thing is for management to recognize that policies of the corporation influence the future in specific, though limited, ways and to reflect carefully on what purposes and impacts management wants that influence to serve. Second, management needs information on the power exercised by the corporation and the effects its actions have. Most executives already have fairly clear notions on these matters. What is usually needed is precise information to confirm or correct the appraisals constantly being made and to bring these data directly into discussions as policy is being shaped. Third, it is important that management be aware that projections of social consequences can be as risky and as wrong as financial predictions. Provision for discovering what actual impact is made, through evaluation, and for modification of policy is crucial here as is always the case in policy. On the one hand, ethical reflection that does not take consequences into account is a truncated, partial ethics. On the other hand, ethical reflection that overlooks the contingent nature of projections of consequences and fails to make provision for corrections is deficient in responsibility.

The composition of a bank's loan portfolio illustrates areas where the policies of the bank have social influence and contribute to the shape of the future: real estate and housing; food production; consumer credit; industrial expansion, productivity, and employment; international development; world hunger and population; and human rights and politicoeconomic liberation. Lending to oppressive governments not only carries financial risk factors; it may not build the kind of world society that management really believes in. Loan policies can open up future markets at home and abroad by freeing people from economic oppression. Urban development plans should be a significant factor in setting policy in the area of real estate and housing. What an industry will produce and what impact it will have on society should be included in loan policy, as well as issues of financial capability. Such considerations alter the way calculations are made about market, economic, and political trends. At the same time, information on larger national goals and the aspirations of emerging groups here and in the Third World help to broaden corporate policy so that it does not represent narrow interests.

To provide a firmer basis for policy formulation, financial institutions may find it necessary, in cooperation with governmental agencies, universities, private research groups, and other banks, to develop comprehensive information about social values and trends. Banks may become places for accumulating and storing such data and making them available to clients as a means for strengthening loan policy. In this way banks would become repositories and distributors of social data as well as sources for money and financial information. Various systems for social policy information and evaluation are being developed, with the capability for feeding data into the policy formulation processes of diverse companies and providing means for the feedback of results to inform policy modification.

This perspective suggests that banks wanting to include social vision in their process of policy formulation should create a Social Policy Loan Committee, or a comparable group, to assemble appropriate information on social values and the social impact of alternative policies and to integrate this into policy planning and development. A social ethics staff group may prove helpful to such a committee, but such a committee must not substitute for the reflection and action of line management and policymakers. Comparable steps in other corporations would have to be adjusted to the needs of their core operations.

Multiple Responsibility in Policy Formulation

Considerable progress has been made in specifying the groups to which corporate management acknowledges responsibility. The spectrum varies from one corporation to another and shifts over time. In the case of a bank, the task is, first, to be clear about the particular groups affected, directly or indirectly, by bank policies and to identify the impact of bank activities on each constituency or group carefully. Second, channels of information must be secured that clarify for management the way policy and its impact will be perceived from the perspective of these groups. And third, the social claim and potential leverage of each group must be assessed in order to provide a basis for policy formulation when there are conflicting interests at stake and trade-offs must be made.

In order to carry out these three tasks, improved methods are needed for gathering and shaping information about groups affected by policy. Here are some ways for making progress in a systematic way on these improved methods:

1. Create a register of constituencies and groups that are to be considered in policy formulation with an ordering as to distance and valence. All top policymakers should be familiar with the register, but it ought to be used routinely by the Social Policy Loan Committee, or comparable group, in feeding recommendations into the policy process based on multiple responsibility.
2. Develop an understanding of the appropriate kind of responsibility the corporation has to each group included in the register. Relate this responsibility to specific policy alternatives and their projected results for that group.
3. Seek reliable information on how policies affecting them are viewed by the groups themselves. The view from the recipients' perspective may be different from that of the boardroom. Experimentation with advisory councils having members from various groups inside and outside the corporation, whose views are not directly represented in policy formulation, will provide fresh, direct reaction to policies in effect or to policies under consideration. Such councils have been used on a limited basis and might be expanded in scope.
4. Make particular members of the top management team responsible for representing the viewpoints and interests of constituencies or groups not represented otherwise and deserving attention with reference to specific policies.

These steps will not solve all of the problems connected with bringing multiple responsibility into policy formulation, but they will provide more reliable data, open up significant, new policy alternatives, and provide a firm basis for the trade-offs of values in shaping corporate action.

Evaluation takes place not only in terms of assessing the importance of the company's responsibility to various groups. Evaluation of personnel for salaries, promotions, and bonuses also takes place in corporations. The criteria and procedures for personnel evaluation and the methods for carrying them out must be kept under constant scrutiny, and suggestions must be continually sought from interested groups for ways to improve them. The top management of one company, well known for its strong culture and corporate ethics, was somewhat shocked to receive a complaint from a large group of middle managers about the personnel evaluations. The criteria actually used in the evaluations, said the complaining group, were very different in content and in balance from the values espoused in corporate statements about personnel. Rather than reacting defensively, the CEO to his credit, investigated the charge himself. He checked out what his office and the directors had promulgated as policy about personnel evaluations. Then he checked on the evaluations themselves, looking not only at the forms but also talking with the senior managers who did the evaluating and the middle managers who were evaluated. It became clear to him that the complaining group was substantially correct. The CEO thanked them personally for calling the matter to his attention and put a task force with an outside consultant to work, charged with the responsibility to look over the evaluation process and instruments in the light of the policy intended and to come up with a pattern of assessment congruent with company intentions.

The consultant, who also taught a course in business ethics, asked the CEO, after the revision of the evaluation procedures had been completed, whether his reasons for responding as he did had more to do with corporate self-interest or altruism. The CEO answered first that he had not really considered it in terms of ethical categories. After a few moments' thought, he added that he thought the entire policy came from a combination of motives and that the decision to change the defective procedures emerged primarily from a sense of corporate integrity that he knew had to be maintained for the sake of the enterprise and everyone in it. The values on which he acted were so ingrained, however, that he had not thought about it much at the time. "Perhaps we ought to be a little more reflective on a regular basis," he concluded. "Then maybe we wouldn't have to wait on complaints to find out what needs to be improved."

Corporate Self-Interest in Policy Formulation

Substantial support is already present in the policy processes of corporations for representing and ascertaining the stake of the corporation in alternative policies and their results. Information is available, and management is usually selected and retained on the basis of their effective carrying out of corporate self-interest. The profit yardstick, as shaped in the market and through a competitively oriented management system, provides the most important criterion in management action and for the measurement of corporate self-interest. It is not clear, however, that this measure alone is adequate. Data on profit reflect mainly financial analysis — and this often in very short-range terms. More is needed in order to identify and support the interests of any company.

Corporate self-interest includes more than profit. Even a narrow conception of self-interest includes corporate survival, and no level of profit would ordinarily be sought if it would result in the demise of the corporate entity and legal or other action against the directors and officers. Avoiding legal difficulties, building up the corporation's reputation and public image, and strengthening the position of the company in relation to markets are elements of self-interest that cannot be appraised accurately with financial data alone. When such interests as maintaining a heritage of excellence in performance, serving the community, encouraging human growth and rights, and preserving the social and natural environment are added, the picture is even more complex. In addition, it is often difficult to assess with accuracy the corporate self-interest in a narrower or broader sense in relation to political candidates, public issues, and community involvement.

Rather than assume that self-interest is taken care of by the market and the profit-and-loss sheet of the annual report, it is important that management give sustained attention to the values the company stands for and wants to maintain, that is, what the corporate interests really are. Then it will be possible to develop information with reference to these interests, shape criteria for appraising them, and discover ways to integrate this deepened conception of corporate self-interest into policy formulation.

Toward Comprehensiveness in Policy

Managerial judgment is already used to integrate conflicting interests and ambiguous data and to fill out from experience and "feel" the areas where solid information is lacking or insufficient reflection has taken place to arrive at a consensus on values and criteria for policy. The same managerial skills that have worked well in solving other problems can be applied to the extension and development of resources for integrating social vision, multiple responsibility, and self-interest into policy formulation. To the extent that this is accomplished, it could lead to the capability for analysis and evaluation of socioethical input into policy as advanced and useful as the present capabilities in financial information systems.

How can we illustrate what it means to integrate all three ethical perspectives into the process of policy formulation? It may be best to speak of a *decision matrix* that is applied to policy planning, formulation, and implementation. Such a matrix would incorporate the following:

1. Examining alternative policies in order to see how they fit into the larger social goals agreed to among corporate policymakers and compatible with the environment of values present in society;
2. Exploring how specific policies will affect particular groups and society in general in the short run and in the long run;
3. Checking to make sure that important social goals are not being ignored or violated by corporate actions;
4. Keeping tabs on groups within and outside the company that are affected by corporate action and how these groups benefit or are affected adversely by potential or operative policies;
5. Giving sustained attention to the interests and goals of the corporation itself, especially as these interests are wider than the maximization of profits, and seeing which policies serve these interests and which affect them adversely; and
6. In cases of conflict among the various interests, responsibilities, loyalties, and purposes established for policy, providing the means within the policy process for developing acceptable compromises and trade-offs, finding ways that various constituencies may share appropriately in the benefits and costs of various policies, and seeking more acceptable policy alternatives that will include a wider spectrum of interests, aspirations, and purposes.

Acting to include such procedures in policy formulation will lead toward increased ethical precision and to policies that encompass a wider spectrum of values. These steps provide an approach useful for varying types of value commitments and different levels of information. Much can be accomplished along these lines through cooperation with a variety of agencies and institutions rather than by one corporation acting alone. Practices that work to improve policy and enhance performance are gradually copied from one company to another. Working together may produce improvement even more rapidly in the management of values.

Whether used as a basis for preliminary discussions or for overall systemic change in corporate management, these suggestions related to ethics and policy formulation provide a strong approach to a comprehensive corporate ethic and one that can be built upon as investigation and experience in this vital area proceed further.

SUGGESTIONS FOR GROUP STUDY

1. Reread the conversation at the beginning of the chapter. From the information provided there and in the chapter, construct a step-by-step program for formulating the corporate policy on affirmative action that will meet the criteria suggested in the text. Carry out a group discussion to see if a consensus on this process can be achieved.
2. Using the information and conclusions of the exercise above, carry out a group discussion that will identify and list the elements of the political aspects of the policy-making process. Can you identify the participants and issues, the identities and loyalties, the negotiation and reconciliation, the leadership role? Examine the process by which your group achieved consensus in the exercise above for elements of these factors at work in the policy-making process.
3. Examine the elements of a policy on affirmative action as outlined in this chapter to identify the ways in which the comprehensive ethic enters into the process. Are there definable considerations of corporate self-interest, multiple responsibility, and social vision present in this policy and the process by which it is formulated? What kind of ethical reflection is involved and what are its results?

Seven

SOCIAL VALUES AND POLICY ETHICS

As soon as we entered the office, it was clear that Jay was deeply agitated. The previous afternoon, after participating in a session of a corporate ethics seminar with the senior management of the company, he had asked us to come by for a talk. He was CEO of a large manufacturing firm, with many divisions operating around the globe.

After greeting Jim and me, Jay motioned for us to take seats on one of the long sofas across the room.

"Thanks for coming on short notice. I've got a dilly of a problem and need to talk," he said, coming around from behind his desk and taking a seat on the edge of a chair that he pulled up to the coffee table. "You mentioned it in passing yesterday. It's the issue of 'peaked-out' employees. That's more than a small problem around here."

"We picked up some concern about it in our interviews with the heads of divisions when we were beginning the seminar," Jim replied. "No one talked about it extensively, though several people suggested it as a possible topic of discussion."

"None of us knows exactly how to tackle it, though it's a nagging problem within the divisions as well as higher up." Jay paused a moment. "Well, there's no reason to hold back. You're certain to find out eventually. The person I'm really concerned about is Sid. The situation has really gotten to me."

"We had noticed that he seemed more defensive and aggressive than the others in the seminar," I said.

"That's partly his style," Jay replied, "but he fits the definition of peaked out in too many ways for me to ignore. Two things have brought matters to a head. The first is the board of directors. Profits have been way down in Sid's division over the past two years. It's clear that his performance is, as we say, inadequate, and the directors are grumbling. What makes it really difficult is that Sid's been . . ."

Jay stopped in midsentence as the door opened and a young man entered, bringing us coffee and pastries. After pouring coffee for each of us, he left.

"You said it's particularly difficult with Sid," I said to start up where Jay left off.

"Exactly," Jay continued. "Sid is now 52 years old, nowhere near normal retirement age. He started with this company as a stock clerk 34 years ago. I had just finished my M.B.A. and was getting familiar with the nuts and bolts of the place. We worked together very closely for three months then and have been good friends ever since. He was plenty sharp and energetic and has worked his way up as the company has grown. Every promotion has been based on his excellent performance in the job he was doing. Three years ago we made him head of the division, and he now illustrates the Peter Principle at work. His poor performance in his present job is clear. But this company has a record of loyalty to the people who have been with us since it was a small family firm. I cannot fire him, and I don't see a decent way to demote him." Jay paused.

"You said there were two reasons it's a big problem now," Jim reminded him.

"The second reason is you," he said with a wry smile. "This seminar has made me think. I see now that managing values is as much my job as managing finances. Look at the different values involved. It's not fair to Sid to let him go on failing. The people in his division are unhappy about missing out on bonuses the last two years. The stockholders deserve better performance from that division and, I see now, better performance from me. At the same time, the government and social opinion are making it harder to force people into early retirement. We've got to find out how to handle conflicting values. That's why I asked you to drop by. What are we to do? It is a dilly, isn't it?"

"Let's begin," Jim said, "by using a peaked-out employee case in the seminar. It's a problem at various levels. That group will have ideas, maybe Sid also."

Jay is an expert and sensitive manager. He handles the policy process well in the company he runs, and he is aware of the value judgments woven into policy and the bearing of corporate values on performance. His concern to find a way to deal with peaked-out employees helps us focus on the importance of social values for policy ethics.

If a corporate ethic is to be useful in managing values in this world of complex organizations and plural perspectives, it must embody several central elements:

1. It must be appropriate for an operating business enterprise; it must be helpful in making the value judgments related to a business context; and it must provide insight with precision for choosing among, balancing, and trading off the actual values present.
2. It must fit the value commitments of a particular business enterprise, its history, its character, its culture, and its purposes.
3. It must provide the means for scanning the environments of values external and internal to the company and bringing those values into the policy process.
4. It must enable management to obtain critical perspective on policy and its implementation, to evaluate what has been done, and to contribute to improved performance.
5. It must be capable of opening up new policy alternatives and projecting their meaning in terms of the interests of the corporation, its multiple responsibilities, and its goals in society.

Corporate ethics, however, will not be effective if it is applied only to external or peripheral activities of a company. To become an instrument for managing values, ethical reflection and insight must be integrated into the central policy process of the corporation and applied to the core operations of the firm. For a bank, for example, that means not only whether to pay dues for executives who belong to clubs that discriminate but, most important of all, how to deal with loan policy. For a manufacturing firm, it means monitoring the patterns of manufacturing and marketing, the quality of employee relations and affirmative hiring, and the amounts contributed to worthy civic groups.

The corporate policy process as the focus of corporate ethics means several things. It means the pattern by which management formulates and implements policy. So it can be understood as the way the company acts in carrying out the entire range of its corporate functions. It also includes the means for evaluating policy in comprehensive perspective and initiating changes. As a political process with different interests and purposes at stake, policy-making clearly has value judgments as a fundamental element. Corporate ethics becomes effective in policy formulation as value judgments are carried out on a reflective, well-informed basis and integrated into the policy process.

This means that top management must be clear about the values it is using and wants to use in shaping policy. In the conversation above with Jay, the CEO of a manufacturing firm, we begin to see the spectrum of values that belongs to this company and that Jay wishes to see embodied in its policies. The heritage of loyalty to those who have served the company long and well is a value that must be maintained. This means that Sid, as a peaked-out employee, must be dealt with both as a human being who has a sense of pride and dignity and as a friend. There are also the values of productivity and profit, of bonuses as rewards for persons in divisions that have done well, and the responsibility to stockholders. The way society views older workers in relation to forced retirement is also a value that must be kept in mind. The pressure of the directors' dissatisfaction makes it clear that something must be done, and the seminar on corporate ethics has expanded the horizon of Jay's perception. His job as CEO is to take leadership in deciding how to handle the situation. But it must be leadership that includes taking a variety of values into account and finding ways to act so as to include them all. Policy toward Sid and other peaked-out employees must be formulated and carried out so that, insofar as possible, all the diverse values, interests, and purposes present can be reconciled and effectively embodied in what the company does.

This way of putting the matter emphasizes the complexity and difficulty of excellence in management today. Jay is challenged and excited by the prospect. He has a grasp of the scope of the problem presented by Sid and all the other present and future peaked-out employees. Given the way that the company developed, there was probably no way to avoid having the problem on an expanding scale. Equally inescapable was the necessity of dealing with it. And it had to be handled in a way that was at once realistic and true to the core values of the company and the society around.

Thus the management of values requires knowing the environment of social values that corporate action must take into account and, in different ways, represent. Social values, no less than a framework of ethical criteria and understanding of the corporate process for policy formulation, are fundamental for policy ethics.

THE CHANGING ENVIRONMENT OF VALUES

In 1950 the U.S. automotive industry built approximately 80 percent of all the cars produced in the world. By 1981 the percentage of autos produced in the United States had dropped below 30 percent. In *The Decline and Fall of the American Automobile Industry,* Brock Yates, senior editor of *Car & Driver* magazine, provides a persuasive account of the continuing errors and miscalculations that produced the precipitous decline among U.S. automakers, after they had dominated production since the first decade of this century.

The basic problem, Yates contends, is that the management of Detroit's Big Three — General Motors, Ford, and Chrysler — made corporate policy in splendid, self-imposed isolation from the society they had to know well in order to thrive. They lost touch with the environment of social values that should have been guiding the process of policy-making. When the oil crisis developed in the early 1970s and gasoline prices soared, Detroit continued to emphasize manufacture of the gas-guzzling models that Americans might "prefer" but passed over in favor of fuel-efficient foreign makes. Even the continuing drop in sales did not bring management around. Industry executives kept on ignoring societal values and opinion. "It was in early 1982," Yates reports, "that [General Motors Chairman Roger] Smith announced that he was cutting his half-million dollar a year income by $135 a week as a personal sacrifice in the face of declining sales. Then, in a sad moment in GM history, Smith and his colleagues voted themselves increased bonuses just hours after the Corporation had extracted $2.5 billion in long term wage concessions from the Union."[1]

Reports of greatly increased sales and profits indicate that some U.S. automakers are making a comeback. The news accounts of high bonuses to upper management, however, suggest that not much has been learned from the past. Social values change, and those changes must inform corporate policy or the world will pass on by, leaving another hulk in the sands of time.

At the center of a corporate ethic capable of supporting effective management is careful knowledge of the environment of values.

One sector of the environment of values is external to the corporation, in the surrounding society. Another sector of the environment of values is internal to the corporation, among the employees, divisions, and other constituencies on the inside. Whether deciding what products and services are in demand or developing relations with employees that ensure productivity, whether building and maintaining the confidence of customers or improving methods of personnel evaluation, keeping tabs on the value climate is essential.

What has become known as Management by Walking Around is one way that managers at various levels can keep up with the environment in the workplace and sense its changes. Marketing departments note carefully what gets response and what does not among clients. These are ways to find out about changing values in the environments crucial to corporate performance. And the need is always present for faster and better methods to learn with precision what the environments of values are now and what they are likely to be in the future.

Wells Fargo Bank has long identified itself with a frontier stagecoach in its advertising, relating both to the values of its history and to the nostalgia of contemporary society for an earlier and simpler time of supposedly more solid values. Successful as those ads have been, they would not have worked if the values customers want today had not been built into the performance and service of Wells Fargo. Knowing the environment of values in various sectors and building on that knowledge are vital for effective policy and implementation.

Awareness of the internal environment of values, or the corporate culture, developing it, nourishing its better elements, and reshaping it to make it stronger are continuing tasks of top management. Of equal importance are the social values of the external environment. These are represented in the various constituencies to which the company relates — customers, clients, stockholders, suppliers, labor unions, professional groups, special interests, social justice activists, and so on. The external environment also includes government at various levels with regulations and laws, society with its social values that give rise to law, the political-economic scene within the nation, communities at home and abroad in which the company operates, and the larger global arena of interaction among nations and peoples.

An increasing amount of significant research is being done on the social values that give shape to the cultural environment in which we and societal organizations exist. It should come as no surprise that this research discloses that social values do not remain static but are continuously changing. As social values change, changes occur in all areas of society: in customs, in laws, in political and economic activity, and in power. As change develops, it produces social trends. The more accurately top managers know the climate of values in society and the shifts that are taking place in them, the more effectively they will be able to manage values in a changing world.

One book reporting on changes in the environment of values is Ronald Inglehart's *The Silent Revolution: Changing Values and Political Styles among Western Publics.*[2] Inglehart's findings are based on survey data from the United States and nine countries of western Europe. He interprets these data primarily in terms of their political implications. It can, nevertheless, be as instructive for corporate leaders as for governmental officials.

Inglehart reports that social values in the North Atlantic community have been shifting from an overwhelming emphasis on material well-being and physical security toward greater interest in the quality of life. "The causes and implications of this shift are complex," he writes, "but the basic principle might be stated very simply: people tend to be more concerned with immediate needs or threats than with things that seem remote or non-threatening. Thus, a desire for beauty may be more or less universal, but hungry people are more likely to seek food than aesthetic satisfaction. Today, an unprecedentedly large portion of Western populations have been raised under conditions of exceptional economic security. Economic and physical security continued to be valued positively, but their relative priority is lower than in the past." This change in priorities is what Inglehart refers to as "the silent revolution."

Such a change may help to explain the widespread interest in quality of life and human rights for persons in other parts of the world by groups in Western society. It might also suggest reasons for greater preoccupation with economic and military security on the part of the Soviet Union. Corporations as well as governments need such information as the basis of policy.

In *Megatrends,* John Naisbitt identifies "ten new directions transforming our lives" in American society. The shift in values represented by these new directions, as they restructure our lives at every level, cannot be ignored by leadership in any sector. The ten overall, critical trends, in Naisbitt's view, are summarized by the author:

1. Although we continue to think we live in an industrial society, we have in fact changed to an economy based on the creation and distribution of information.
2. We are moving in the dual direction of high tech/ high touch, matching each new technology with a compensatory human response.
3. No longer do we have the luxury of operating within an isolated, self-sufficient, national economic system; we now must acknowledge that we are part of a global economy. We have begun to let go of the idea that the United States is and must remain the world's industrial leader as we move on to the other tasks.
4. We are restructuring from a society run by short-term considerations and rewards in favor of dealing with things in much longer-term time frames.
5. In cities and states, in small organizations and subdivisions, we have rediscovered the ability to act innovatively and to achieve results — from the bottom up.
6. We are shifting from institutional help to more self-reliance in all aspects of our lives.
7. We are discovering that the framework of representative democracy has become obsolete in an era of instantaneously shared information.
8. We are giving up our dependence on hierarchical structures in favor of informal networks. This will be especially important to the business community.
9. More Americans are living in the South and West, leaving behind the old industrial cities of the North.

10. From a narrow either/or society with a limited range of personal choices, we are exploding into a free-wheeling multiple-option society.[3]

Whether we are inclined to agree that all these changes are occurring or that, if they are indeed happening, they are to be regarded as good or desirable, Naisbitt makes a persuasive case for them. Corporate management must be aware of them and prepared to take account of the changing environment of social values producing these trends.

It is not sufficient, however, to make judgments about the shifting cultural climate by having top management hold their fingers up to the wind or by reading books such as *The Silent Revolution* and *Megatrends,* important and beneficial as that may be. Corporations must develop ways to assemble accurate information about social change, to assess the social values underlying change carefully, and to integrate this knowledge into the formulation and implementation of corporate policy. The changing environment of social values must inform policy ethics and the management of values.

It may be some comfort to the U.S. automotive industry today to recall previous failures to pay adequate attention to society's changing values. Philip Selznick tells the story of what happened to the Ford Motor company in the 1920s:

> A characteristic crisis is the shift from a production orientation to an emphasis on sales and public relations. The Ford Motor Company, among others in the auto industry, went through a crisis of this sort. The organization that produced the famous "Model T" was dedicated to the goal of producing more cars per day at an ever lower cost per car. In this it was highly successful. But the organization that made this achievement possible failed to recognize or respond to changes in the market. Consumer preference was shifting to comfort, styling, and performance. By 1926, when sales were off disastrously, Ford permitted his company to engage in a national advertising campaign. He accepted this technique grudgingly, only under the pressure of a major crisis.

But much more than advertising was needed to permit sales an adequate role in the organization. Design and engineering had to be influenced as well. Finally, in 1927, production of the Model T was stopped, and Ford undertook the monumental task of retooling for a completely new automobile and rebuilding factory interiors so that it could be manufactured. It was now clear that the very techniques that brought about the great production achievement of the Model T were stumbling blocks when the need was speedy and efficient changeover. Huge, single-purpose machines had been built into production lines where more flexible machines were needed to keep up with periodic model changes. When the policy that "the customer could have any color he wanted so long as it was black" gave way to color styling, the old finishing process became completely obsolete.[4]

Keith Sward adds this postscript:

> Nearly every piece of the company's monolithic equipment, laid out on the assumption that the Model T would linger forever, had to be torn down and rebuilt. The staggering changeover necessitated the replacement of some 15,000 machine tools, the total rebuilding of another 25,000, as well as the redesigning and rearrangement of $5,000,000 worth of dies and fixtures.[5]

The total process of conversion needed to shift to the Model A cost $100 million and required 18 months. Even so, Ford did not go through with the reorganization in the depth needed to adjust to the changing values of the market. It was not until after World War II that the company went through the major overhaul that was required. By that time the company had paid a heavy price for ignoring the social environment. More than dollars, it lost its lead in the automotive industry, a lead it has never recovered.

SOCIAL VALUES SYSTEMS ANALYSIS

The environment of social values in our society and around the world is changing rapidly, and corporate management must understand these changes in order to formulate policy effectively. From such understanding can come a clear perception of the conditions to which corporate policy and action must adjust and the ways to carry out the purposes and values of the company. Because social values are changing, information about them must not only be accurate and realistic but also timely.

It is a common observation that the values of business have in recent centuries been widely accepted in Western industrial society. The dominant social values have been associated with individualism, with productivity as a measure of individual worth, and with the market mechanism as the best way to allocate goods, services, and investment.

Over the past few decades, it has become increasingly clear that this business value consensus is under intense pressure and may be dissolving. We live in a society that is becoming more pluralistic than was the case a century ago and in which there are increasing conflicts among the diverse values of individuals and groups. The environment of social values is undergoing change, and these shifts underlie the plethora of new social legislation, increasingly active regulatory commissions, and the rise in direct social pressure on corporations. The definitions of *social responsibility* change. The sphere of corporate freedom of action is altered in texture and horizon. The problems to which executives must give attention have broadened. The management of values has been much more complex.

The problem of social values is often posed as how to relate business and society. In the search for a model or integrating framework, it is tempting to divide society up into subsystems defined by academic disciplines and then seek ways to relate the parts. Michael Novak, for example, sees three spheres — the economic, the political, and the cultural — interacting with one another through institutions representing each sector.[6] Human wholeness does not yield to such division. Political, economic, and technological factors permeate all societal institutions. Churches are political and economic as well as religious. Corporations are political and have value systems as well as being "economic" entities. All societal organizations exist and operate

FIGURE 7.1   *Field of Cultural Values*

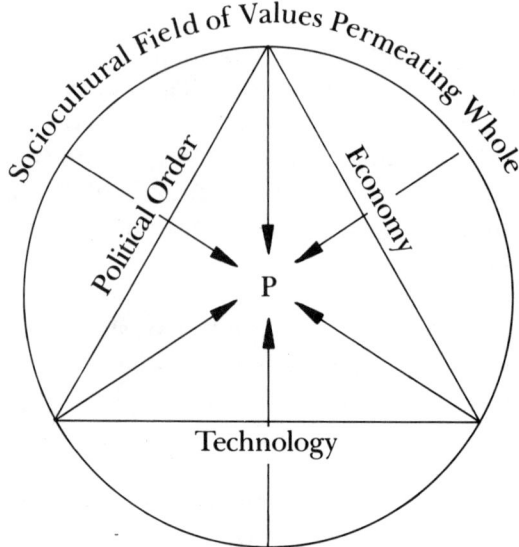

P = any policy-making center in a societal organization

in a field of cultural values. Depicted graphically, the field to which business and society gives attention might look like Figure 7.1.

Understanding Social Values Systems Analysis

For any corporation the ability to perceive the changing field of values surrounding it and anticipate the impact of those values can be crucial for shaping effective corporate policy. A company that wants to be a leader in performance must have the means to understand the changing environment comprehensively, continuously, and on a timely basis. One way to track shifting values is with an instrument called Social Values Systems Analysis.

Its focus, first, is social, interpreting the society around us in which all of us must live and within which corporations carry out their economic and social functions. This analysis is concerned, second, with social values, interests, and commitments that are widely held in society. These values reflect the ways society defines what is good and right and what purposes are worthwhile. Social values are subject to changes that can usually be traced to specific forces at work in the world; at the same time, social values are shaping human action and society.

Third, it is possible to grasp these shifting constellations of values as social values systems and to understand them fairly accurately by means of social values systems analysis. The pluralistic values of Western society cluster in identifiable patterns or systems, each system given shape and relation by a particular social perspective. By discovering these systems and describing their distinctive pattern, it is possible to understand what at first appears to be confusing complexity and overlapping of values. Analysis of each system, once it is identified and described, reveals the implicit and explicit assumptions underlying it and what these assumptions mean in terms of policy and action.

Social Values Systems Analysis can provide corporate management with a clearer view of the environment of values, the probable impact of this environment on the company, and the relation of this environment to alternative courses of action. When available to management and used within the policy process, it can become a powerful and valuable instrument for the effective management of values.

Value Trends and Social Forces

At this point in history there appear to be a bewildering variety of interpretations of contemporary social change. Most shifts in social values can be related to definable social forces at work in society. Recently, for example, a decisive globalization of culture has taken place, brought on by dramatic improvements in communications and travel. Changes in the environment of social values for Western society is caused in part by the greater awareness of other peoples and cultures. We learn more about the problems of other sectors of the world and about the impact of Western society upon them. What happens in any country can be known almost instantly everywhere and can influence actions and events rapidly. Ideas from one culture permeate others, and above all it becomes clear that we share a fragilely interdependent existence on spaceship Earth.

Given the global perspective, what does Social Values Systems Analysis reveal about the constellations of values in North Atlantic society? Three interpreters of social change provide useful background.

1. Daniel Bell, who provided an early description of the movement into a postindustrial society, speaks of the change in social values now in progress in *The Cultural Contradictions of Capitalism.*[7] In this wide-ranging inquiry into and analysis of the contemporary scene, Bell reaches the conclusion that there is a radical disjunction between the current technoeconomic order and the existing culture. The economic system of the Western industrial nations embodies such principles as efficiency, market-dictated decisions, and organizations that treat persons as "things." At the same time, culture is characterized by an anti-rational, anti-intellectual temper in which the self is taken as the source of cultural judgments, and the effect on the self is the measure of experience. The character patterns handed down from the nineteenth century emphasize self-discipline, delayed gratification, and restraint. Though relevant to the demands of the technoeconomic structure, these characteristics clash sharply with a culture in which middle-class values have been rejected — in part, paradoxically, because of the success of the capitalist economy.

    The core values that once dominated culture in the industrialized nations could be summarized by such terms as *the Puritan temper* and *the Protestant ethic*. The environment of values in that era emphasized the virtue of achievement defined as doing and making; humans displayed their character in the quality of their work.

    By the 1950s the pattern of social values was showing the result of comprehensive change, according to Bell. Rather than work and achievement, value was now placed on spending and enjoyment. Western society, especially in the United States, was becoming hedonistic, concerned with play, fun, display, and pleasure. The technoeconomic order of capitalism was left without a transcendent ethic.

2. George Cabot Lodge also makes a case for the change of social values in Western society. In *The New American Ideology*,[8] Lodge describes how "the ideological basis of legitimate authority" is being radically transformed, with "profound implications for our society in general and the great corporations in particular." This transformation is a change in ideology. By *ideology*, he means the

framework of ideas by which a community defines and applies values. Thus, an ideology is the foundation upon which a society judges the actions of its institutions — whether they are acting for or against the common good. As the social values that informed the past undergo change, the old ideas and assumptions that once made societal institutions (including corporations) legitimate are being eroded and replaced by ideals that are different and unsettling.

First, individualism is giving way to communitarianism. For most people today, Lodge says, fulfillment occurs through participation in an organic social process. In our complex, highly organized society, few can or wish to live a life of rugged individualism. The old idea of equality of opportunity is being transformed into equality of result and equality of representation. A corporation, therefore, must respond to inequalities in the surrounding community and accept new criteria for the rightness of corporate conduct.

Second, property rights are being replaced by rights of membership. The right to survive, to enjoy income and health, to secure employment, and so on — rights arising from membership in the national community (or in the corporate community) — have superseded property rights and rights based on holding property. Increasingly, it is clear that large public corporations are no longer private property. The 1.5 million shareholders of General Motors may in an abstract legal sense still own the company, but they do not control it or have a real sense of responsibility for the company. The corporation has become a kind of social collectivity, floating in philosophical limbo, dangerously vulnerable to charges of illegitimacy and lack of responsiveness to community direction.

Third, the methods for controlling the use of property are changing. Where we once entrusted this function to open competition in the marketplace, we are now more inclined to apply criteria of community need in order to allocate resources. This represents a decisive shift in social values from the older idea that the public interest emerges from free and vigorous competition among numerous aggressive, individualistic, and preferably small companies attempting to satisfy the needs of consumers.

Fourth, the role of government is expanding so that the notion of the state as planner for the entire society is increasingly accepted as a social value. As arbiter of community needs and purposes, the government takes on the tasks of coordination, the setting of priorities, and comprehensive planning. Societal institutions exist more and more on government subsidies, grants, allowances, and contracts — to corporations, to farmers, to the disadvantaged, to the schools and universities, and to every type of community agency. Individuals receive social insurance, medical care, unemployment benefits, housing allowances, and food stamps. The allocation of these entitlements reflect more the power vectors of political interests than any coherent long-range plan.

Fifth, there is growing acceptance of holism, perceiving reality as a total system rather than viewing it as parts to be dealt with separately. The old idea of scientific specialization is giving way to a consciousness of the interrelatedness of all things. Ideas such as Spaceship Earth, the limits to growth, and the fragility of the life-supporting environment have all dramatized the ecological, philosophical, and theological truth that everything exists in symbiotic relation with everything else.

Lodge suggests that the change in social values has already taken place. And there is no going back to the old values.

3. Neil Chamberlain is even more explicit than Bell or Lodge about the significance of the changing environment of values for business management. In *The Place of Business in America's Future: A Study in Social Values,*[9] Chamberlain defines *social values* as shared beliefs about what is "good" within society. Values characterize the spirit of an age, establish broad social purpose, serve as norms for social conduct, and function as sanctions controlling individual and organizational behavior.

Three general types of values operate in society, says Chamberlain. First are the *focal values* that define the "good life." Although primary emphasis has been placed on private consumption and material welfare (values closely associated with business), anti-materialistic values are becoming increasingly strong, especially among younger people. Second, there are *constitutional values* defining the individual's relation to government, the amount of coercion that is acceptable, and the degree of conformity necessary for social order. Values of individual autonomy are giving way to values of a more structured social order. This shift is responsive to the perceived need for coordination of individual and institutional activities toward service of public objectives. Third, *distributive values* concern how power, status, and material advantages are to be distributed in society and the extent to which differences of privilege are accepted as socially justifiable. Society is experiencing a shift from the traditional values of equality of opportunity (meritocracy) toward equality of condition as the primary characteristic of distributive value.

Business has been the group with the greatest influence on social values over the past several centuries, according to Chamberlain, with government, church, and education serving to institutionalize and support dominant social values. It is possible that a creative group of "thrusters" in business will provide leadership as social values are being reshaped for the future, but it may also happen that other groups will assume the dominant position that business has previously occupied.

Patterns of Change

Apart from the issue of whether we agree with the views of these three analysts, the lesson emerging clearly from their discussions is that corporate management must give careful attention to the environment of values in which it operates and to the changes occurring in those values. Such awareness is an essential part of a corporate ethic and of the effective management of values. Further, business executives should exercise leadership in shaping social values.

Using the work of Bell, Chamberlain, and Lodge as the basis for social values systems analysis, we can derive a table of the changing environment of social values such as Table 7.1. More comprehensive study would modify and refine this analysis, and continuing research is needed in order to keep pace with ongoing change. In the following section three social values systems are identified that are present in the contemporary environment and the relations among them explored.

THREE SOCIAL VALUES SYSTEMS

In contemporary Western society there are three systems that deserve special attention by corporate policymakers. Each of the three

TABLE 7.1 Summary of Social Trends

	Bell		Chamberlain		Lodge	
	From	Toward	From	Toward	From	Toward
Protestant ethic; self-discipline; delayed gratification		Self-indulgence; consumption now; luxury	Material abundance linked to work ethic	Divorcing of abundance and work ethic	Individualism	Communitarianism
Thrift		Installment buying	Success measured primarily in material terms	New meaning of success in more nonmaterial terms	Property rights	Rights of membership (survival, health, income)
Emphasis on how to achieve		Emphasis on how to spend	Equality of opportunity	Equality of condition	Competition (consumer desire)	Community need
Individualism		Communal society emphasis on social planning and participation	Relatively decentralized forms of social authority	Greater hierarchical and systemic order	The limited state	State as planner and coordinator

TABLE 7.1 (*cont.*)

National center of economy	Globalization of economy	Great confidence in "superiority of American way of life"	Greater tolerance for non-American styles	Scientific specialization	Holism — the total system approach
Abundance of resources	Resource shortages; problems of resource management				
Decentralized control	More central authority and regulation; greater demands on public sector				
Faith in technology	Loss of faith in technology				

has deep roots in tradition and is embodied in strong or emerging social forces. Each provides an internally consistent understanding of what is "good" and "right" in societal policy and action, and each represents a distinctly different social perspective and constellation of values. The changing environment of social values comes into focus through an examination of conflict and accommodation among these systems and becomes available for use in policy formulation.

The three social values systems are: (1) a Smithian social values system, (2) a humanitarian social values system, and (3) a communitarian social values system. The Smithian system, named after Adam Smith, author of *The Wealth of Nations* (1776), represents the strong tradition of business values passed down in the societies of Western industrial nations. More than the other two, it embodies the social values inherited by business leaders and underlying contemporary corporate policy processes. The humanitarian and communitarian systems have bases in traditions passed down in other institutions and, in various ways, are becoming stronger within the business community, to overlay and to modify but not to replace the Smithian system. This process of interaction among these constellations of social values has been going on for a long time in Western society, and all three are present, often deeply ingrained, in the personal value commitments of corporate managers.

Owing to a combination of forces shaping global culture and having an impact on Western societies, humanitarian and communitarian values have been gaining power. Their rising influence in the industrial nations is apparent, as evidenced in Bell, Chamberlain, and Lodge. These values are also becoming increasingly represented within corporations. As significant elements in both the external and internal environment, they must inform policy. Social Values Systems Analysis makes it possible to include consideration of social values with more precision in the management of values. Table 7.2 presents a schematic summary of these three social value systems in parallel form.

The Smithian Social Values System

This system derives from the teachings of Adam Smith (1723–90), the Scottish moral philosopher, influential political economist, and implicitly one of the founders of policy studies. Responding to the emergence of the industrial revolution in England, Smith opposed the heavy-handed control of commerce by governments, a political economy known as *mercantilism*. Not money but productive capability must be regarded as the true "wealth of nations," Smith affirms. The focal values of his system are individualism and productivity. When individuals pursue their own self-interest in the marketplace, they contribute to the good of society. In a thinly veiled theological doctrine of providence, Smith holds that the individual entrepreneurs, in seeking their own interests, are led by an "invisible hand" to promote an end that was not part of their intentions. Although Smith in his ethics regards propriety, prudence (or self-interest), and benevolence as coordinate virtues, self-interest is most appropriate in the marketplace and more likely to produce beneficial results for the entire society than altruistic intentions. Even more important, perhaps, productivity is a focal value of the Smithian system. A central criterion of goodness and rightness is productivity. When persons fail to be productive, they do not pursue what is good for themselves or for society.

In the nineteenth century, social Darwinism built upon and became intertwined with Smithian values. This view posits a "natural law" governing economic affairs: the fit survive, the unfit fail. Productivity and success are goods that are attained by some and withheld from others. Good people — those who are virtuous and fit — are productive; lack of productivity is seen as a sign of unfitness and lack of virtue. While this view is no longer embraced with the fervor it commanded a century ago, its ways of defining *success* in terms of productivity and wealth retain latent power in our time.

As Smithian values flowed into the development of corporate business, they supported the market system. As individuals were to pursue their own self-interest and thus contribute to the general welfare, so also the corporation ought to pursue its own interest in the marketplace and in that way benefit society. An ethic of corporate self-interest, as these interests are woven together by the market, will generate wealth, allocate capital goods and investments, and distribute goods and services for the ultimate benefit of all. The interests of stockholders and managers, as represented in maximized profits, are justified in terms of transcendent ethical principles.

The Humanitarian Social Values System

The focal values of the humanitarian system are the rights of individuals and equality among persons in society. These values find historical roots in federal political philosophy as represented in the American Declaration of Independence and the U.S. Constitution and in a somewhat different way in English utilitarianism and reform movements. Though having impact on the political economy as a whole, the influence of humanitarian values is especially apparent in the democratizing tendencies in the political order. In the economic sphere humanitarianism has worked to protect individuals from the harshness of the market system and to produce tendencies toward greater equality of opportunity. The values of this system have modified Smithian values in Western industrial nations — for example, in the abolition of slavery, in the improvement of working conditions, in laws protecting the rights of children and women, in supporting the developing labor movement, and in various forms of social legislation regarding health, retirement, unemployment insurance, and the rights of minorities and women.

The pace at which humanitarian values have modified or been superimposed on Smithian values has increased in recent decades. To the extent that laws confirm the general acceptance of particular social values, we may say that we have been experiencing in Western society a revolution in values of significance proportions. The legal protection of unions and the right to collective bargaining were humanitarian issues of the 1930s with impact in the economic sphere that had to be taken into account in the formulation of corporate policy. Equal employment opportunity and affirmative action were comparable issues of the 1970s.

Not only have many humanitarian values become socially valent and found expression in law, but they have also come to be part of the values of persons who become corporate executives. What had been more prevalent in the external environment now becomes part of the internal environment of values in business corporations. Managers, directors, and employees have been shaped by the society around and bring their values with them to their roles within the corporate community. The March 20, 1981, issue of *Business International* has an article that underscores this development: "In the coming decade," says the author, "companies interviewed by BI believe that strong pressures to integrate new ethical standards into corporate policy will arise within the organization itself." Experience with corporate executives in projects in both the western and eastern United States confirms this view. Management is finding itself influenced increasingly by this changing internal environment.

The Communitarian Social Values System

More recently than humanitarian values but just as decisively, communitarian values have become an emerging force in Western societies. Its central idea is that the "good" and "right" are to be defined from the perspective of the whole society rather than in terms of individuals or social collectivities on any level less than the whole. George Cabot Lodge suggests that communitarian values are gathering strength as a result of the increased interrelatedness and interdependency among persons and institutions in society. Gone are the days when "rugged individualism" could be regarded as a viable basis for policy. The single-minded pursuit of self-interest narrowly defined is viewed by few today as a certain path to the common good. Instead, it is said more and more, policy must be shaped from the perspective of the advantage of the total human community.

In the corporate sphere the communitarian view, like the humanitarian perspective, can be expected to modify rather than replace Smithian values. As managers of major institutions, corporate executives find themselves increasingly constrained by external and internal pressures to guide policy by criteria related to the good of the whole as well as the interests of the corporation. Indeed, it is being argued often that corporate interests are closely aligned with the interests of the larger community.

The proliferation of governmental regulatory agencies, to a significant degree, is informed by communitarian values and designed to encourage or even impose these values on corporations even though it is not always clear that the actual operation of such agencies carries out the intentions that led to their being founded. In addition, it is possible to see a shift from humanitarian values toward communitarian values as the affirmative action movement has gone from advocating redressing unfairness to individuals toward affirming the benefit to the whole society to be derived from overcoming injustices to entire groups.

Communitarian values are also reflected in the emerging view that rights of entitlement derive from membership in a group rather than from one's status as an individual. Belonging is becoming more important as the basis for rights and relationships, including the belonging to corporations. "Job as right" is one form in which this shift appears. "Consensus" as modifying "authority" in organizational relations is another.

As Lodge points out, the move toward communitarian values is clearly under way, but the precise patterns of the change are often confusing. Forces at work on the global scene, however, are working in a communitarian direction and influencing the environment of social values in every industrial society. Recognition of the social values system can be helpful in policy formulation and for the management of values in the corporation.

A Comparative View

Examination of the three social values systems in comparative terms discloses likenesses and differences. Each system, for example, defines a basis for corporate power. In the Smithian system the productive involvement of the corporation in the market system and its active pursuit of corporate self-interest validate and legitimate the corporation. Corporate power arises from individual property rights and the ability of the corporation to fulfill social needs through the market. In the humanitarian system corporate power is curbed when individual rights are impaired by imperfections of the market or by too narrow a conception of corporate interests. Corporate power arises from the ability of the corporation to contribute to individual life and fill, as Daniel Bell has argued, a broad range of wants that arise with increasing affluence. Under the communitarian system the power of corporations will rest increasingly on their ability to assist in achieving the goals of the whole society. When the automotive industry, for example, and the market system as well, were pitted against the needs of the total society for fuel conservation and safety, communitarian values won — or at least substantially modified Smithian values.

The environment of values in society continues to change. The analysis given above is based on research done in the 1970s. One wonders how much Daniel Bell, George Cabot Lodge, and Neil

Chamberlain have changed their minds about the climate of values as we have moved into the 1980s. A study completed in 1982 by the Public Agenda Foundation and the Aspen Institute confirms the emergence of a new configuration of social values in the industrialized countries, especially among younger and better educated people.[10] Keeping up with changes in values is a continuing imperative for leaders in all sectors of society.

Perceiving humanitarian values and assessing what is good for the whole from the perspective of corporate management are neither easy nor simple tasks, yet doing so is increasingly important for those who will guide the policy of modern corporations. The challenge to understand the changing environment of social values and to discover the meaning of social values systems for policy formulation must be met by executives who seek to manage values well.[11]

POSTSCRIPT

What happened to Sid? Some readers may be asking this question in relation to the outcome of Jay's concern about peaked-out employees in the conversation opening the chapter. The discussions on the topic of what to do about employees promoted beyond their capabilities or no longer able to function effectively were held with a group of senior managers in the company where Jay was CEO. Sid participated in the group and made many helpful contributions. The policy that emerged from these discussions and that was, with modifications, adopted by the company appears in Appendix I. Six months later, in connection with the performance evaluation process initiated under the new policy, Sid carried out a rigorous self-assessment in the course of which it became clear that he was as much aware of his problems as others. At his request, Sid and Jay, in conjunction with the director of personnel, began to explore the best ways to utilize Sid's extensive talents and experience. He shifted into the role of troubleshooter, stepping on a short-term basis into the kind of positions at which he had excelled earlier or advising managers with problems he was skilled and experienced at solving. His last five years, before retiring after 40 years of service with the company, were the most productive of his career. Jay was also pleased that a way had been found to handle a very sticky issue in accord with the

TABLE 7.2 Three Social Value Systems

	Smithian	Humanistic	Communitarian
Focal values	Self-interest; productivity	Respect for individuals; equality	The good of the whole society; rights of membership
Roots	Adam Smith and the industrial revolution; social Darwinism; Protestant ethic	U.S. Constitution; Jeremy Bentham and utilitarian philosophy	Recognition of increasing interdependence of individuals, groups, and institutions — nationally and globally
Highest social good	Results from individuals acting in their own self-interest	Creation of equality of opportunity	Contributing to the achievement of goals and priorities established nationally and internationally
Impact on corporation	Conceptual basis for the market system; justifies corporate self-interest	Protection of individuals and groups against the imperfections of the market system	Corporations expected to help achieve national goals; corporate policies/actions seen in larger social systems

TABLE 7.2 (cont.)

Corporate power	Derived from property rights; legitimized by filling the material needs of society	Derived from ability to meet human wants (material and social)	Derived from meeting community needs; consensus as the basis of authority
Value of persons	Based on individual's productivity and material success as measured by the market	All are created equal; individual is responsible for own performance	Personhood derived in relationships to the larger community
Distributive values	Governed by the market as the distributive mechanism	To each according to productivity if: (1) equality of opportunity; (2) compensation for past injustices are present	Each person has the right to fulfillment of basic needs; equality of condition

commitment of the company to the welfare of its employees and loyalty to those with proven allegiance to the firm.

SUGGESTIONS FOR GROUP DISCUSSION

1. Reread the conversation at the beginning of the chapter with Jay about Sid, a peaked-out executive. Then examine the policy statement developed to guide management decisions on peaked-out employees in Appendix I. Also read the brief from Christopher Stone's book entitled *Where the Law Ends* (Appendix J). Reflect carefully on what he has to say about "policy as process." In class discussion identify the ways in which the policy statement in the appendix conforms to the objectives of polity-as-process. Discuss how this policy would work in a situation with which you or other persons in the group have firsthand knowledge.
2. What eventually happened with reference to Sid does not come out in the conversation that opens the chapter but is given briefly in the "Postscript." In the light of your reflections and discussions on corporate policy for peaked-out employees, develop a scenario for what *you* think Jay should have done in relation to Sid, and others like him in the company, that would have been responsible to the values and character of that corporation.
3. Reread the megatrends identified by John Naisbitt as outlined in the text of this chapter. See if you and the members of your study group can verify or discount the validity of these trends from your own life experience. Can you also identify the current or potential impact of them on a company with which you are familiar? If you were president of the company, what would you do to ensure that the implications of these trends are carried into the policy decision-making process?
4. In group discussion see if you can distinguish the value systems that have been at work in the automobile industry and how they are related to its current problems. What specific elements of Smithian, humanistic, and communitarian value systems do you find? How has the industry responded to the conflicts caused by value system changes that have been taking place over the past decade? In what ways can this method of identifying constellations of values help in the management decision-making process?

Eight

INSTITUTIONALIZING CULTURE, VALUES, AND ETHICS

Phillip Owens was well known to me as president and CEO of Owens Industries, but I had never met him. Jim and I went to see him, therefore, with considerable interest in him as a person, as well as curiosity about the project he had mentioned on the telephone that he wanted to discuss with us.

"Let me give you a little background first," he began after we had exchanged greetings and were comfortably settled in his office. "Owens Industries has been a company of our family for almost a century. During all that time, we have prided ourselves on being good citizens and trying to make sure that the firm was also socially responsible. I suppose that if we applied standards of today to earlier eras the company might not come off so well. But I believe each generation tried in its own time to be responsible and succeeded fairly well."

"You have certainly acquired a good reputation over the years, and the firm always gets high ratings for corporate social responsibility," Jim agreed.

"We try. Happily, the business analysts and reporters don't know all the problems that crop up. They only see our solutions, which with a little ethical sensitivity, a moderate amount of work, and a lot of luck usually look pretty good when compared with other businesses." He laughed softly. "I could tell you a few stories that I hope will never be published."

"We'll wait to read your memoirs," I said, as we joined in his laughter.

"Anyway," Owens continued, "the company has done some good and has done very well. It has grown enormously. A crowd of recruits fresh out of business school is required every year. New people come in from all directions.

They don't know our tradition of corporate ethics, and I'm not sure they are learning it from the older hands. The problem is further compounded by the fact that I retire in six years, and for the first time, the head of the company will probably not be a family member."

He paused before going on.

"In the light of all this," he continued, "I want you to develop a project for us aimed at building a sense of ethics and responsibility into the fabric of the company. If you find some ways that work, then we won't have to be so concerned about the leadership passing out of the family. Is that a project that interests you?"

"It certainly does," Jim responded. "It takes us in exactly the direction we want to go. We have some ideas on what we have called 'institutionalizing corporate ethics and social responsibility,' but we need a real business context to work them out."

"That's it exactly," Owens said, sitting up in his chair. "I want to find ways to institutionalize corporate ethics and social responsibility so the traditions of the family will continue, even without one of us sitting in this seat."

"We'll be willing to try," I said. "Whatever we can find out here will be useful elsewhere — in business schools as well as in other corporations."

"I am convinced that it is impossible to have continued high levels of performance without continuing emphasis on ethics," Owens added. "When we've slipped there, we've always slipped in our overall showing."

"Many executives we've worked with think just that," Jim replied, "and the research on culture and values seems to be pointing in that direction."

"We know a lot here about institutionalizing productivity and profit quotas. Let's see if those insights help in relation to corporate values," Owens concluded.

O wens voices a concern shared by many corporate executives: How can value commitments be built into the patterns of company operation so that they are not dependent on continuing pressure from the CEO? How can issues of corporate social responsibility and ethics become concerns for middle management, first-line supervisors, and all employees, as well as top management? To be most effective the management of values must not be the job only of senior executives; it must get out of the executive suite and be taken on at every level of company activities. Only as this process of institutionalization takes place will ethics contribute fully to corporate performance.

In this chapter we shall explore the institutionalization of culture, values, and ethics. In the next chapter we shall continue the same theme by examining the importance of communication, participation, and commitment, for performance.

When Vladimir Horowitz gives a piano concert, a magnificent array of technical skills, artistic sensitivities, and cultural values is united into a musical performance. Not piano keys struck at random but a carefully composed and practiced series of notes played together in their connectedness constitute the concert. What appears on stage as the performance and is heard and seen by the audience seems deceptively easy. The performance is like the tip of an iceberg. There is much more beneath the surface and behind the scenes than appears to the audience. That is the case with every kind of human activity, including the performance of a corporation.

Michael Polanyi, the great Hungarian-British physical chemist turned philosopher, speaks of the tacit dimension underlying and making possible complex, coordinated human action. In every situation of doing, "we know more than we can say," Polanyi reminds us.[1] The performance of the pianist has behind it a tacit dimension of practice, learning, and discipline, with more detail than can be specified. A musical performance is highly individual, but it is also intensely communal. Underlying the career of the individual pianist are years of study, apprenticeship to master instructors, and endless practice. Behind pupil and teacher are a heritage of musical knowledge and skill, a culture within which performing music has meaning and value, and a society that sustains the entire enterprise. The same is true in similar ways with all human activities. Speaking a sentence, riding a bicycle, and managing an organization have comparable ranges of the tacit behind them, far more than we are aware of or can specify, but we rely on this dimly understood wholeness in all that we do.

As with Horowitz, a bicycle rider, or a speaker, the performance of an organization represents the integration of many elements, most of which are invisible to the "audience" and are tacit in the awareness of the policymakers shaping the performance. One way to view the performance of a corporation is to look at its policies, actions, and their results. If we wish, however, to understand the tacit dimension of performance that makes it possible and provides the meaning of the quality of that performance, it is necessary to probe further than what appears "on stage" to the observing public. Many elements of the tacit dimension that make performance possible have to do with labor productivity, adequate capital, technological innovation, and managerial energy and skill. Equally important elements underlying performance relate to corporate culture, values and ethics, and the understanding of social environment.

In exploring the institutionalization of these latter aspects, we shall be dealing with factors that are crucial for performance but that are woven into tacit background rather than appearing explicitly in the foreground of corporate operations. It becomes clear that institutionalization requires (1) developing the corporate culture, (2) working through all the corporate structures, and (3) integrating values and ethical reflection into the entire process of formulating and implementing policy. Responsibility for managing values must be extended from the board and top management through middle management to the first-line supervisors and workers. Beyond institutionalization, this achievement requires communication of, involvement with, and commitment to the values of the corporation at all levels. These are the directions in which Phillip Owens was pointing when he gave us our assignment.

DEVELOPING CORPORATE CULTURE AND VALUE COMMITMENTS

A few years ago, it would have been necessary to explain the importance of corporate culture and value commitments for the performance of a company. This is no longer the case. Recent discussions in widely read books have clarified what is meant when we speak of the culture or ethos of a corporation and also the central role such a culture and its values play in shaping corporate performance for better or worse.[2] The developing and shaping of its culture and value commitments are crucial for the institutionalizing of ethics and for enhancing corporate performance. How to do it is the difficult problem.

Even so, ways to strengthen culture in organizations is not a subject to which much attention has been paid in the literature on business. Books by management scientists are more likely to provide analytic frameworks for understanding various aspects of organizations than to deal with building commitment to corporate values. Writing on business ethics is most apt to deal with ethical theory — with deontological, utilitarian, or teleological ethics — or with enumerations of corporate misdeeds such as bribery, fraud, and expense account padding. Criteria of justice and truth are presented, with case studies to be used in discussing ethical principles. When there are illustrations of "good" corporations, we are given little to help us understand how they got that way. And there is a notable absence of material exploring how ethical reflection can be institutionalized, that is, integrated into the patterns of policy formulation and implementation. But it is just such building of ethics into the processes of operation that relates corporate culture and values to corporate performance.

In their helpful book Terrence Deal and Allan Kennedy list five elements shaping corporate culture: the business environment, the values, the heroes, the rites and rituals, and the cultural network.[3] The importance of the environment for shaping culture and for making policy has been dealt with above. We shall accept Deal and Kennedy's view about the centrality of values, expand their notion of rites and rituals, transpose their heroes into leaders, and add the element of existing resources. We now have the elements for developing, shaping, and strengthening a culture within a corporation.

Infusion with Value

When we speak of developing a corporate culture and value commitments, we are not referring to something peripheral to the company, pronouncements of senior management, or written directives. On the contrary, culture is meaning that is embodied in actions.

"Truly accepted values must infuse the organization at many levels," writes Philip Selznick, "affecting the perspective and attitudes of personnel, the relative importance of staff activities, the distribution of authority, relations with outside groups, and many other matters. Thus if a large corporation asserts the wish to change its role in the community from a narrow emphasis on profit-making to a larger social responsibility (even though the ultimate goal remains some combination of survival and profit-making ability), it must explore the implications of such a change for decision-making in a wide variety of organizational activities."[4]

For a corporation to be infused with value means, first, that it has a high level of integration in its total operation. Throughout its various divisions and layers of management, there are common understandings that provide a sense of community and relationship. Communication is possible because there is a community of purpose.

It means, second, that there is a sense of corporate identity. Not everyone has the same tasks to do or the same authority, but everyone possesses a firm knowledge that they are part of the same organization and contributing in different ways to shared goals.

Third, to be infused with values is to have corporate integrity based not on conformity to external directives but on an inner cohesion based on common commitments. As this integrity becomes increasingly institutionalized, there are distinctive outlooks and habits that are reflected in agreement and coordinated action beyond that produced by chains of command or reams of regulations.

Fourth, there is then a fabric of support in which persons participate, both to receive support for decisions and possible innovations and to give support to one another. It is a fabric of community able to sustain persons when they make mistakes as well as guide them toward success and make it an occasion of common rejoicing.

Fifth, there are ceremonies and celebrations that both represent the culture and strengthen the infusion of values throughout the corporate community. The times when achievements are recognized in small and large ways form part of these cultural rituals, as do parties and fun times. Thomas Watson, Sr., leading IBM employees in a company songfest may seem more than a little corny. But it was part of a pattern that helped develop and sustain a strong corporate culture, inspired loyalty that could endure frequent transfers, and empowered people toward innovation and accomplishment.

Building on Existing Resources

In developing corporate culture and value commitments, it is never necessary to begin from ground zero. People bring much from their own experiences in various sectors of society and from their own natural abilities with them into the setting of the corporate community.

The task is not so much creating something out of nothing as it is a matter of tapping the energies and resources already present — "waiting" as Peters and Waterman put it, "for motivation."

The first and most important resource is human nature itself. If management operates with the notion that human beings must be coerced and threatened, it will fail to notice and make use of the resources people bring with them. If management takes the view that everyone working for the company is a cool, rational human being, it will tap only a fraction of the energies available. Humans are rational — but not very. Nowhere but in the economists' ideal and the philosophers' theory does the "rational man" exist. Real human beings enjoy activity, especially if their efforts are noticed and praised. Commitment to common objectives comes as naturally as breathing to people; indeed, finding contexts where persons can devote their energies may be among the most universal of human quests in life. To speak of these characteristics is an alternative way of saying that human beings are creatures of community by nature and respond to challenges to action that derive from the community and give them a sense of belonging to the community.

Humans as communal beings are convivial. As Michael Polanyi reminds us, "Pure conviviality, that is, the cultivation of good fellowship, predominates in many acts of communication; indeed, the main reason for which people talk to each other is a desire for company. The torment of solitary confinement is that it deprives one not of information but of conversation, however uninformative."[5] Conviviality is the central theme of one of the most successful ad campaigns of the past decade. Sponsored by Miller Beer, these TV commercials depict energetic young adults gathering for good times after work. The glowing scenes emphasizing the deep, ineradicable conviviality of humanity has attracted viewers and propelled its product toward the top of the sales charts.

Second, when humans expend their energies in a community and find there a context of conviviality, the interaction of persons sparks insights and responses that would never have occurred to one person alone. A process sometimes called *synergism* happens when people are together. Their natural resources are multiplied. It can be called teamwork or whatever. The fact is that persons in relation, bouncing off each other, make resources available in a situation far beyond the sum of the resources of the individuals on their own.

Third, everyone comes from a setting in which culture and

value commitments have been instilled in them from birth. Most of the employees and virtually all of the people in management have been raised in communities permeated by social values and have been deeply influenced by one or another religious community. In Western society they almost certainly will have been active in a Judeo-Christian religious community and very likely will regard it as important in their lives. The prevalent notion that religion is fading away cannot endure even minimal exposure to the statistics on the growth of and participation in religious communities. Nor are ethical awareness and commitment disappearing. Only those with perfectionist expectations for human performance and no knowledge of human history could suggest that society is more corrupt than it was in those "good old days" that never existed. Both the cynics and the perfectionists have been saying at least since the time of the Babylonian Empire that the next generation was going to the dogs. And humanity staggers on.

What all this means for the development of corporate culture and value commitments is that the basic materials are already present among the people who work in corporations. The individual ethics that people bring is not enough and needs shaping in the distinctive community of a particular corporation, but their backgrounds, permeated by values, are an important resource.

Meaning and Action

Nothing motivates people more powerfully than a sense of meaning in which they participate, and the meaning that involves and motivates is that which is embodied in action. In one sense, meaning is shared values, but these values must be acted out in specific ways. It is through actions that embody values and meaning, therefore, that corporate cultures can be developed, strengthened, and sustained.

One form that meaning-bearing action takes is storytelling. Regardless of age or location, people love a compelling story that is well told. Because a story with artistic dimensions draws persons in and involves them in its world, stories are one of the important ways to develop a corporate culture. And then people who are impressed by a story tell it to others. In so doing, they both pass the culture on and affirm themselves as part of it.

But the stories will help develop the culture only if they grow out of, and are backed up by, corporate actions that demonstrate the same meaning. There must be an integrity at the core of a corporation as the foundation of a culture. Then it can spread and come to pervade the entire organization. Policies that have consistency of value and purpose will aid in developing and building a culture. In addition, rituals and ceremonies must become part of the actions of the community. Some of these have to do with the identity of the corporation and the sharing of everyone in that identity. Slogans, symbols, the repetition of goals — all these can provide the means for instilling a culture. So also can the methods of personnel evaluation and reward. In all these ways value commitments are projected and caught by those involved. Still another kind of occasion involves celebration and conviviality. The beer-busts, the songfests, the softball games, the company picnics, and times to cheer when quotas are met or exceeded illustrate events that aid in developing corporate culture.

Jerome Bruner, the psychologist, tells us that people are more likely to act themselves into feeling than feel themselves into action. And they are even more likely to act themselves into thinking than think themselves into acting. Nothing will contribute to the building of a corporate culture unless the actions throughout the corporate community represent a coherent meaning, that is, unless there is a sufficient unity of value commitments spreading out from the center of the company to convey integrity.

Leadership

Some may wonder why leadership was not named first. It is not because it is less important but rather because leadership must be seen in terms of what it means to develop corporate culture and value commitments rather than as striking out into a vacuum. It is all too easy to emphasize the personal element in leadership and neglect what effective leadership accomplishes. "Values are the bedrock of any corporate culture," Deal and Kennedy remind us. "As the essence of a company's philosophy for achieving success, values provide a sense of common direction for all employees and guidelines for their day-to-day behavior.... In fact, we think that often companies succeed because their employees can identify, embrace, and act on the values of the organization. . . . Shared values define the fundamental character of their organization. . . . Moreover, values are a reality in the minds of most people throughout the company, not just senior executives."[6] Because a corporation is distinguished by its value commitments, by the assumptions of policymakers and employees as to the nature of the enterprise, the central problem of leadership has to do with control of the core of value commitments and the continual care of them. It has to do with the balancing of various purposes, integrating values into policy, encouraging innovation, and shaping this particular time in the organization's life history. In this perspective we may say that the central task of management is to develop corporate culture and the value commitments informing and giving substance to that culture.

James MacGregor Burns in his book *Leadership* emphasizes this role in saying that "transforming leadership ultimately becomes *moral* in that it raises the level of human conduct and ethical aspiration of both the leader and the led, and thus has a transforming effect on both" and "is dynamic leadership in the sense that leaders throw themselves into a relationship with followers who will feel 'elevated' by it and often become more active themselves, thereby creating new cadres of leaders."[7] Or, to return to Selznick:

> The inbuilding of purpose is a challenge to creativity because it involves transforming men and groups from neutral, technical units into participants who have a peculiar stamp, sensitivity, and commitment. This is ultimately an educational process. . . . The art of the creative leader is the art of institution building, the reworking of human and technological materials to fashion an organism that embodies new and enduring values. . . . The institutional leader . . . *is primarily an expert in the promotion and protection of values.*[8]

It is probably inadequate to say, as many have, that IBM is the lengthened shadow of Thomas J. Watson, Sr. Rather than the extension of anything so insubstantial as a shadow, IBM embodies a culture carefully developed by Watson and value commitments that were integrated into and nurtured within the company by Watson, his colleagues, and their successors. At the core of effective leadership is the management of values. An essential aspect of managing values is developing a corporate culture that sustains and enhances performance

INTEGRATING VALUES INTO CORPORATE STRUCTURES

Although developing the corporate culture and strengthening the value commitments that shape the corporation at all levels provide part of the answer to Philip Owens's question about institutionalizing ethics, much more is required for a complete answer. An operative and effective corporate ethics must be integrated into all the institutional structures of a company. Only as the culture and values of a corporation permeate all units does corporate culture provide a real alternative to centralized control. But it can provide an alternative, and one that overcomes the problems of too tight a rein at the top that inhibits or preempts decisions at appropriate levels. Integration requires, however, that values be embodied in the patterns of action and interaction rather than residing only in codes and managerial rhetoric.

Culture and Control

For more than half a century, Ind-Ill Company, a firm in the midwestern sector of the United States, had done well in regional distribution and marketing of the products. As cash reserves accumulated in the 1960s and early 1970s, management pondered how to invest wisely and expand in ways that would strengthen the already successful operation. On sound strategic grounds, it was decided to move into manufacturing of the products marketed in order to ensure supplies at costs permitting continuing profits, and to acquire sources of raw materials in order to back up the manufacturing units. As this expansion took place, the company grew from a moderate-sized regional firm with a homogeneous culture into a national corporation with international connections and diverse divisions having very different cultures and operating values. Many of the holdovers in management from the old days longed for the centralized decision-making patterns of the smaller company. Perceptive executives oriented toward the needs of the enlarged company and sensitive to the promise of the future looked for new ways to ensure adequate control while permitting necessary diversity.

The details may vary, but the overall story of the growth of Ind-Ill Company with its problems resulting from expansion is a familiar one. Decentralization and differences in values arise in part through growth and acquiring new operational divisions, but many of the same changes probably occur because of the increasing pluralism of Western societies and the rapid development of new generations of technology.

Decentralization and diversity are increasing. In one sense they can no more be made to disappear than King Canute could stop the ocean tides. Decisions can no longer be made in central offices on many issues because the choices to be made involve specialized knowledge and insight available only to managers in particular situations far distant from the CEO's executive suite. Geographical, societal, and technological differences conspire to assure that those situations in which managerial decisions must be made and overall policy implemented are quite varied.

All this is undoubtedly true, but the problem of maintaining control over far-flung corporate operations remains very real for top management. Many are discovering that a strong culture and firmly held value commitments can provide a means for ensuring coherence and control of a large, diverse organization without exercising a centralized decision-making authority on issues better left to on-site managers. One CEO told us about a decision to buy a particular kind of pipe that came to him through 16 levels of management. Upon investigation, he learned that only the lower 2 levels had enough first-hand information and on-the-job expertise to make the decision. The other 14 levels could only trust the judgment recommended from the actual situation and approve the purchase. In the meantime valuable time was lost getting unnecessary signatures. This CEO decided that an effectively institutionalized culture would better serve the purposes of managerial control than cumbersome centralization.

Corporate culture and value commitments will not provide the control needed for management if they are verbal forms or based on executive expressions of moral sentiments. To be effective, values must be integrated into the entire range of corporate structures and embodied in the action patterns of management at every level. A policy whose practice is enforced with meaningful sanctions can be distinguished easily from those that are enunciated for one or another constituency but never backed up in practice.

Culture and Rules

There is another aspect of the institutionalization of corporate culture that must be considered. As a culture and value commitments are integrated into the structures of a corporation, the result may be to inhibit the ability to deal with change. Jeffrey Pfeffer writes of the institutionalization of organizational culture:

> Instead of questioning the distribution of power, the making of certain decisions, or the following of certain rules of operation, these aspects of the organization become defined as part of the organization's culture and are seen and accepted by participants in the organization as a natural part of their membership in that particular social system. Organizational change, including change in the distribution of power and control, is made more difficult by the tendency to develop shared beliefs, world-views, or organizational cultures which legitimate and institutionalize present practices, structures, and influence distributions.[9]

Quite clearly, the institutionalization of culture and values tends to stabilize the operation of an organization and to lend a coherence to its actions that tends toward greater unity. While excessive cultural control can lead to a type of groupthink that does prevent different alternatives from being considered, the support that comes from social cohesion also provides the basis for persons and groups within it to take risks, try out new ideas, and venture into unknown territory. A strong culture can put a damper on change or it can offer a springboard for innovation. What is the difference?

The institutionalization that inhibits newness and change is that which tries to control actions within the organization by specific rules and rigid directives from the central authority of the organization. Overspecification of behavior prevents persons from taking responsibility in their own sphere of operation and action that is creatively responsive to the immediate situation. Such a method of control not only makes innovation unlikely; it also makes it difficult for those who have on-site knowledge and expertise to take appropriate and timely action.

The institutionalization of culture seeks agreement on the basis of a shared view of what the history, purposes, and character of the corporation are. This is demonstrated more in what the company has done, is doing, and plans to do than in bureaucratic rules. To the extent that there is social control in the organization and unity of perspective and action, they derive from a community of shared interpretation and common value commitments. Such a culture is difficult to develop and sustain in any human community — but especially in large organizations. When it is present and appropriately institutionalized, it becomes the basis of creative interaction, meaningful participation, and continuing innovation. It does not require adherence to rigid codes or rules but sharing in a significant enterprise that provides fulfillment for all participants and important services for the larger community.

Through the Operational Patterns

Although support functions may provide help in the institutionalization of culture, values, and ethics, the effective management of values must have its center in the intentions and actions of the CEO and flow outward into the structures of the corporation. Managing values is the task of every level of management. The heads of all units should take their cues from the CEO and undertake to infuse the corporate culture and value commitments into the practices and understanding of those with whom they work. There may be difficulty at first to find the right language to use, to find illustrations, and to find the appropriate places to deal with values. Once it is clearly understood that values and overall perspectives are no less important for performance than technical skill and sound equipment, the work of learning can begin.

When we speak of all the corporate structures, units, and operational patterns, we mean *all* of them: the corporate office of the CEO, strategic and operational planning, human resources development, education and training, personnel evaluation, recruitment and orientation of new hires, operating divisions, plants, transportation, exploration, legal, purchasing, distribution, marketing, sales, advertising, and the like. Institutionalization must flow through them all and reach every level.

To some, it may seem like overkill if they have been accustomed to think that culture and values ought always to stay on the unspoken level of implicit understandings and be exhibited only in actions. People need to share also in explicit understanding and overt discussion. Emphasis on slogans without stories, illustrations, and cases may become boring, and tiresomeness is a peril to dealing effectively both with values and with performance. Each unit of a corporation has its own distinctive characteristics. The culture and value commitments common to the entire corporation must be made applicable to that particular context and illustrated with examples and particular situations drawn out of the operational experience of the people who make up that unit. Unless the culture is brought alive in a specific community of those who work together, it has not been effectively institutionalized.

RELATING VALUES TO THE POLICY PROCESS

We have already discussed the central role that policy plays in the management of complex organizations such as large corporations. Policy is not formulated in isolated decisions — although decisions may mark "decisive" points of adoption and announcement — but rather is the result of an involved policy process. Every part of this process emerges from and is shaped by the culture and the value commitments of the corporation. Value judgments and ethics are thus present inevitably in policy formulation and implementation. To the extent that management is aware of the evaluative dimensions of policy and has deliberately shaped the criteria for value judgments, we may speak of an explicit corporate ethics. Now we shall explore how the operation of values can be strengthened within the policy process. In so doing, we show in greater detail the close relationship between ethics and performance, giving attention to the organizational patterns and processes connecting them.

Beyond developing a strong corporate culture, building that culture into all the organizational patterns and units, the institutionalization of culture may also take place by integrating values into the policy process (1) by means of ethics codes and social audits, (2) by changes in or additions to the organizational patterns, and (3) by widening and deepening the involvement of all employees in value judgment and implementation.

Codes and Social Audits

Among the means for relating values and policy, the code of ethics is perhaps the instrument used most pervasively for the longest time. Corporate codes appear to have originated as a response to the reform movements in the late nineteenth century that resulted in antitrust legislation and the rise of regulatory agencies. These codes began as very general statements and, gradually over the decades of this century, have become more detailed, with statements or codes covering a wide spectrum of business and legal practices.[10] There are now codes for entire industries and codes for professions, as well as codes for corporations. A recent survey of 611 companies found that 77 percent had a corporate code of conduct. It is also worth noting that only 40 percent of the smaller companies in the study, those with annual revenues under $60 million, had codes, whereas 97 percent of the companies with annual revenues above $4 billion reported having codes. Bernard White comments about the value of corporate codes of ethics or conduct, especially for large companies:

> The immense size of many corporations, along with decentralized and geographically dispersed operations, has created senior management concerns over how to build a shared management philosophy, and insure predictable and appropriate behavior in ambiguous circumstances and in situations where corporate and personal motives may not be congruent. The code of conduct has been a tool in this effort.[11]

Codes of ethics confirm the meaningfulness of moral action in corporate contexts and indicate the concern of management to develop clear standards of conduct. The conversation with Phillip Owens at the beginning of the chapter exemplifies this concern at its best. To the extent that codes are adequately promulgated and enforced, they will clearly have some impact on action. It is doubtful, however, that rules can significantly affect the behavior of persons at all levels of management unless they are reinforced by the culture and value commitments of the corporation and by corporate policies and practices throughout the divisions and levels of the company. Where a code emerges from a strong culture and is updated as the internal and external environments of social values change, it can give public statement to the ethos and provide guidance for those committed to the ethos.

Codes usually apply to the individual behavior of persons in the corporation rather than to corporate policy. They also deal with actions that are clearly reprehensible and give little guidance for morally ambiguous or new situations. Codes tend to deal with things such as: offer of bribes, concealment of information related to bribes, acceptance of bribes and dubious gifts, participation in decisions related to possible individual profit, conflict-of-interest situations, conduct that would injure the company, price-fixing, and falsification of records. Areas like these need attention, and managers and employees at all levels need to be reminded not to violate clear standards. Various pressures and temptations will still lead persons to succumb at times, but that does not alter a widening area of consensus about right and wrong.

One of the most successful uses of a code has been the *Credo* of Johnson & Johnson. Formulated over a generation ago by General Robert Wood Johnson, it has provided Johnson & Johnson with a succinct statement of its corporate culture and value commitments. Several things are noteworthy about it. First, it focuses on the constituencies to which the company is responsible and states clearly the ordering of priorities to be followed in making value judgments about company policy and operation. Second, it mandates action for the company as a whole, in its entire policy process, rather than only for individuals. It provides clear guidance and support for individuals as they act as part of the company. Third, the *Credo* has had the backing of top management from its beginnings, and management has acted in conformity with the code and enforced it through policy channels. Fourth, management has worked to make it known and followed from the boardroom to the farthest representative of the company. In the 1970s extensive discussions of the *Credo* were carried out to update its language, to increase understanding of it, and to deepen the level of commitment and ownership of it throughout the corporation.

The discovery of poison in a number of packages of Tylenol, a

Johnson & Johnson product, demonstrated in a dramatic way that this company had effectively institutionalized its culture and values and that there is a close relation between ethics and performance. Codes can be helpful — but only when they permeate the company as an operative culture rather than being formulated and sent out as part of a public relations campaign.

Codes of ethics and conduct are becoming more widespread. If standing alone, they can at best be regarded as minimally useful in relation to performance. They become an effective instrument for the management of values in the business corporation when they are integrated into the entire policy process and fit in with the culture and value commitments of the corporation.

Another way to relate values and policy has been by means of appraising corporate performance. The Weyerhaeuser Corporation, for example, not only has policy statements equivalent to a code of conduct but also commissions someone from outside the company to provide a careful critique of its social policies and actions. This critique is published as part of the annual report of the corporation.

A type of appraisal that received considerable attention in the 1970s was the social audit. Using the financial audit and report as model, interested persons developed methods for measuring success in areas of social responsibility. The methods of measuring may be either quantitative or qualitative. Clark Abt of the Cambridge, Massachusetts, consulting firm Clark Abt Associates developed a way to state social costs and benefits of corporate operations in monetary terms. Any social benefit such as better health or security, more equality, or an improved environment can be quantified in dollars and reported along with the financial statement.[12] Others have advocated a qualitative method for social audits, using various criteria to measure performance with reference to working conditions, consumer relations, investor relations, employee and community welfare, and so on.[13]

In commenting on the pros and cons of the social audit, Thomas Donaldson says:

> Even without a thorough look at the various forms of social audit, certain strengths and weaknesses are apparent. The obvious strength of the social audit is its affinity to traditional corporate procedures. Like everyone else, business people are creatures of habit

> and accept change less grudgingly when it is packaged in familiar colors. If corporations accept *financial* audits, then why not *social* audits? . . .
>
> The weakness of the social audit probably lies in the failure of the analogy between financial and social audits. Social audits are not, after all, financial audits, and instead of working with easily quantifiable sums of money, they work with difficult to quantify areas of human conduct. . . .
>
> Even when stripped of its quantitative packaging, the social audit has problems. It or any other form of social audit is only as powerful as the tendency of corporate executives to take it seriously and act on its conclusions, and to date, social audits have been treated primarily as public relations efforts.[14]

The social audit, even in its better forms, tends to emphasize responsiveness and responsibility to the value agenda of society and powerful or vocal groups within it. We have suggested here that it is important for management to become proactive, to develop its own ethical criteria to be institutionalized, and to engage in the management of values as an integral part of excellence in management that results in enhanced performance.

Organizational Change

In addition to codes of ethical conduct and some form of social audit, approaches to integrating values into the policy process by means of changes in patterns of organization appear promising. Without going into them in detail, let us enumerate a few of these.

Corporate Committees on Social Responsibility and Ethics. One organizational change designed to relate values and policy more effectively is the formation of corporate responsibility committees or corporate ethics committees. These may be at the level of the board of directors or at the senior and middle management level. Neither will work if not backed up by the other and carefully coordinated. It is also crucial that matters be addressed that are at the center of corporate operations and interests as well as those at the edges. Such committees will be far less effective if they deal only with "issues" and fail to grapple with patterns of policy formulation and implementation. Committees for corporate ethics and social responsibility have become very common. They can be helpful, however, only to the extent that they are taken seriously and give attention to the entire spectrum of corporate structures and relations.

Organization and Operation of Boards of Directors. A second organizational change to relate values and policy better involves the board of directors of the corporation. Two patterns that are emerging deserve mention.

First, there is the movement to change the composition of board membership so that it represents a wider spectrum of constituencies or stakeholders than was the case previously. This involves bringing onto the board persons who represent important perspectives that might otherwise be missing. The point of view and interests of groups falling within the scope of the corporation's responsibilities will be included in the policy-making process. Persons with special insight or resources needed for policy formulation can be brought onto the board. By this method directors bring to the shaping of company actions a greater awareness of what is going on in society than would be the case with a less representative membership. Changes in the environment of values are brought into the policy process quickly and directly. Management is rendered more sensitive to social issues and trends that might otherwise be overlooked. If such persons are added to the board, however, it is important to ensure that their contributions and insights are put to good use.

Second, an emerging pattern involves changing the relations between the board and areas of operation inside the company. The standard relations keep company personnel and activities separate from the board except as reported by the CEO. The newer way relates the Board and its committees directly to various sectors and personnel in the company without the presence or mediation of senior management. This change in organization acquaints members of the board more closely with corporate activities, ensures that board policy will be based on better knowledge of company operations, and improves the sense of mutual responsibility between outside board members and managers. It can also provide a means for developing a more integrated corporate culture. This change in organizational patterns has been used successfully by Connecticut General as well as by other corporations.[15]

Additional Structures and Functions. There are numerous additional possibilities for relating values and policy more closely in the processes of a business organization. A writer on business ethics who emphasizes the importance of organizational restructuring is Richard DeGeorge. He also draws together a list of changes worth attention.

"Organizational theory is only beginning to turn its attention in this direction," he writes. "Yet a number of innovative organizational changes have been tried in the United States or in Europe and deserve serious consideration."[16] He cites ten specific possibilities:

1. If a board of directors is to be morally responsible it cannot simply be a rubber stamp of management....
2. More than half the board, as well as the chairman of the board, should not be from management....
3. At each level a determination should be made about how much disclosure is appropriate and to whom....
4. There should be channels and procedures for accountability up, down, and laterally....
5. Develop input lines whereby employees, consumers, stockholders, and the public can make known their concerns, demands and perceptions of a corporation's legitimate responsibilities....
6. Develop a mechanism (possibly a department) for anticipating the various demands, for seriously considering them and weighing them, and for proposing appropriate action.
7. Develop techniques for disseminating to those interested the basis for decisions affecting the general good....
8. Responsibility should be enforced with sanctions both within an organization and, where compatible with antitrust laws, throughout an industry....

9. A corporation that wishes to preclude the necessity of whistle blowing should provide procedures, mechanisms, and channels whereby any member of the organization can file moral concerns . . . and get a fair hearing and possible action without fear of negative consequences. . . .
10. The corporation should hold some highly placed official in the corporation responsible if insufficient attention is paid to a legitimate claim of product safety and so on.[17]

It is a varied list and provides productive points of beginning for discussion of changes in patterns of organizations that might more effectively relate values and policy.

Several years ago, as the result of discussions among its top executives on corporate ethics, a prominent bank formed a Social Policy Loan Committee. The idea for the committee emerged during a management seminar initiated by the president and CEO that involved 14 senior officers and 5 outside members of the board of directors. The Social Policy Loan Committee focused on the central activity of the bank, lending money. It was made up of the senior loan officers in every division of the bank's organization. The committee dealt with the way loans were actually made, examining the criteria used and whether these criteria were adequate. Within the bank's organization, the final decision on each loan was made by a single responsible loan officer, but there were guidelines to follow and loan officers were given support in using social ethical criteria in evaluating loans and making judgments among them. Eventually, the bank integrated ethical reflection and criteria into its overall credit policies and decentralized the decision making on particular loans even more.

Rather than leaving value judgments beyond profitability to the unguided consciences of individuals deciding on each loan, this bank regards the varied values going into loan policy as important, provides a means for raising these values to consciousness, and has developed organizational mechanisms for integrating values into loan policy and its implementation.

One thing became clear early in the work of the committee that has wider applicability than to just this bank. While there are many laws and regulations governing making loans and overall profitability is necessary, there is not only latitude for criteria beyond profitability but also the necessity of using additional values in making choices among a great variety of loans that would all probably be profitable. Indeed, many other values had already been part of the process of evaluating loans, values of which management was only partly aware. In banking or in any other business, it is important to be clear about the values influencing policy, to work through the network of formal and informal relationships in management to develop guidelines for relating values to policy, and to strengthen the corporate culture that sets limits and gives support to managers at every level as they make choices and value judgments. When this is done, the overall result can be a deeper awareness on the part of management of the necessity for reflecting on the values shaping policy, for institutionalizing ethics into corporate processes, and for developing the ability to manage values at all levels in the company.

Widening the Involvement

A highly decentralized manufacturer of industrial products, operating in 50 countries, recently added a Public Policy Committee to the organizational structure of its board of directors. The committee was added, said the CEO, "because of the company's perception that being — and being seen to be — socially responsible and ethical was both natural for the company and was also good business." The question for the committee, as perceived by the board and senior management, was not whether but rather *how* to integrate ethics and a sense of social responsibility into the ways policy is developed and carried out.

The committee first compiled an inventory of corporate social responsibility programs throughout the company on a multinational basis. An investigation was also carried out as to the extent the values assumed by top management were present throughout the firm's operations. The committee reluctantly concluded that:

- Most of the so-called social responsibility programs were mainly cosmetic;
- Programs existing at company headquarters were generally absent in the operating companies, especially in locations distant from headquarters;

- Organizational charts showing committees on ethics and responsibility, codes of conduct passed by the board of directors, and programs administered through bureaucratic routines lead to little substance in terms of specific achievements; and
- The values affirmed by the directors, the chairperson, and the president were only sporadically present in company policy and action outside corporate headquarters.

The committee identified four reasons for this state of affairs:

- Even in highly centralized companies with strong cultures, attempts of corporate headquarters to force-feed value commitments and notions of social responsibility to operating managers and their employees are almost universally disastrous.
- Line managers trained to be concerned with efficient day-to-day operation of their divisions cannot suddenly and without preparation add new managerial functions and dimensions related to values, even if they are in general agreement with the purposes intended.
- Headquarters-originated programs, good enough in themselves, are often totally inappropriate for the geographic, political, cultural, and social environment in which the various divisions operate.
- Thinking and acting in terms of a wider spectrum of values cannot be assumed to happen easily in various divisions without careful preparation and training, any more than people would know how to use computers without training even though they might agree with the need for them.

Based on these findings, the committee reported to the board and senior management that their perception of the extent to which corporate ethics was institutionalized had been much too optimistic. To get the reality more into line with what was wanted, the committee recommended — and the board approved — a corporate strategy for integrating its values more completely into the operations of the entire company. Setting aside a full year for the process, the corporation as a whole, including each of its divisions and operating units, would discuss at every level the company it wanted to become, the value commitments it believed were present and should be strengthened, what these values meant for policy, operating plans, and action in their own location, and how to get these values embodied in specific processes and programs. The activities flowing from this decision led to the opening up of a year-long conversation among the company's operating units and between them and corporate headquarters about institutionalizing ethics in appropriate ways at every level and in every sector. The objectives of this conversation were:

1. To raise consciousness throughout management of the relationship between ethics and corporate performance and of the importance for managers at various levels to consider ways to integrate values beyond productivity and profit into company policy processes;
2. To encourage and provide training in every unit, at every level, for developing understanding of corporate values for their own context, for taking account of the internal and external environment of values related to their location, and for formulating guidelines of ethics and responsibility applicable to their situation, with examples and cases familiar to the people in each unit;
3. To ascertain what programs might be continued, developed, or dropped in their unit that would strengthen the relation between ethics and performance and provide opportunities as time and resources permitted to embody corporate social responsibility;
4. To discover ways that corporate headquarters could assist in the development of such programs and give support to managers trying to integrate corporate values into policy processes in their particular unit; and
5. To deepen the consensus among the various parts of the corporation as to the culture and values shared and how these were to be expressed adequately in different locations and societies.

As the conversation progressed, it became apparent that some of the objectives were being accomplished — even though in varied ways and at different strengths in the many units of the company. Most satisfying for the Public Policy Committee, however, was evidence that corporate ethics was getting a firmer base than the chairman's whims, cosmetic gestures, or a corporate culture shared generally but not institutionalized throughout the company.

SUGGESTIONS FOR GROUP STUDY

1. Suppose that you are a consultant who has been retained by Phillip Owens to advise him on the problem posed in the conversation at the beginning of the chapter. Develop some ideas for the institutionalizing process, using the text of this chapter as a starting point. Organize a discussion that will pool the ideas of the group members. See if a consensus emerges.
2. Read the case study in Appendix K on the use of committees. With the other members of your group, evaluate the use of such committees as a means of building an awareness of social and ethical implications of company policy and fostering participation. In the group discussion see what other ideas emerge for carrying out the process of institutionalization.
3. Read the *Corporate Responsibility Creed* of Wells Fargo and Company in Appendix L. You may want to compare this example with others from companies familiar to members of your group. In a group discussion explore the strengths and limitations of this way of gaining understanding and acceptance of company policies. Ask members of the group to tell about their own experiences in living under these types of guides to ethical behavior.

Nine

COMMUNICATION, PARTICIPATION, AND COMMITMENT

The CEO's executive assistant, Larry, escorted Jim and me into an office that was attractive and modern in its furnishings, its works of art, and its relative bareness. The desk was completely clear except for a telephone and a folded copy of the Wall Street Journal. Bernie, chair and CEO of the upper-middle Fortune 500 company, was looking out at the winter landscape surrounding the firm's suburban headquarters. We had met with him several times before, so he greeted us very informally and waved us toward the three armchairs near his desk. Bernie sat down at his desk, leaned back, propped one foot up on the edge of the desk, and cocked his head on one side as he gave us a smiling welcome.

"How are things going?" he began. "I've always been wary of talking about ethics, especially in the company. It sounds moralistic. But I may be changing my mind — a little."

"The seminars have been exciting so far," Jim said. "Everyone's been helpful. We're learning a lot, and I think the questions we're asking are challenging the senior executives to give more careful thought to the culture and ethics of the corporation."

"It's the corporate culture I've been convinced needs developing," Bernie responded. "And now I see that the corporate ethics can be thought of as the value commitments of the corporate culture, not a bunch of moral rules."

"Exactly. If the corporate culture really permeates the company," I added, "then it will shape the reflection about values, the criteria for deciding alternative directions, the way people perform and interact within the company, and the way the company interacts with society."

"The response from everyone has been very good," Larry interposed, "and the people in personnel are getting some ideas for training."

"But training is not enough," Bernie said, slapping the desk with the palm of his hand. "I'm convinced this entire outfit has more possibilities than we've gotten out of it so far. Performance has been fairly good, especially when you consider the economy. But we can do better. And I mean in many more ways than profit."

"We picked up a story from Bill that may interest you," Jim replied. "On his recent trip to the Ohio plant, a worker complained to him that the men's room for their section had been out of order for three weeks. They had to go to the next building. Bill asked a few questions, and the place was fixed before he left the next day."

"Sure," Bernie exploded, leaning forward, "the issue isn't profit. It's human decency in the workplace. Things like that, big and little, add up to the corporate culture and the commitment of everyone to performance in an overall sense. A strong culture makes a difference in everything, including capital return."

"That is Bill's view," Jim continued. "He thinks the corporate culture ought to be strong enough not to require a visit from an executive vice-president to get the 'john' fixed." We all laughed.

"I suppose that developing effective communications and participation up and down the company are important elements for deepening the commitment to our corporate culture and values," Bernie said, poking fun at our academic-sounding language but indicating understanding and approval.

"That's it and more," I responded.

"I know a strong corporate culture can't be produced by orders from my office," Bernie added. "That's the reason I like the questions you are asking us at headquarters about projecting what we mean in action as well as talk. It's important, too, to get participation among managers and employees from top to bottom. Let's keep at it."

Although written in the 1930s, Chester Barnard's *The Functions of the Executive* remains among the most perceptive books on management. Barnard sees clearly that managing values is at the core of the excellent executive's job. "It is precisely the function of the executive," he writes, "to facilitate the synthesis in concrete action of contradictory forces, to reconcile conflicting forces, instincts, interests, conditions, positions, and ideals." He understands an organization as a means for coordinating the activities of persons. "An organization comes into being when (1) there are persons able to communicate with each other (2) who are willing to contribute action (3) to accomplish a common purpose. The elements of an organization are therefore (1) communication; (2) willingness to serve; and (3) common purpose."[1]

Because the CEO and the senior management of a corporation are able to see the interacting elements required for decision making, they are most aware of the wholeness of the policy process. This wholeness appears vividly in the actions of the company as a corporate entity. The heads of divisions feel a primary responsibility for their sector, but top management must oversee how all of the parts fit together and mesh with the market and the social environment to produce that encompassing action known as *corporate performance.*

Because they are responsible for the total performance, senior managers are more aware than other management levels of the value judgments permeating the policy process. Senior management must make the choices that shape corporate priorities, action, and performance. They know that ethics and performance are inseparable because they are accountable for weighing the values that produce alternative results.

There is, however, more than meets the eye in this wholeness. Corporate culture, ethics, and performance, interwoven as they are, cannot be dictated from the office of the CEO or from headquarters. They must permeate the company, involving the energies and loyalties of managers and employees in every sector. To be effective, one perceptive executive said in a corporate ethics seminar, the culture must flow up and down through all the institutional channels of the firm. Middle managers need to get a sense of the total performance, rather than seeing issues narrowly in terms only of the sector for which they are responsible. Employees at every level should be made aware that their performance and commitment to excellence in what they do contribute not only to the productivity of their unit but also to the excellent performance of the entire company.

In Chapter Eight we explored what it means to institutionalize corporate ethics as a way to enhance corporate performance under three headings: developing and shaping corporate culture and value commitments, infusing values into all the operational structures of the corporation, and integrating values into the policy process. In this chapter we shall look at three additional elements important for excellence in corporate performance: first, communication in the company and the relation of information and values as these must be part of the tacit dimension of corporate performance; second, participation as a management style that encourages ownership of the corporate culture and values; and third, commitment and imagination as crucial for the effective management of values.

COMMUNICATION: INFORMATION AND VALUES

"Every organization is held together by communication," Karl Deutsch says is the viewpoint of the new science of cybernetics.[2] In corporations there are systems of communication that provide the basis for their policies and their implementation. Some of the communication takes place through the official systems of the company. Much of it takes place by means of the jungle grapevine operating in all organizations. A substantial portion of communication in corporations takes place through actions and what they are perceived as meaning rather than through the officially sanctioned declarations or informal reporting. Still another form of communication occurs through the stories told about significant events and actions of corporate life, stories often focused on company leaders.

All these systems of communication, formal and informal, convey information. It is, however, not always clear that communication involves information shaped and given valence by the values that are transmitted and received. In one sense there is the issue of information perceived as false or unreliable because of the value context in which it is transmitted and received. Assuming sufficient trust to provide credibility, there is still the issue of depth of commitment evoked by a communications system. One level of communication in a corporation provides understanding. A deeper level of communication based explicitly on awareness of the inseparability of values and information provides the means for developing ownership of corporate values, commitment to its culture, and loyalty to the corporate community. Both levels must be given attention in order to enhance performance.

The information and values communicated in any particular system, the quality of understanding achieved, and the effectiveness of ownership and use in the corporate policy process have tremendous impact upon performance. Inventions and technical innovation often provide the basis upon which corporations are founded and keep ahead of the competition. Financial data have always been of crucial importance, and financial information systems have gradually forged a central role for themselves as corporations have become larger and more complex. Sound legal information has emerged as increasingly important. Now it is becoming equally clear that management must have a firm grasp of social values, ethics, and culture.

When we consider ways to develop and strengthen a corporate culture related to performance, it becomes clear that one means is a corporate communications system that recognizes the importance of values. A central component of such a communications system is information on the values in the corporate environment, on social issues important for corporate policy, and on the meaning of these values and issues for performance. Individual sensitivity to ethics and individual knowledge must not be omitted. But these must be supplemented with data assembled on a systematic basis, made available as the common information base of those concerned with policy formulation and implementation, and utilized in the routines of evaluation and decision making. Just as a corporation would not rely exclusively on the perception of individuals about the financial or legal scene, so also must reliable data about issues and values become part of an institutionalized ethics.

We shall explore three aspects of such a communications system in order to suggest how it supplies crucial information, operates on deeper levels of communication, and thus becomes part of the management process as related to performance. First, we shall look at social values information as a means of effective management. Second, we shall discuss the life cycle of social issues as they have bearing on corporate performance. And third, we shall indicate the shape of a social values information system that is based on involvement of corporate personnel.

Social Values Information in Communication and Management

Once the close relation between ethics and performance is seen clearly and the integration of values into the policy process is under way, information on social values becomes an instrument by which management can enhance the precision and quality of its corporate ethical reflection and action. Here are a few of the ways this will work.

As a Basis for Common Understanding and Discussion. Managers in senior positions are concerned directly with the overall performance of the corporation and not merely with a particular unit of it. Like the conductor of a symphony orchestra, top management must give attention to the integration of multiple factors and the balancing out of many values. Policymakers understand that more is needed than technical know-how and organizational skills. They are aware that considering values, setting priorities among alternative purposes, and making difficult choices compose the core of their function. Although corporate executives know this, they are usually more at ease discussing production schedules and financial projections than the priority of values in formulating policy. In addition, they also usually lack a vocabulary and frame of reference for careful consideration as a policy-making group of social values and responsibility.

In marketing, manufacturing, and finance, for example, communications within management groups is greatly facilitated by standard terminology, practices, and information systems that are generally understood. Information can be rapidly and effectively transmitted, shared, and brought to bear as issues are discussed and decisions arrived at. When questions of conflicting values are involved, however, the vocabulary of managers is less likely to be adequate. As a consequence the discussion of values within the management group will probably be lacking or very limited in scope.

The first way that social values information can serve as a tool of management is by deepening executive ability to consider value alternatives and to develop frames of reference for choosing among these alternatives. As the information is shared and becomes part of the common understanding, it enters routinely into the policy process and emerges as an integral component of the tacit dimension underlying the corporate ethic.

As a Means for Accurately Scanning the Environment of Values. We have spoken earlier about the importance of the context in which corporations operate. Organizations, like human beings and animals, exist in symbiotic relation with their surroundings. There is an interdependence within the world of nature and in society that cannot be ignored.

For corporations there is an internal environment as well as an external one. In each case it is an environment of values as well as of things, people, and other organizations. Because those values describe the interests and purposes of persons and groups in those environments, policymakers must be aware of them and shape the actions of the organizations they direct in terms of these social values.

Just as the driver of an automobile must continually scan the highway ahead, behind, and around in order to operate a vehicle safely, so policymakers must be able to scan the total environment in which the corporation moves in order to steer it properly. In the case of automobile drivers, their performance will be excellent not only in terms of their skills in turning the wheel and stepping on the accelerator or brake but also in terms of the precision of their knowledge of the territory in which they are driving. The internal environment of the car is part of it; so also are the immediate surroundings — other vehicles, pedestrians, traffic lanes and lights, stop signs, and so on. Driving in a city requires knowing the layout of the streets. And traveling to a distant city requires information about the highways. Drivers may know many of these environments through past experience and good memories. But conditions even in well-known places may change. And we are always likely to enter territory that is new to us. In any event our knowledge needs to be extended and made more precise by maps, directions, and up-to-date information. One becomes especially aware of the need for good, accurate, and current data when driving in a foreign country.

Even for experienced managers, the territory is partly new and changing. Social values information is crucial as a tool of effective management because it provides the means for scanning the environment of social values. Even more, if it is a good source of data, it provides more precise information about the surroundings through which the corporation must be steered than any individual policymaker can pick up through experience, more current information than even the recent past can offer, and information about territory that is new and perhaps strange.

The need for such information as a tool of management is clear enough for the more familiar terrain of a Western industrial nation. For a corporation that is attempting to operate in a non-Western culture, it is imperative that the environment of values, often very different from those where headquarters is located, be known in detail. Social values are too important to leave to chance experiences. They need to be built into the information systems that are shared by those controlling the policy process and constantly integrated into the reflection shaping corporate action.

As a Way to Discover and Develop New Alternatives. As social values become a part of the common understanding and discussion among policymakers in a corporation and as policymakers use social values information to become aware with greater precision of the environment within which the company operates, new alternatives can be discovered and developed. In one way social values information opens up new alternatives by suggesting different perspectives from which to look at problems and proposed policy. In another way social values information helps policymakers listen to people with different values from their own or to the recipients of policy who may have alternatives to propose that would not otherwise have been considered. In these ways communication about social values within the company can become a basic and continuing source of innovation.

In Chapter Seven three value systems were presented that are found in the societies of industrial nations — the Smithian, the humanitarian, and the communitarian. As part of a corporate ethics project of the Berkeley Center, a group of top executives in a manufacturing firm were discussing the problem of peaked-out employees. The purpose of the discussion was to explore the factors that ought to be considered and the components of a policy for dealing with this increasing problem. At first the proposals all emerged from the Smithian value system, representing the values of profitability and productivity. It soon became apparent, however, that this value system, which represented the values they were most accustomed to discussing in relation to corporate decisions, did not contain all of the values that were important to these policymakers or to the company. To open up different perspectives and alternatives, they were asked to view the problem in two ways: first, with a viewpoint informed by the humanitarian values system; and second, in terms of the communitarian social values system. Not only did new ways to deal with the problem occur to them, but the people participating agreed that a policy based on this wider spectrum of social values would be more satisfactory to them, represent the values of the corporation better, and probably work better in terms of human relations, employee morale, and productivity.

Out of the discussion came an additional idea: It is not only important from the standpoint of human dignity to let peaked-out employees participate in discussions about their future; in many instances they may also have insights and suggestions pointing to good solutions for themselves and the company. A policy on peaked-out employees, the group concluded, ought to involve early consultation with persons peaking out as well as consultation again when the problem becomes more serious. At both points the employees concerned will have the opportunity to suggest possible solutions and even develop new career expectations.

As a Method for Projecting Probable Results and Responses.

Policy decisions nearly always require trade-offs among varied purposes, divergent values, and conflicting interests. Social values information provides a means for balancing these and setting realistic priorities by aiding in projecting the probable results of alternative policies and calculating what the probable responses will be on the part of the groups affected. Like a nautical chart that gives information about currents and shoals, social values information provides a view of the value currents and rock-bottom interests through which specific policies must steer the company. By understanding in some measure the values and interests of groups who will be affected by policy, management can avoid unnecessary conflict, locate potential allies, and prepare to meet opposition when there is no way around it.

As a Way to Understand and Use Information on Social Issues.

Information on social values can become an important tool for management by identifying social issues before they become immediate problems, by providing understanding of social issues, and by thus making data available necessary for effective policy. Questions of social responsibility will emerge or become clearer as social issues are identified. And the earlier such issues are identified, the better the opportunity for developing appropriate policies.

When social values information is understood not only as scanning the immediate environment but also as tracking shifts in social values over periods of time, it can delineate the emergence, rise to dominance, and decline of particular social issues. This possibility of developing and using information on the life cycle of a social issue in policy formulation is sufficiently important for corporate performance to deserve special treatment.

The Social Issue Life Cycle and Corporate Performance

Social issues having significant impact on corporations have an identifiable life cycle. Appropriate actions through policy and implementation are different, depending on the stage of development of a particular social issue as it progresses through its life cycle. The shifts in social values that shape this life cycle as well as the changes taking place from stage to stage can be understood through social values information.

A clear view of social issues as they arise, as they have impact on societal institutions, and as they are integrated into the fabric of accustomed practice can be of great help to management. As such understanding becomes a part of the policy process, it constitutes a central means for managing values and enhancing corporate performance.

To explain more fully the significance of this important notion, we shall look at the concept of the social issue life cycle, then we will trace the recent history of Equal Employment Opportunity (EEO) as an illustration.

The Concept of Social Issue Life Cycle. Most social issues, when carefully examined, follow a pattern that is predictable within limits — so says Robert Ackerman in *The Social Challenge to Business*,[3] a book growing out of research on two large corporations, carried out at Harvard Business School from 1972 to 1975. There is a time, Ackerman suggests, when a social issue is unnoticed or not regarded as important. Indeed, those who support the issue at this stage may well be subject to various kinds of social sanctions. If interest in the issue increases and is sustained, however, it passes through phases of awareness, rising expectations, demands for action, and ultimately enforcement by law and other means. Once new patterns of action relating to the issue have become accepted and are ingrained in the usual conduct of affairs, the issue will no longer be a matter of active social concern except that now social sanctions will be exercised against those whose conduct violates the new norm. Viewed in this way, social issues have a life cycle analogous to the life cycle of a living organism or the life cycle of a commercial product.

Equal Employment Opportunity as Example. To understand with greater precision what the social issue life cycle means, it will be helpful to look at a particular illustration. EEO is a major social issue with a well-documented history. And it is one that has affected most business organizations in the United States, as well as having impact in all Western industrial nations.

Though the notion of equality is an old one in the Western tradition, it has emerged with increasing valence over the past two centuries. During the nineteenth century its impact was primarily against major social inequalities: slavery and class. In the twentieth century there has been a rising recognition that even though equality has been established as a general goal, many groups have been systematically excluded from access to multiple sectors of society. Through protests, social movements, and court decisions, the notion of equal opportunity has emerged with increasing power. When the U.S. Congress passed the Equal Employment Opportunity Act of 1964, this social issue emerged, not as one that management could give attention to and take action on if it chose but as one that every corporation in the United States had to confront. Because the legislation was general and somewhat ahead of the emerging consensus of values on the subject, the late 1960s provided a "zone of discretion" for corporate management, a time when a wide variety of responses could be tried out and ways found to deal with EEO that would fit with corporate needs and purposes as well as with the changing environment of values.

As minorities acquired higher expectations and began to exert pressure for immediate action to rectify past injustices, dramatic alterations took place in the way EEO was defined and enforced, with reference to opportunities for advancement and redress for treatment of minorities and women. Major problems of compliance developed for most large corporations in the 1970s, even for corporations with good records in hiring and promotion practices on lower and intermediate levels. Now in the 1980s, the social issue has attained the status of general consensus, and equal employment practices have become mandatory for all levels and for most types of positions.

EEO clearly illustrates the life cycle of a social issue. It also exemplifies an issue about which social values information could have provided advance warning and given management the opportunity to develop responses that might have enhanced performance rather than endangering it.

A Corporate Social Values Information System

Development and implementation of comprehensive management informations systems have become central characteristics of excellence in large organizations, including corporations. In the past these informations systems have been comprised, usually, of quantifiable data related to financial accounting, cost-benefit analysis, funding, marketing, and so on — the kinds most compatible with computers. Such data have greatly enhanced the quality and timeliness of corporate decisions and thus contributed to improved corporate performance. Data on social values, by contrast, are seen as more difficult to quantify and therefore less available for systematic reporting and use. Managers have tried individually and with mixed success to keep up with public issues, social trends, and changing values through the business press or the generalized views of society.

Here we suggest that a corporate social values information system is possible that will make available in organized form comprehensive and timely information on social trends and issues of importance for policy and performance. What is proposed is closely integrated with the corporate policy process and shaped to assist in the effective management of values.

Choosing Social Value Trends and Issues. Selecting the information to be included is the first step in developing a useful social

information system. Ackerman concludes, in the studies reported in *The Social Challenge to Business,* that management can, at any given time, give adequate attention only to a limited number of social issues.[4] This is, of course, also the case with financial data. Probably no more than two or three "mature" issues currently having impact on the corporation can be examined carefully. In addition, several social trends significant for longer-range planning need to be monitored, and overall scanning needs to take place in order to maintain awareness of trends and issues that may be emerging as important for the corporation in the future. Priorities in this process of selection must be based upon corporate ethics and strategy, and the social data must be understood as a means for integrating ethics into policy with greater precision.

Sources and Methods for Gathering Information. To cope with the bewildering variety of sources for data on social values, trends, and issues, someone in top management with expertise must search for sources that fit the needs of corporate planning. Increasingly, through the work of polling organizations and social research, data that can be quantified, relating to social values, are available. The methods employed by John Naisbitt, as reported in *Megatrends,* indicate the improvement under way in means to discover social trends and the changing values underlying them. That his book remained on the best-seller list so long is clear evidence that information on social values and trends is in demand and believed to be useful. Publications such as the *Wall Street Journal* and *Business Week* are offering more and more articles reporting on social issues. The Conference Board and business research organizations are responding to the needs of corporations for better social information. For corporations interested, there are an increasing range of authoritative results becoming available. A corporate social information system searches out and organizes information from these various sources and places this information in the hands of managers in forms that will be useful for different levels of policy-making and implementation.

One approach to a comprehensive social information system is the Trend Analysis Program sponsored by the American Council of Life Insurance. Its method can be adapted for use by other industries or for a single corporation. Volunteer participants at various management levels are recruited to scan one or more publications or other relevant information sources. The sources fall under specific areas of concern. Guidelines are provided for the information sought and ways to report on what has been found. The volunteers send what they have found to a small staff committee. This committee screens what the volunteers provide, supplements it with additional data, and compiles the results for reporting to management.

This method has several advantages. First, it broadens and supplements information available to senior management and assembled by staff persons. Second, it involves many persons at various management levels in shaping the value perspectives of the corporation and thus leads toward greater ownership of the corporate culture. Third, it can ensure, if organized carefully, that diverse social and ethnic perspectives are represented and so improve the knowledge of changing values, trends, and issues upon which policy planning is based. Fourth, it enhances the probability that the information assembled will be relevant to the management of values and useful in shaping corporate action.

Organizing and Disseminating Social Values Information. Of no less importance than the method for gathering data are the processes by which they are assembled, analyzed, and disseminated throughout management. The pattern and criteria for organizing the information are provided by the selection of prime issues needing attention, the social trends that seem important for corporate policy and planning, and the need for continuous general scanning for changes significant for the corporation. At every point possible the connection must be made between this social information and corporate operations. And it is crucial to organize the data systematically so that they take shape as information about social values and trends related to what the company is actually doing rather than as isolated bits. The methods of disseminating are likewise important. Insofar as possible the social information should be disseminated as part of the entire corporate information system so that data on social values and trends will be available for decision making in the same way that information on financial matters is available. It may be helpful to hold training sessions focused on integrating social and financial data into the policy process and conducted by top line executives.

As the social information system becomes an accustomed element of the policy process, the management training program of the company will emerge as a significant channel for disseminating social information to managers building their careers within the company and industry and for developing further the ways in which social and financial information are brought together for policy formulation and implementation.

When viewed in this way, information about social values, trends, and issues can be seen as crucial for carrying out a corporate ethic. Even more, it becomes clear why corporate ethics that is informed and integrated into the policy process can be as important for enhancing corporate performance as technical and financial information.

PARTICIPATION: MANAGEMENT AND HUMAN NATURE

A social revolution has taken place in the United States, says Alexander Trowbridge, who has served as president of the Conference Board and as chairman of the U.S. Chamber of Commerce. He contends:

> This social revolution not only manifested itself in changing value systems, but it also brought new attitudes toward work and altered ethical and social behavior throughout society. In offices and factories, workers who previously had been docile were now seeking greater involvement in the decisions affecting their work, and were demanding more satisfying work experiences. . . .
>
> Most businessmen were not well prepared to cope with these and other new demands society was placing on them and their enterprises. Even those who had been professionally trained in business schools often felt inadequate in dealing with special-interest groups, hostile media, anti-business government officials, and the new work force. They have been making what has been for some a most difficult transition in their fundamental philosophy and management style. They are really seeking a new philosophical base for, and another operational approach to, the new realities that confront their companies.[5]

Experience with corporate executives confirms their agreement with Trowbridge that decisive changes are under way in society and in business corporations. The shifts have probably been a long time in the making rather than a sudden revolution. To those who had not been aware they were under way, the changes have appeared to have occurred rapidly. An automobile coming up in a blind spot as we are driving along seems to be going much faster than it actually is because we are taken by surprise and must react quickly. It is nonetheless true that what Trowbridge calls "a new philosophical base" for management is sought and needed — a base better suited to the realities of human nature within contemporary corporations and to the environment of values forming the context of business.

Participation as a Style of Management

The new philosophy of management that is needed now must be based on an adequate understanding of human nature, must serve the realistic needs of corporate goals, and must strengthen the corporate culture and value commitments within all levels of management and among all employees. Because it is based upon commitment and involvement, this new philosophy may be called *participative management*.[6] But it must be distinguished carefully from mere manipulation, on the one hand, and industrial democracy, on the other.

One way to delineate it is to compare it with other styles of management. In a well-known book — *The Human Side of Enterprise* — Douglas McGregor contrasts two styles of management that he calls "Theory X" and "Theory Y." Theory X is autocratic and rational; Theory Y is humane and personal.

Theory X assumes:

1. Average human beings have an inherent dislike of work and will avoid it if they can.
2. Because of this human characteristic, most people must be coerced, controlled, directed, and threatened with punishment to get them to put forth adequate effort toward achievement of organizational objectives.
3. Average human beings prefer to be directed, wish to avoid re-

sponsibility, have relatively little ambition, and want security above all.[7]

The style of management required for Theory X is highly structured. Supervision is authoritarian. Instructions are detailed. Work rules are rigid. And punishment is used for motivation.

With Elton Mayo's Hawthorne experiments in the 1930s, the "human relations" style of management (McGregor's Theory Y) emerged, based on different assumptions:

1. The expenditure of physical and mental effort is as natural as play or rest.
2. External control and the threat of punishment are not the only means for bringing about effort toward organizational objectives because persons will exercise self-direction and self-control in the service of objectives to which they are committed.
3. Commitment to objectives is a function of the rewards associated with their achievement, and satisfaction of ego and self-actualization is the most significant of these rewards.
4. The average human being learns, under proper conditions, not only to accept but to seek responsibility.
5. The capacity to exercise a relatively high degree of imagination, ingenuity, and creativity in the solution of organizational problems is widely, not narrowly, distributed in the population.
6. Under the conditions of modern industrial life, the intellectual potentialities of the average human being are only partially utilized.[8]

The style of management called for by Theory Y is human relations oriented. It is designed to bring out the best efforts of people by treating them as responsible individuals. In this style, psychology in handling people became the basis for effective supervision. Realizing the human potential of employees for the good of the organization became a primary objective of management.

Fred Twining, a Berkeley colleague with wide experience in management consulting and training, formulated the notion of "Theory Z" in 1976 for one of our corporate ethics projects. Published in 1978 in a paper of the Berkeley Center, it is not to be identified with the William Ouchi's *Theory Z*, published in 1981 and modeled on Japanese managerial patterns.[9]

Twining's Theory Z says that management is shifting toward new assumptions about human nature:

1. Persons working within corporations recognize that the values of our society are changing and want organizations where they work to respond to these values.
2. Persons within large organizations want value commitments and will perform better in a corporate culture with clearly defined values and recognized processes for resolving conflicts among values.
3. Human beings want to view the work they are doing as meaningful in societal perspective, with the traditional corporate values of growth and profits related to the environment of emerging social goals and values.
4. There will be positive reactions throughout the organization to the explicit consideration of values and their integration into the policy processes of the company; these positive reactions will be enhanced among people who are informed and involved in initiating and implementing programs of corporate ethics, and this participation will contribute to the performance and innovative potentialities within the company.
5. Relating values and policy in corporations will unlock energies and creativity that can lead to higher performance and productivity within the company as well as benefit society.

Participation is the management style suited to this understanding of human nature in large contemporary organizations. As Stephen Fuller reports, based on a study of four General Motors plants, "There is a close relationship between an organization's performance and how the employees feel about the organization. . . . The project showed that we could improve performance and human satisfaction by creating conditions in which people can become more involved, work together, and experience personal growth."[10]

Participative Management in Operation

Although the participative style means a decisive shift from authoritarian, autocratic management, it does not imply that top management abdicates its responsibility for company policy and leadership.

Participative management does not mean corporate democracy. It does imply the recognition that different levels within the corporate structure have contributions to make to policy. "Participation, it is clear," writes Rosabeth Moss Kanter, "needs to be managed just as carefully as any other organization system, and it creates new problems demanding attention in the course of solving others."[11] When participative management is seen not in isolation or as an end in itself but rather as part of the management of values in a corporation, continuing assessment of its meaning and results is essential.

Participative management means involving different levels of management in policy formulation and evaluation. In particular, persons and units that will have the responsibility to implement policy will ordinarily be consulted about that policy prior to its final formulation and promulgation. They will also be included in subsequent evaluation of that policy and its possible revision. When participation takes place in these ways, several results can be anticipated. First, it is probable that the quality of policy made will be improved because it includes the perspectives and knowledge of those best acquainted with the problems of putting it into operation. Second, those who participate in formulation are more likely to understand the policies made, comply with them, and implement them with greater accuracy and enthusiasm. Third, policy formulation and implementation becomes a means for communicating the culture and value commitments of the corporation so that various levels of management come to own the culture as well as understand it and thus reflect its values more in the actions and interactions within their units.

In large corporations with divisional forms of organization, participative management provides for the coordination between headquarters and the divisions that is required for effective control. This will prove true with reference to all aspects of company operations, but it is especially so with reference to the management of values. An overall corporate ethic will permeate the company only by ensuring that priorities and value judgments are in accord at different levels of responsibility in the corporation. By recognizing the various social pressures in the different divisions and integrating these perspectives into policy formulation, realistic performance goals will be set and the quality of performance enhanced. This aspect is important for operating in any environment, but it is of crucial importance for multinational corporations where different divisions may be operating in other cultures with environments of social values different from that at headquarters.

Attention to a participative style can provide a counterbalance to the tendency of rational styles of management to place strong emphasis on quantification, on simplified goals, and on standards of performance related to production and profit. Although Management by Objectives (MBO), for example, began as a means to increase participation in policy formulation and goal setting, MBO often seems to end by depersonalizing the policy process and restricting it to a narrow range of values. Participative management provides a vehicle for ensuring that a wider spectrum of values is utilized, so that the trade-offs among various purposes and goods are made on the basis of awareness and adequate reflection.[12]

By tapping energies and insights within the company on a wider and deeper level than other styles, corporations that utilize a participative style of management tend to improve their ability to be innovative on a continuing basis and to respond to changes in the internal and external environments. This ability is important not only with reference to shifting social issues but also in relation to changing demand, new markets, and technological innovation. By these means, participation can enhance the performance of a corporation in many sectors and in various ways.

A participative style of management is not without costs and problems. As more people are drawn into the process of policy formulation, the time required is greater, and more time must be allowed in the planning cycle. Communications must be increased to provide better bases for participation and to explain how and why suggestions are being acted upon by top management. But the potential for enhanced performance at all levels seems clearly to compensate for these costs many times over.

COMMITMENT: IMAGINATION AND INNOVATION

Recent literature on excellence in management emphasizes the importance of the culture and values of a company for the quality of its operation and production. Managing effectively not only requires having culture and values understood; it also necessitates building commitment to corporate values into the actions of people at all levels. This requires ownership of corporate culture and values. Only in a context of commitment is it possible to achieve the imaginative and innovative elements essential to excellent levels of performance.

Corporate Covenants and Commitment

Organizations are not machines. Corporations might be easier to manage if they were completely rational, orderly, and mechanical. They are, however, too permeated with the passions and unpredictable possibilities of persons to be described adequately by metaphors borrowed from the spheres of machinery or logic.

Organizations, however, are not persons. In spite of the well-established precedent to regard corporations as *persona ficta* before the law, and in spite of the personal elements that saturate them, there are too many impersonal and transpersonal characteristics of organizations to describe them as persons writ large. Thomas Hobbes was more accurate in using the image of the great monster Leviathan for the organization known as the *state*. But the organic, natural metaphors miss the distinctively human characteristics of large organizations.

Organizations are social. The image of society with individual persons interacting with one another in patterned relationships is better than images of a machine, or logic, or a great natural organism. Corporations, like all organizations, are composed of persons in relation and are therefore decisively and inescapably personal. But they operate on a more comprehensive level than individual personality through the patterns that guide and shape the social interaction of the participants. It is these patterns in their regularity that make organizations in part capable of description in terms of machines and reason. When organizations are small, the personal elements are most apparent; but this will not obscure the social and structural elements for the perceptive observer. The larger and more complex the organization, the more its structures appear as most important; but this should not deceive us into ignoring the personal and social elements and reducing it to its mechanical and logical elements.

Because organizations are social, they are also covenantal. There are agreements made upon which they are founded. For a government this is its constitution. Some foundational covenants have no fixed point of beginning or explicit statement, e.g., the British constitution; most of it is implicit and undergoing gradual change.

Other such agreements have specific founding dates and formal statement; but even the most explicit have a multitude of implicit understandings surrounding them.

Like all other social groups, corporations are based upon covenants that define the patterns of interaction and limitations. Corporate charters are the most explicit form of the covenants by which business firms operate, but there are other agreements through which the foundational covenants are spelled out. Corporate covenants are based upon the covenants of the society in which the companies are chartered and operate. These social covenants contain common purposes and values that shape the environment in which a corporation operates and that permeate its own goals and ethical judgments. Societal commitments are most explicit in laws and in the allocation of resources, but they are no less forceful in the implicit moral directives and customs that determine societal action. The commitments of the larger social order and of the internal society of the corporation — commitments never completely spelled out or encompassed in any contractual statements — disclose a corporation as a covenantal community.

The "traditional" assumptions and methods for management within the corporation have over the past half century faced serious questioning. The view that most humans dislike work and must be coerced and threatened is no longer persuasive so far as the evidence is concerned. And what may be of greater importance, it will not be accepted by workers and therefore will not work. The attempts to replace this traditional approach with scientific methods of management that were assumed to be value free and treated people as though they were machines rather than recalcitrant animals continued for a time. Although scientific management with its time-motion studies made many contributions to efficient operations, it failed to do justice to the human dimensions of the corporate community.

Human relations management rediscovered the ancient lesson that humanity and every context of human interaction are inevitably permeated with values, commitments, and purposes. Executive leadership must build upon this basic nature of human situations and find ways to evoke loyalty, responsibility, and imagination within the corporate enterprise. This perspective, however, did not so much displace or envelop the scientific view of management as overlay or supplement it. Increasingly, human relations management was interpreted as psychological understanding, conditioning, and manipulation. The insight that the management of values was central for the executive role tended to be forgotten. As more and more quantifiable tools of management emerged and were refined by means of computer technology, the human relations approach to management seemed to be disappearing.

But a funny thing happened to human relations and values on the way to the graveyard. Some observers began to notice that corporations performing well were paying attention to value commitments and human aspirations whether or not management theorists talked about them. While there is no attempt being made to discard or displace the array of technical wares available to management, it is becoming ever clearer that complex machines and organizational techniques work well only when operating within a corporate culture that recognizes and builds upon the values prized in the human community within the company and in the society around.

Profit, productivity, and survival are not values to be ignored by managers. But these corporate values must be placed in relation to such values as safe and clean workplaces, equal opportunity for minorities and women, products with quality appropriate to their use, mutual trust, common purposes, pride in shared accomplishments, personal work satisfaction, feelings of community, and a conviction of contributing to the larger society. These values may be expressed differently and may not be the same for every corporation. But there must be a network of values woven together into what can be called a *corporate culture* and sustained by specific policies, implementation, and activities. The criteria providing the basis for setting priorities, making trade-offs among values, and shaping policy can be called a corporate ethic. In order to be durable and effective, this ethic must be embodied in the culture, integrated into the policy process and all corporate institutional structures, supported by comprehensive and accurate social values information, and built into the actions of all levels through participative management.

Corporate performance is measured in terms of all these values as they are balanced off and utilized in the sum total of corporate action. The management of values means the conscious activity of recognizing the variety of values present, of undertaking to decide among them and develop a corporate culture on the basis of value commitments, and of integrating those values into the policy process and ensuring that they have a firm foundation in the corporate community. This is a beginning toward the management of values internally for performance.

Commitment and Imagination

At various points we have used the metaphor of driving an automobile or steering a ship. When speaking of the overall task of managing values for performance, there is something especially appealing about the image of the captain and senior officers of a ship integrating the activities and energies of all the persons and machines in different parts of the vessel, taking account of changing conditions with imaginative solutions, setting the course in light of the purposes of the voyage, overseeing and adjusting each element to fit the whole operation, and taking responsibility for the value judgments permeating every part of the process.

At times it may seem to the busy division head or deckhand that the senior officers are doing nothing. The focal concern of management is not with particular tasks related to engine room or galley but rather with the central task of the voyage — making the judgments of basic direction, resolving conflicting interests and values, and integrating the varied functions of the entire enterprise. Executives are engaged in the difficult task of managing values for the sake of the total performance.

The context in which management must steer the company safely is the surrounding social environment, with its currents of values and its legal shoals. The corporation exists as an agent in society. A primary reason for organizing and operating it is to participate in commercial activities and make a profit. But financial values can never be considered apart from internal functions or in isolation from the legitimation and expectations of society. It is unlikely that a profit can be made, especially on a long-term basis, unless there is a good or service that is desired enough for people to pay for it. This further requires that the value of product quality be considered, because the public will not pay for a shoddy imitation of what it wants. The product must also be competitive in relation to other suppliers. The value of production efficiency enters as a balance to the value of product quality. And quality, of course, is not merely excellence unrelated to specific uses and standards; for example, customers do not want expensive, though excellent, bond paper if the purpose for which it is being purchased is to provide scratch pads.

Steering the company requires attention to more than the values of the marketplace, though those must never be neglected. Corporate actions must also fit in with such valent social values as EEO, manufacturing procedures that do not endanger workers or the surrounding community, respect for the natural environment, operation within accepted legal and moral guidelines, and so on. The management of values involves a complex process of navigation that requires attention to basic social realities and the ability to shape corporate action in the light of those realities.

Such navigation demands expert insight among top management. But the tasks of steering these difficult times cannot be accomplished without committed and imaginative involvement at all levels. In the end managing values must be achieved through the efforts of an entire covenanted community. The task will be performed with greater excellence to the extent that the values of the corporation are understood and owned at all levels. The ownership becomes deeper when communication is accompanied by participation and when commitment is seen both as commitment to shared values and as commitment of persons to one another in a common enterprise. Commitment is no less from top management to the community of employees than from them to the company. Practices that violate this covenant impair relations and undermine performance.

As the covenant and the mutual commitments in a corporation become firm and reliable, they release the energies and the imagination of persons. New possibilities of performance emerge. A plant manager in a large corporation with over 300 locations in the United States noticed a decline in the quality of work by one of his best supervisors. A conversation in which the manager expressed personal concern revealed that the supervisor's wife had a life-threatening illness requiring treatment at one or another medical center hundreds of miles distant. The manager took the problem to a conference of regional plant managers and arranged for the supervisor to be transferred to a place where his wife could be treated. The transfer cost the company a modest amount. But, as the manager said later, he would much rather work for a corporation in which he can be humane to the people who work for him and certain that the senior management and the entire corporate culture support him. He also said that the increased loyalty, energy, and imagination evoked in that supervisor and among those acquainted with what was done in his situation probably repaid the company many times over in improved performance.

Managing amid Change

Corporations exist and conduct their business in societies that are in a period of rapid social change — change on the levels of technology, patterns of living, and basic values. Indeed, social change is rooted in changing social values that are correlated with conditions as experienced by identifiable groups in society. These social changes are having major impact on all societal organizations, including corporations. Understanding these changes and the shifts in values underlying them is essential for the management of values that will produce effective corporate performance. The promise of adequate communication and participative management is nowhere greater than in the perspective of the management of change and the imaginative innovation that such management requires.

First, having various levels of management participate in formulating and evaluating policy is one of the surest ways to stay close to the changing values of society. To the extent that management represents diverse groups in society, including the age spectrum, it is less likely that policy will become trapped in the social perspective represented by top management. From product development to marketing, from dealing with social issues to being attuned to new social values, there is no better resource immediately available than those with a stake in the success of the company today and tomorrow. What is true in the original formulation of policy is equally true for reappraisal and modification. If invited in and listened to, management at middle and lower levels can be among the most constructive critics of corporate policy and of the criteria by which it is evaluated. From the standpoint of changing social values, participative management can make powerful contributions to the enhancement of corporate performance.

Second, the formulation and implementation of policy lead inevitably to conflicts of value. Not all purposes can be accomplished simultaneously. Resources and energies devoted to pursuing one goal cannot be used to reach another. By involving management in the policy process, such conflicts are more likely to be perceived before they are built into company policy rather than coming to light later in destructive clashes. Furthermore, the chances are enhanced that solutions will be suggested that encompass more desired values at a higher level. Additional policy alternatives will be introduced into the policy process, and improved patterns of implementation geared to policy are more likely to appear. The management of change with reference to the enactment of policy in relation to multiple purposes and in relation to better implementation will enhance performance.

Third, communication with depth and participative management can be viewed as ways to build a strong culture, with agreed-upon values flowing through the operation of the company. In this perspective the ability to roll with the punches in times of crisis and manage change as a cohesive team is greatly improved by involvement and participation. In this way also, they can enhance performance.

On the basis of a wide range of experience with corporations meeting the challenges of performance in the midst of change, Kanter emphasizes the importance of integration and innovation:

> American corporations are at a critical watershed because they face a transforming economic and social environment which has emerged since the 1960s. This new context for corporate America makes past responses less effective; it changes the tasks of management at all levels and encourages the search for better ways to involve the entire work force in innovative problem solving.
>
> But where segmentalism prevails, companies are likely to stifle their own potential for greater innovation, making it all but impossible for any but a few hardy individuals to contribute to solving problems — and highly unlikely that the company can even take advantage of those innovations in structure and practice that do occur.
>
> There is hope, however, in the experience of several leading, innovating American firms that already operate in an integrative mode, thereby encouraging entrepreneurial behavior and employee involvement leading to productive, responsive change.[13]

As culture and values give cohesion and unity to actions at all levels and the parts of the policy process are seen as interacting components rather than as separate entities, it becomes possible to manage values effectively. Communications, participation, and commitment in management emerge as instruments for achieving higher levels of performance in the most comprehensive fashion.

SUGGESTIONS FOR GROUP STUDY

1. Read the book brief on Robert Ackerman, *The Social Challenge to Business* (Appendix M). Also reread the conversation on equal employment opportunity at the beginning of Chapter Six in the light of the social issue life cycle analysis. Assign to members of your group the task of preparing a report on a single social issue that has had an impact on a corporation they know, using the appendix material as a guide. Then, examining the history of that company's policy, see what changes were made and how these changes are related to the life cycle of the issue involved. Was the company a leader, one of the pack, or a "lagger" in the timing of its policy shifts? Share your individual conclusions.
2. In group discussion identify the elements of a corporate social value information system suited to the needs of a company with whom the group is familiar. Identify the available sources of this information and outline how it would be gathered, processed, and presented to various individuals and groups in the corporate setting. What kind of an organizational unit is needed to support this system? Where should it be located organizationally?
3. From the personal experience of the group, evaluate the validity of Theory Z as outlined in the text. Are the assumptions about human nature true? Is the feeling of involvement in an organization that is recognized to be socially responsible a positive reinforcement of productive behavior for its employees? Can you see evidence of the effectiveness of participative management?
4. Based on readings provided in this book and sources the group has discovered, discuss ways to institutionalize corporate ethics and thus improve communications, encourage innovation, and enhance performance.

Part Four

CONCLUSION

Ten

THE ETHICAL DIFFERENCE

Ten senior vice-presidents of a major industrial corporation with over 200 locations scattered over the United States were meeting. The topic for discussion was how to make the corporate code and its ethics more effectively operative throughout the company.

"The real problem, as I see it," Tom was saying, "is whether we do the right thing when issues arise or do what will mean more profit. It's okay to have a code of ethics, but we are first of all in business to make money. If the profit is rolling in, we can afford to put our values into operation."

"I don't think it's that way at all," Bill replied. "We can't make a profit over the long run unless we have a strong culture with value commitments that we are always trying to practice better. One of the main reasons I like working for this company is that I believe we have values and try to build them into what we do."

Chris leaned forward in his seat. "That's what the CEO at Johnson & Johnson was saying in the videotape we saw last week. A corporation has to put the concerns of people first, or society will rebel and pass laws compelling corporations to act in approved ways."

"That was James Burke," Cliff added, joining the conversation. "He made a speech last year in New York comparing the long-term profits of corporations having strong cultures and ethical codes with corporations that did not. According to his report, it's having value commitments and practicing them throughout the company that ensures good performance."

"Well," Tom said, retreating a little, "it may be something of a chicken

and egg thing. You can't tell which comes first. But I'd like some examples of how we put our ethics to work here."

"I'll give you an illustration," Frank, who had been silent up to now, said. "Last year our southwest region had just locked some of our major suppliers of raw materials into three-year contracts when the market for their products shot way up. We could have held them to the lower price legally. But I discussed it with our managers in the region, and we decided to renegotiate the contracts. We still came out well with reference to the current market but not as well as we could have in terms of the original contracts."

"If it was mushy do-gooding," Tom replied, "I'd say you were wrong. If it will turn a profit, I'd say you did right."

"I don't think those sharp alternatives are the correct ones," Frank responded. "I used to think so, but no more. The discussions we have been having over the past year about our corporate culture and ethics have given me a different perspective on the way we make decisions here. In this case we took a careful look at the different values that were involved — our long-term relations with these suppliers in the past; our plans to keep buying from them in the future; the confidence we had developed in the quality of the materials we were getting from them; the importance of their confidence in us as reliable purchasers; the times they had gone out of their way to help us and will again; and the reputation of this company in the entire region."

"It sounds to me," Bill said, "as though you looked at the trade-offs among values carefully and came up with a solution that was sound management because it combined humane values and business values."

"I agree," Bob chimed in. "I'm proud to work for a company that has those commitments. When we have similar decisions, we work them through and know that the CEO we've got will support us and so will most of the top management. Did you check with your executive vice-president before making the final arrangements?"

"No," Frank replied. "We included it in our reports. A note came down on that item commending us and wanting to use it as an illustration if it could be done in a way that would not embarrass anyone."

"I can think of decisions like that we've made in our division," Cliff said. "We are gradually learning that ethics is not doing something perfect but rather weighing values and working through to the best combination of trade-offs we can come up with."

"Those are illustrations of what we might call **managing values for excellence**," Bill suggested.

"There really is such a thing as business ethics," Irving Kristol wrote several years ago.[1] Leaders in the corporate community and in business schools could have been the ones to bring Kristol to this conclusion. Once the misunderstandings of ethics — such as moral perfectionism and rational precision — are overcome, it becomes possible to see what a statement like Kristol's means. Better still, listen to some corporate managers like the ones presented in the conversation above and watch them wrestle seriously with the value judgments inescapably woven into making and implementing company policy. They are constantly engaging in ethical reflection, balancing various goals and goods, and seeking how best to manage values in their particular sector of responsibility.

Not only are executives in all companies grappling with issues of value and corporate ethics, there are also many business leaders who believe that the survival and future health of business in the North Atlantic community and around the globe depend upon the quality of ethical awareness informing corporate policy. In no way does this imply diminished need for other qualities. Management of the modern business enterprise must possess technical knowledge, financial competence, innovative imagination, *and also* ethical understanding, discerning judgment, and moral courage. The need for the first three is generally acknowledged. What is becoming clear to perceptive leaders is that the latter three are equally crucial for excellence in management and performance. Possessing the last three capabilities can be called the *ethical difference*.

The ethical difference in human affairs can never be reduced to an old saw like "Honesty is the best policy." Both idealists and cynics attempt to demonstrate or discredit the presence of ethics in social context with such reductionism. Honesty, like lying, is far too complex to use in this manner, even though honesty, understood and carried out with concern for persons, cannot be too highly prized. Because policy represents by its very nature a balancing of values, all of which are desirable, the best policy can never be summed up by naming only one value.

In a world of rapid change, corporate management succeeds according to its safe navigation through channels defined by multiple values and purposes and understood by means of ethical reflection and insight. The close relation of ethics and performance is emerging in the experience of operating managers with increasing clarity. To those who deal with the problems of running corporations, the ethical difference seems very real.

THE TESTIMONY OF JAMES BURKE

The story of the Tylenol poisoning crisis and Johnson & Johnson's successful handling of a difficult situation has become well known. It is fascinating to get the perspective of James E. Burke, chairman and CEO of Johnson & Johnson, on what lies behind the ability of that collection of companies to perform so well both in situations of success and circumstances of adversity. In November 1983, on the occasion of receiving an award for his leadership, Burke gave an address in which he offered his views on the relation of ethics and performance. He does not believe that Johnson & Johnson is unique. Burke suggests that "those companies that organize their businesses around the broad concept of public service over the long run provide superior performance for their stockholders."[1]

The strong corporate values of Johnson & Johnson go back a long way. Right after World War II, Robert Wood Johnson, longtime CEO, said: "Institutions, both public and private, exist because the people want them, believe in them, or at least are willing to tolerate them. The day has passed when business was a private matter — if it ever really was. In a business society, every act of business has social consequences and may arouse public interest. Every time business hires, builds, sells or buys, it is acting for the people as well as for itself, and it *must* accept full responsibility for its acts." This view sees clearly the common interests and interacting values of corporations and the larger society, and it affirms that corporations are moral agents.

Robert Wood Johnson developed Johnson & Johnson's *Credo* and sought to ensure that its principles were understood, accepted, and operative throughout the corporation during his years at its helm. The *Credo* enunciates core values and provided an ordering of priorities. As a maker of pharmaceuticals and other health care products, the first responsibility of the company, said the *Credo,* is to the consumers: doctors, nurses, patients, and mothers who buy the firm's products and services. Second in order of priority are the company employees whose creative energies are responsible for its products and services. Third are the communities where the company operates and humankind. Fourth are the stockholders who have invested in the corporation. Burke and his predecessors have insisted that this is the correct ordering, for if the first three responsibilities are carried out, the shareholders will do well. The record of Johnson & Johnson would support the view that ethics and performance, in this case at least, have gone hand in hand.

In the 1970s, with the *Credo* nearly 30 years old, questions arose as to whether it was really being followed in the large, complex, international corporation that Johnson & Johnson had become, and whether it was outmoded in language. In a series of meetings, beginning with upper management and eventually reaching into every level of management around the world over a three-year period. the *Credo* was discussed, examined carefully as to its meaning and applicability, and reconsidered with reference to its precise wording. Burke says, "What we discovered was that we had a set of guiding principles far more powerful than we had imagined." By 1979 the revised *Credo* had become again the focus of the corporation's culture, understood and also accepted by the management throughout the company.

It was Johnson & Johnson with a strong and revitalized culture that was hit in September 1982 by the Tylenol crisis in which a product of a subsidiary company was used as an instrument of random murder. In a time when people had to make decisions quickly, often too quickly for conferring with headquarters and thinking through all the details, the people at Johnson & Johnson, according to Burke, are today convinced that the guidance of the *Credo* was the most important factor in making sure that priorities were kept straight, value judgments made consistently and well, and actions taken that brought great credit to the corporation. And Tylenol has won back its consumers and regained most of its share of the market.

In his address Burke takes the lesson further and suggests that ethics makes a profound difference in performance. "I have long harbored the belief," he says, "that the most successful corporations in this country, the ones that have delivered outstanding results over a long period of time, were driven by a simple moral imperative — serving the public in the broadest possible sense." His staff conducted research and found 15 public companies that have written codes with service to the public central and that had promulgated and practiced the code for at least a generation. These companies had far outstripped other companies, the general growth of the economy, and the Dow Jones average. "The results," as Burke put it, "are at the very least provocative."

The measure of performance that Burke takes for this example is primarily financial. When one looks at the list of companies he is examining, it is likely that more comprehensive evaluations of performance would yield similar results. From the testimony of James Burke, the ethical difference is clear and impressive.

EVALUATING CORPORATE PERFORMANCE

For the second year, *Fortune* magazine has conducted a survey to ascertain which are "America's Most Admired Corporations." To get its results, "*Fortune* polled over 7,000 corporate executives, outside directors, and financial analysts; half responded." They were asked to rate corporations on eight criteria: "quality of management; quality of products or services; innovativeness; long-term investment value; financial soundness; ability to attract, develop, and keep talented people; community and environmental responsibility; and use of corporate assets."[2] These may not be sufficient to satisfy everyone as to criteria of corporate performance. It is interesting, however, that financial measurements do not dominate and are interwoven with other values.

To be the most admired cannot be identified with having a strong corporate ethics. And reputation is not always in line with actual character and practice. But these criteria that *Fortune* used in asking for evaluations ties perceived performance closely to perceived ethics.

In this light the concluding paragraph of the story is especially interesting: "The most admired U.S. companies believe that their ultimate success depends on how they are perceived by the public. 'Consumers trust certain companies,' says August Busch III, chairman of Anheuser-Busch. 'Consumers trust IBM. Consumers trust an Anheuser-Busch product. They trust a Boeing airplane.' Repeatedly, corporations with first-class reputations are seen to put quality, integrity, and respect for the customer alongside profits on the bottom line."[3]

Another perspective from which to evaluate companies is provided in a book reporting on "the 100 best corporations to work for in America." The research was carried out by asking employees, not executives in other businesses or the public, about the companies they worked for. The results derive from the perspective of those who work in a company: best paying, best for benefits, best for job security, best for ambience, best for women to work in, and best companies for blacks. Criteria behind the ratings include making people feel part of a team, encouraging open communications, informing people about what is going on, encouraging and welcoming complaints and suggestions, promoting from within more than from outside, encouraging people to feel pride in their work, and keeping stress at a minimum.[4]

While these criteria may be inadequate for a thorough evaluation of corporate performance, they represent a spectrum of values in which the humane and the economic are interwoven. As with the *Fortune* criteria, these also point clearly to the imperative that corporate executives be able to understand and manage values effectively.

ETHICS AND PERFORMANCE: A SUMMARY

Drawing on wide resources and emphasizing the insights of those in the policy arena, we have discussed in this book many dimensions of the close relation between ethics and policy and diverse perspectives on the management of values. We shall summarize the main elements.

Corporate Culture and Character

To speak of the ethical difference means, first, attention to the culture and value commitments of the corporation. Corporate culture radiates out from top management. For better or worse a strong chief executive can influence the entire tone of a company. But this influence will be enduring only as it shapes the culture and permeates the institutional structures of the corporation rather than remaining primarily in a vision of the CEO. To the extent that similar characteristics, purposes, and values pervade the actions of a corporation, it is possible to speak of a corporate culture.

Reginald Jones, formerly CEO of General Electric, emphasizes the importance of character at the core of corporate management:

> The people rightfully expect something more than technical competence in the managers of our large corporations. They look for a moral center — some evidence that we are operating from higher principles than expediency or narrow self interest. These are entirely reasonable expectations, and if they are ignored they quickly become a matter of law. So if the manager of the future wants to hold the respect of his peers and keep his company out of the toils of the law, he will be absolutely scrupulous in matters of law and ethics, and make sure that these same standards are upheld at all levels of the organization.[5]

In making certain that compliance takes place at all levels of management, values begin to pervade the culture. The culture reflects these value commitments as they become part of the policy process, of personnel practices of recruitment and training, of evaluation and promotion, of production and marketing, and so on. When compliance is no longer so much because there is careful monitoring from senior management but rather because the values have been internalized, it becomes possible to speak of corporate character.

The ethical difference with reference to corporate culture and character is coherence and economy of action. It is no longer necessary to expend enormous amounts of energy ensuring product quality or humane relations with employees and customers. There is not as much time wasted on sorting out conflicting purposes, resolving internal differences, or repairing external relations. Continuing support and monitoring continues, especially as changes occur, but policy and action emanate from a shared center.

Corporate Ethics

Once there is a community of values and purpose, it is possible to have meaningful corporate ethics. This means having criteria for policy and implementation that are relevant to the operations of the company and related to the actual processes by which decisions are made and actions taken. Corporate ethics is not a code of behavior, though it may include one. Codes have clarity, but they must either be very general or, if specific, constantly updated in order to be relevant to company operations. Ethics provides methods and criteria for reflecting on the significance of action at appropriate levels and emerges from the actual processes of policy-making and implementation. As suggested in Chapter Five, overall criteria such as self-interest, multiple responsibility, and social vision provide a framework for corporate ethics with comprehensiveness and the possibility of informing corporate policy formulation and implementation.

The ethical difference for a corporate ethics involves the deliberate choice and use of criteria rather than letting these operative values come from external pressure or emerge amorphously from a general context of corporate culture. It is the difference illustrated when travelers have maps and directions for a common destination rather than depending on hearsay or on a conversation at the starting point as to where the group is going. If there is no agreement on the goal and meaning of the trip, maps may go unused. Where there is community of purpose established, explicit guidance can be crucial in ensuring that everyone travels by the best routes and reaches the destination with economical expenditure of energy.

The Environment of Values

Managing a business requires knowing the territory in which the company operates. In the same way, the management of values demands that managers know the territory. The effective extension and use of corporate ethics involves constant and careful scanning of the environment of social values within which policy is being formulated and carried out. This environment is both external to the corporation and internal to it.

The internal environment of values is embodied in the corporate culture and character. It is important for management not only to take leadership in shaping, developing, and supporting a strong corporate culture and value commitments but also, on a continuing basis, to listen to and be aware of the internal environment as it exists and changes. This is a way to monitor the effectiveness of efforts to shape the corporate culture, to ensure compliance with the values intended, and to get feedback on changes in content and method and new perspectives that may be useful in policy development.

The external environment of values involves the customs and concerns of the immediate community, the social values of the larger society that shape the laws and provide clues to emerging trends important for company operations, and the global culture with its particular sectors that may be related to corporate activities as well as the general course of changes that have significance for the political economies of all industrialized nations.

The ethical difference means knowing that the total environment of values enables corporate management to anticipate possible problems, foresee probable results, and evaluate actual consequences in relation to the factors that produced them. Just as the good captain of a sailboat knows the rules of the road, the direction and strength of the wind, the set of the currents, and the courses of other vessels, management must know the environment of interests, purposes, and values in which the company is to be steered.

Setting Priorities and Shaping Policy

Once there is a stable character, an ethics with relevant criteria, and accurate information about the environment of values, it becomes possible to order priorities with greater confidence and precision and to shape policy with a firmer sense of direction and purpose. No amount of ethical reflection can remove the hard work of planning, coordination, and development that management requires. Nor does ethics diminish the awareness of responsibility for actions taken. On the contrary, the more serious and comprehensive the ethics, the more it will require increased work in taking greater pains and getting better information. And as ethical sensitivity is heightened, the feeling of responsibility becomes deeper and wider. The ethical difference means being oriented and knowing where the company is going; it is not an excuse to do less.

The integration of ethics into the entire policy process must not be neglected. In one way this means formulating criteria that relate to and are drawn from the actual activities of the company. In another way it means making sure that ethical consideration with appropriate criteria takes place throughout all the institutional structures of the corporation and at every level. The ethical difference can mean not only enhanced quality of performance but also the encouragement of the moral imagination that combines know-how with the willingness to innovate. That endeavor can result in more than quality; it can even produce excellence.

Acting with Integrity

A. W. Clausen, formerly CEO of the Bank of America and now chair of the World Bank, has said: "Integrity is not some impractical notion dreamed up by naive do-gooders. Our integrity is the foundation for, the very basis of, our ability to do business."[6] What Clausen said with reference to the banking industry is equally true for every business enterprise. In this perspective, ethics not only is important because it provides the basis for performance with quality; ethics, of a minimally acceptable nature is essential for performing at any level.

The understanding of corporate ethics presented in the preceding chapters underscores the fundamental importance of integrity as Clausen articulates it. What we have done is to spell out more completely the meaning of *integrity* as involving the character of the entire company, not just senior management; to develop operative criteria for a comprehensive ethics; to show how it can be integrated into the entire policy process and thus provide corporate integrity with a broader and firmer base; to delineate the kinds of information systems needed to ensure integrity of action as well as intention; and to suggest ways to carry that integrity throughout the institutional structures.

The ethical difference has to do, therefore, with the permeation of the entire corporation, so that intention, policy, and action have a cohesiveness, an integrity, a unity. It is a mistake to regard integrity understood in this way as perfection or as a static ideal. We have shown, rather, that integrity is a process of development of corporate character and ethics and of integrating that ethic more consciously and thoroughly into the entire top-to-bottom operation of the company.

Correcting for Error

Nothing confirms the fallibility of individual and corporate agency more than the necessity of admitting mistakes — intentions not carried out well and intentions that need improvement. And nothing confirms the strength and adequacy of corporate character and ethics more than the capability to see mistakes, to evaluate the results, to discover what went wrong, and to correct for error. Character, ethics, integrity, and their presence in organizations and individuals involve living process and critical development, not static norms and rigid rules. Quality control requires monitoring to maintain agreed-upon standards and to evaluate those standards for change and improvement. *Corporate ethics* implies the presence of (1) comprehensive, inclusive quality control with which to evaluate the entire enterprise from intention to action to consequences and (2) the constant review of information so that criteria are regularly appraised, related more closely to every level of operations, and utilized to correct the course and to enhance performance.

Ethics and Performance

The management of values requires the continuous exercise of moral imagination, but the inseparability of ethics and performance is far from imaginary. Here are some of the linkages suggested in this close relationship:

- Selection of the criteria for what is regarded as an excellent performance is itself a product of ethical reflection.
- Corporate culture as a network of value commitments empowering and shaping action in the corporate community can be understood only when ethical reflection and other perspectives are utilized.
- A corporate ethics with consciously articulated criteria applicable to the policies and actions of the particular firm is necessary if management is to take over the management of values rather than merely react to external or internal pressures.
- The criteria for a comprehensive corporate ethic include self-interest but must encompass many more values important for corporate performance.

- If corporate ethics is to have impact on performance, ethical reflection must be integrated into the corporate policy process and made to permeate all of the institutional structures of the corporation.
- The effective management of values requires accurate knowledge of the internal and external environment of values in which the company operates and the capability of bringing that information into policy formulation and implementation.
- Ethics will have maximum effect on corporate performance when patterns of participative management are used that communicate values throughout the organization and involve all levels of managers and employees in affirming and shaping excellence in all activities.
- In quite specific ways, ethical reflection and information on social values contribute to corporate performance by shortening the response time between (1) the emergence of new social issues and a changing context and (2) appropriate corporate action through policy and implementation.
- Conscious and careful attention to ethics and values enables management to distinguish transitory shifts in public sentiment from long-term changes in social perspective that are important for corporate policy.
- Corporate ethics and criteria for value judgments provide a basis for making important decisions that can be justified to internal and external constituencies because that basis reconciles profit and growth values with humanitarian and communitarian values.
- A basis in ethics and values gives cohesion and unity to actions at all levels of the company, which contributes to performance by building community, infusing the culture with purpose and pride, and maintaining good relations and receptivity in society at large.

Such a list only makes a beginning. But it can be sufficiently suggestive to evoke others to modify it and make additions.

Ethics is, in these multiple ways, clearly related to performance. Indeed, if we understand the scope of ethics in the inclusive ways described here, it is possible to say that performance depends upon the quality and comprehensiveness of the ethics of a corporation. This requires that we not forget the interdependence of all the many factors that go into any performance, whether that of a concert pianist, a skilled technician, an organizational management, or an entire corporation.

Plato tells a delightfully instructive story about the world on the eve of creation as the gods were making final preparations for its beginning. The brothers Prometheus and Epimetheus (meaning "forethought" and "afterthought") were charged with the responsibility for equipping the creatures-to-be for survival. Epimetheus took on the task. Some creatures were given teeth and claws, others the ability to run fast or fly or burrow into the ground. When he came to humans, however, Epimetheus discovered that he had nothing left with which to endow human beings for surviving. The resourceful Prometheus saw that this would never do, so he entered the workshop of the gods surreptitiously and stole from them technology and energy (fire) to give humans the means for defense. He did too well. Humanity was well equipped to defend itself against animals, but humans also banded together against one another and appeared headed for extinction at their own hands.

Needless to say, Zeus was annoyed at the botched job Prometheus and Epimetheus had done. So he sent Hermes to give humans two additional skills. The first was respect for one another. The second was insight into and desire for justice. And he instructed Hermes to give them to all people, not just to a few experts. So the perils of technology and energy were in part overcome and their possibilities in part realized by the ethical powers of humanity. The ethical difference makes human survival possible and provides the basis for the great achievements of the human community.[7]

SUGGESTIONS FOR GROUP STUDY

1. Reread the conversation at the opening of the chapter. Explore in the study group the values represented in the illustration discussed by these managers. How does the balancing of values relate to corporate culture and ethics? What is the meaning of *the ethical difference* in the context of this discussion of the management of values?
2. After the group has read and pondered the speech by James Burke (Appendix N), have a discussion in the group of the importance of corporate culture and ethics for the performance of Johnson & Johnson in the Tylenol crisis. What is the group's evaluation of Burke's case that ethics makes a great difference in the performance of corporation?

3. Read the EastWest Bank case in Appendix O. What actions do you think should be taken by the bank's management in response to the situation that they face as stated in the case? In the perspective of corporate ethics given in the previous chapters, develop an analysis of the possible lines of action that the bank might take. In a group discussion, formulate what you believe would be the appropriate international loan policy for an institution like EastWest Bank. Do you see anything in such a policy that could be called *the ethical difference?*

Appendices

MATERIAL FOR GROUP STUDY

A

SUGGESTIONS FOR USE OF STUDY MATERIALS WITH GROUPS

Charles S. McCoy and Fred N. Twining

1. *Management of Values* may be read straight through for its overall perspective. This use requires minimal attention to the "Suggestions for Group Study." The book may also be used for group or class study. The suggestions can aid in examining carefully the issues raised in each chapter and make the book useful in business ethics courses, in business and society courses, or in management discussion groups in corporations.
2. When using *Management of Values* in study groups or as the text in courses:
   a. Have each person read the chapter carefully, noting important points, especially those that present new insights or open up innovative perspectives.
   b. Go over the chapter in the group, making sure that the central issues are emphasized and that participants have the opportunity to mention ideas that impressed them.
   c. Focus on *each* suggestion for group study. Some will require advance planning. Use the suggestions as a means to go more deeply into particular issues and to ensure that all members of the group have made the material their own.
3. Suggestions regarding case study discussion:
   a. Examining cases is a good way to relate classwork to actual situations and to problems in operational settings. Cases also give

a sense of living wholeness rather than academic fragmentation. Getting the most out of the case discussions requires experienced, expert leadership and practice on the part of participants.

b. Each person should read the case slowly and thoughtfully. Try to dwell in the situation. Imagine more details than the case relates. Prepare to ask questions about the context and circumstances as well as to suggest solutions.

c. Focus on the value judgments and ethical considerations involved in the cases as well as descriptions of what happens or can happen. Use the insights on corporate ethics emerging from group study and discussion to probe more deeply into the cases.

B

THE SOCIAL RESPONSIBILITY OF BUSINESS IS TO INCREASE ITS PROFITS

Milton Friedman

When I hear businessmen speak eloquently about the "social responsibilities of business in a free-enterprise system," I am reminded of the wonderful line about the Frenchman who discovered at the age of 70 that he had been speaking prose all his life. The businessmen believe that they are defending free enterprise when they declaim that business is not concerned "merely" with profit but also with promoting desirable "social" ends; that business has a "social conscience" and takes seriously its responsibilities for providing employment, eliminating discrimination, avoiding pollution and whatever else may be the catchwords of the contemporary crop of reformers. In fact they are — or would be if they or anyone else took them seriously — preaching pure and unadulterated socialism. Businessmen who talk this way are unwitting puppets of the intellectual forces that have been undermining the basis of a free society these past decades.

The discussions of the "social responsibilities of business" are notable for their analytical looseness and lack of rigor. What does it

---

From "The Social Responsibility of Business Is to Increase Its Profits," The New York *Times Magazine,* September 13, 1970. © 1970 by The New York Times Company. Reprinted by permission.

mean to say that "business" has responsibilities? Only people can have responsibilities. A corporation is an artificial person and in this sense may have artificial responsibilities, but "business" as a whole cannot be said to have responsibilities, even in this vague sense. The first step toward clarity in examining the doctrine of the social responsibility of business is to ask precisely what it implies for whom.

Presumably, the individuals who are to be responsible are businessmen, which means individual proprietors or corporate executives. Most of the discussion of social responsibility is directed at corporations, so in what follows I shall mostly neglect the individual proprietors and speak of corporate executives.

In a free-enterprise, private-property system, a corporate executive is an employee of the owners of the business. He has direct responsibility to his employers. That responsibility is to conduct the business in accordance with their desires, which generally will be to make as much money as possible while conforming to their basic rules of the society, both those embodied in law and those embodied in ethical custom. Of course, in some cases his employers may have a different objective. A group of persons might establish a corporation for an eleemosynary purpose — for example, a hospital or a school. The manager of such a corporation will not have money profit as his objectives but the rendering of certain services.

In either case, the key point is that, in his capacity as a corporate executive, the manager is the agent of the individuals who own the corporation or establish the eleemosynary institution, and his primary responsibility is to them.

Needless to say, this does not mean that it is easy to judge how well he is performing his task. But at least the criterion of performance is straight-forward, and the persons among whom a voluntary contractual arrangement exists are clearly defined.

Of course, the corporate executive is also a person in his own right. As a person, he may have many other responsibilities that he recognizes or assumes voluntarily — to his family, his conscience, his feelings of charity, his church, his clubs, his city, his country. He may feel impelled by these responsibilities to devote part of his income to causes he regards as worthy, to refuse to work for particular corporations, even to leave his job, for example, to join his country's armed forces. If we wish, we may refer to some of these responsibilities as "social responsibilities." But in these respects he is acting as a principal, not an agent; he is spending his own money or time or energy, not the money of his employers or the time or energy he has contracted to devote to their purposes. If these are "social responsibilities," they are the social responsibilities of individuals, not of business.

What does it mean to say that the corporate executive has a "social responsibility" in his capacity as businessman? If this statement is not pure rhetoric, it must mean that he is to act in some way that is not in the interest of his employers. For example, that he is to refrain from increasing the price of the product in order to contribute to the social objective of preventing inflation, even though a price increase would be in the best interests of the corporation. Or that he is to make expenditures on reducing pollution beyond the amount that is in the best interests of the corporation or that is required by law in order to contribute to the social objective of improving the environment. Or that, at the expense of corporate profits, he is to hire "hard-core" unemployed instead of better qualified available workmen to contribute to the social objective of reducing poverty.

In each of these cases, the corporate executive would be spending someone else's money for a general social interest. Insofar as his actions in accord with his "social responsibility" reduce returns to stockholders, he is spending their money. Insofar as his actions raise the price to customers, he is spending the customers' money. Insofar as his actions lower the wages of some employees, he is spending their money.

The stockholders or the customers or the employees could separately spend their own money on the particular action if they wished to do so. The executive is exercising a distinct "social responsibility," rather than serving as an agent of the stockholders or the customers or the employees, only if he spends the money in a different way than they would have spent it.

But if he does this, he is in effect imposing taxes, on the one hand, and deciding how the tax proceeds shall be spent, on the other.

This process raises political questions on two levels: principle and consequences. On the level of political principle, the imposition of taxes and the expenditure of tax proceeds are governmental functions. We have established elaborate constitutional, parliamentary and judicial provisions to control these functions, to assure that taxes are imposed so far as possible in accordance with the preferences and desires of the public — after all, "taxation without representation" was one of the battle cries of the American Revolution. We have a system of checks and balances to separate the legislative function of imposing taxes and enacting expenditures from the executive function of collecting taxes and administering expenditure programs and from the judicial function of mediating disputes and interpreting the law.

Here the businessman — self-selected or appointed directly or indirectly by stockholders — is to be simultaneously legislator, executive and jurist. He is to decide whom to tax by how much and for what purpose, and he is to spend the proceeds — all this guided only by general exhortations from on high to restrain inflation, improve the environment, fight poverty and so on and on.

The whole justification for permitting the corporate executive to be selected by the stockholders is that the executive is an agent serving the interests of his principal. This justification disappears when the corporate executive imposes taxes and spends the proceeds for "social" purposes. He becomes in effect a public employee, a civil servant, even though he remains in name an employee of a private enterprise. On grounds of political principle, it is intolerable that such civil servants — insofar as their actions in the name of social responsibility are real and not just window-dressing — should be selected as they are now. If they are to be civil servants, then they must be elected through a political process. If they are to impose taxes and make expenditures to foster "social" objectives, then political machinery must be set up to make the assessment of taxes and to determine through a political process the objectives to be served.

This is the basic reason why the doctrine of "social responsibility" involves the acceptance of the socialist view that political mechanisms, not market mechanisms, are the appropriate way to determine the allocation of scarce resources to alternative uses.

On the grounds of consequences, can the corporate executive in fact discharge his alleged "social responsibilities"? On the one hand, suppose he could get away with spending the stockholders' or customers' or employees' money. How is he to know how to spend it? He is told that he must contribute to fighting inflation. How is he to know what action of his will contribute to that end? He is presumably an expert in running his company — in producing a product or selling it or financing it. But nothing about his selection makes him an expert on inflation. Will his holding down the price of his product reduce inflationary pressure? Or, by leaving more spending power in the hands of his customers, simply divert it elsewhere? Or, by forcing him to produce less because of the lower price, will it simply contribute to shortages? Even if he could answer these questions, how much cost is he justified in imposing on his stockholders, customers and employees for this social purpose? What is his appropriate share and what is the appropriate share of others?

And, whether he wants to or not, can he get away with spending his stockholders', customers' or employees' money? Will not the stockholders fire him? (Either the present ones or those who take over when his actions in the name of social responsibility have reduced the corporation's profits and the price of its stock.) His customers and his employees can desert him for other producers and employers less scrupulous in exercising their social responsibilities.

This facet of "social responsibility" doctrine is brought into sharp relief when the doctrine is used to justify wage restraint by trade unions. The conflict of interest is naked and clear when union officials are asked to subordinate the interest of their members to some more general purpose. If the union officials try to enforce wage restraint, the consequence is likely to be wildcat strikes, rank-and-file revolts and the emergence of strong competitors for their jobs. We thus have the ironic phenomenon that union leaders — at least in the U.S. — have objected to Government interference with the market far more consistently and courageously than have business leaders.

The difficulty of exercising "social responsibility" illustrates, of course, the great virtue of private competitive enterprise — it forces people to be responsible for their own actions and makes it difficult for them to "exploit" other people for either selfish or unselfish purposes. They can do good — but only at their own expense.

Many a reader who has followed the argument this far may be tempted to remonstrate that it is all well and good to speak of Government's having the responsibility to impose taxes and determine expenditures for such "social" purposes as controlling pollution or training the hard-core unemployed, but that the problems are too urgent to wait on the slow course of political processes, that the exercise of social responsibility by businessmen is a quicker and surer way to solve pressing current problems.

Aside from the question of fact — I share Adam Smith's skepticism about the benefits that can be expected from "those who affected to trade for the public good" — this argument must be rejected on grounds of principle. What it amounts to is an assertion that those who favor the taxes and expenditures in question have failed to persuade a majority of their fellow citizens to be of like mind and that they are seeking to attain by undemocratic procedures what they cannot attain by democratic procedures. In a free society, it is hard for "evil" people to do "evil," especially since one man's good is another's evil.

I have, for simplicity, concentrated on the special case of the corporate executive, except only for the brief digression on trade unions. But precisely the same argument applies to the newer phenomenon of calling upon stockholders to require corporations to exercise social responsibility (the recent G.M. crusade, for example). In most of these cases, what is in effect involved is some stockholders trying to get other stockholders (or customers or employees) to contribute against their will to "social" causes favored by the activists. Insofar as they succeed, they are again imposing taxes and spending the proceeds.

The situation of the individual proprietor is somewhat different. If he acts to reduce the returns of his enterprise in order to exercise his "social responsibility," he is spending his own money, not someone else's. If he wishes to spend his money on such purposes, that is his right, and I cannot see that there is any objection to his doing so. In the process, he, too, may impose costs on employees and customers. However, because he is far less likely than a large corporation or union to have monopolistic power, any such side effects will tend to be minor.

Of course, in practice the doctrine of social responsibility is frequently a cloak for actions that are justified on other grounds rather than a reason for those actions.

To illustrate, it may well be in the long-run interest of a corporation that is a major employer in a small community to devote resources to providing amenities to that community or to improving its government. That may make it easier to attact desirable employees, it may reduce the wage bill or lessen losses from pilferage and sabotage or have other worthwhile effects. Or it may be that, given the laws about the deductibility of corporate charitable contributions, the stockholders can contribute more to charities they favor by having the corporation make the gift than by doing it themselves, since they can in that way contribute an amount that would otherwise have been paid as corporate taxes.

In each of these — and many similar — cases, there is a strong temptation to rationalize these actions as an exercise of "social responsibility." In the present climate of opinion, with its widespread aversion to "capitalism," "profits," the "soulless corporation" and so on, this is one way for a corporation to generate goodwill as a by-product of expenditures that are entirely justified in its own self-interest.

It would be inconsistent of me to call on corporate executives to refrain from this hypocritical window-dressing because it harms the foundations of a free society. That would be to call on them to exercise a "social responsibility"! If our institutions, and the attitudes of the public make it in their self-interest to cloak their actions in this way, I cannot summon much indignation to denounce them. At the same time, I can express admiration for those individual proprietors or owners of closely held corporations or stockholders of more broadly held corporations who disdain such tactics as approaching fraud.

Whether blameworthy or not, the use of the cloak of social responsibility, and the nonsense spoken in its name by influential and prestigious businessmen, does clearly harm the foundations of a free society. I have been impressed time and again by the schizophrenic character of many businessmen. They are capable of being extremely far-sighted and clear-headed in matters that are internal to their businesses. They are incredibly short-sighted and muddle-headed in matters that are outside their businesses but affect the possible survival of business in general. This short-sightedness is strikingly exemplified in the calls from many businessmen for wage and price guidelines or controls or income policies. There is nothing that could do more in a brief period to destroy a market system and replace it by a centrally controlled system than effective governmental control of prices and wages.

The short-sightedness is also exemplified in speeches by businessmen on social responsibility. This may gain them kudos in the short run. But it helps to strengthen the already too prevalent view that the pursuit of profits is wicked and immoral and must be curbed and controlled by external forces. Once this view is adopted, the external forces that curb the market will not be the social consciences, however highly developed, of the pontificating executives; it will be the iron fist of Government bureaucrats. Here, as with price and wage controls, businessmen seem to me to reveal a suicidal impulse.

The political principle that underlies the market mechanism is unanimity. In an ideal free market resting on private property, no individual can coerce any other, all cooperation is voluntary, all parties to such cooperation benefit or they need not participate. There are no values, no "social" responsibilities in any sense other than the shared values and responsibilities of individuals. Society is a collection of individuals and of the various groups they voluntarily form.

The political principle that underlies the political mechanism is conformity. The individual must serve a more general social interest — whether that be determined by a church or a dictator or a majority. The individual may have a vote and say in what is to be done, but if he is overruled, he must conform. It is appropriate for some to require others to contribute to a general social purpose whether they wish to or not.

Unfortunately, unanimity is not always feasible. There are some respects in which conformity appears unavoidable, so I do not see how one can avoid the use of the political mechanism altogether.

But the doctrine of "social responsibility" taken seriously would extend the scope of the political mechanism to every human activity. It does not differ in philosophy from the most explicitly collective doctrine. It differs only by professing to believe that collectivist ends can be attained without collectivist means. That is why, in my book *Capitalism and Freedom,* I have called it a "fundamentally subversive doctrine" in a free society, and have said that in such a society, "there is one and only one social responsibility of business — to use its resources and engage in activities designed to increase its profits so long as it stays within the rules of the game, which is to say, engages in open and free competition without deception or fraud."

C

CASE STUDY: PENN SQUARE BANK

Penn Square began its existence in 1960 as a shopping-center bank, mainly to meet the financial needs of the residential neighborhood in which it was located. But, beginning about 1974, when the bank had deposits of only $30 million, some dramatic changes began to be made. Scores of bright young men and women were hired away from other local banks (including Bill Patterson and 57 others from Oklahoma City's First National). And the bank opened a separate oil and gas loan department that eventually was put in Mr. Patterson's charge.

Penn Square's directors and principal stockholders included some of the biggest wildcatters in Oklahoma. According to the charges made in some of the current suits, loans were made by the bank to enterprises controlled by these bank insiders.

Named as a defendant in many of the suits is Carl Swan, the co-owner of Longhorn Oil & Gas Co., a holding company that, among other things, operates drilling funds that solicit investments from the public. According to 16 lawsuits filed by more than 30 such investors in at least 11 states, Penn Square made millions of dollars of loans to Longhorn drilling funds, secured by the investors' personal notes.

Condensed from Tim Metz and G. Christian Hill, "Wildcat Banking: Penn Square Blowout Ended a Lending Spree as Risky as Oil Drilling," *Wall Street Journal,* July 27, 1982. © Dow Jones and Company, Inc.

The notes were backed by letters of credit that the investors obtained from their own banks. Now the investors face the unpleasant and unexpected prospect of having these notes called, immediately transforming the letters of credit into actual loan obligations to their banks by the investors.

MR. SWAN'S VENTURES

Mr. Swan is a Penn Square director and is a close business associate and friend of Mr. Jennings, the bank's chairman. Regulatory filings by Penn Square's holding company, First Penn Corp., show that Mr. Swan operated seven businesses in early 1980, including Longhorn, a coal company and a travel agency. By the end of 1981, he had become a local tycoon, with 38 companies, branching out into cattle ranching, a commuter airline, bars, real-estate developments and other ventures. His partner in five of these enterprises was Mr. Jennings. They shared ownership in Trans-Central Airlines, another company that owned aircraft, a real-estate partnership and a property-management concern.

According to recent investigations by the Tulsa *Tribune,* court records indicate that Penn Square made more than $70 million of loans to various Swan enterprises, including Longhorn. That amount is equal to more than 20% of the bank's total loan portfolio and was about twice its total capital. Federal law prohibits a bank from lending an amount exceeding 10% of its capital to any one borrower, but in practice sometimes this has been circumvented by setting up a legally separate entity as the borrower.

A Longhorn investors' lawsuit, filed in state superior court in San Francisco, alleges that Penn Square did more than just lend money to Mr. Swan's enterprises. It charges that the bank's ebullient Mr. Patterson helped promote the partnerships, attending meetings with investors where he allegedly asserted that Longhorn had considerable oil and gas reserves that would preclude any need to call in the letters of credit.

From conversations with other Oklahoma oilmen, it's apparent that one hardly needed to be a bank insider to get a loan from Mr. Patterson. One borrower of $7 million from Penn Square says that the day he met with Mr. Patterson to propose a large, unsecured loan, the banker was wearing his Mickey Mouse cap. "He just listened and said, 'I think we can handle that' " — all the while "tugging on those strings on each side of the hat that made the ears wiggle."

SOME SHAKY LOANS

The same borrower, who says he has never been in default on any of his loans from Penn Square, says, "I was a good bet. But golly, you should see some of the other loans that Bill made. Once I introduced him to a friend of mine who had put a second mortgage on his house and lost all the money in a drilling program. Then he lost his job and had missed two house payments by the time I introduced him to Bill. But Bill chatted with him for a half an hour and gave him a $100,000 credit line at Penn Square."

If this screening procedure was typical, it isn't hard to see why Penn Square's loan portfolio exploded. A filing in the U.S. district court here shows that on March 31, the latest date for which any Penn Square figures are available, the bank's loan portfolio reached $323.5 million, up from $218.9 million a year earlier and more than triple the figure at year-end 1980.

Penn Square's deposits were mushrooming, too, but not nearly fast enough to support the loans the bank was authorizing. So Mr. Patterson apparently turned his main efforts to passing the loans Penn Square was writing "upstream" by selling participations (often 100%) to other banks. Banking sources estimate that at the time Penn Square collapsed, some $2 billion of its loans had been laid off in this way. In a participation, the participating bank gets the income from the loan payments, but the originating bank continues to service the loans and, often, to keep the borrower's deposits.

In late 1981, natural-gas prices had begun to fall, eventually dropping almost 40%. Meanwhile, the Longhorn partnerships apparently weren't finding much natural gas. The lawsuits allege that certain Longhorn reserves were overstated by six times, to begin with.

BANK MOVE IS BLOCKED

As Mr. Swan's empire began to crumble early in 1982, it began dragging Penn Square down with it. In May, Penn Square tried to call the drilling funds' letters of credit to repay the loans, but the Longhorn investors' attorney, Raymond Erlach, successfully obtained preliminary injunctions against repayment in six states. In New Mexico, a state judge ruled that "the underlying transactions giving rise to the issuance of the letters of credit were induced by fraud."

It isn't known how much cash was tied up by these legal actions, but in its March 31 condition statement, Penn Square listed as "cash and due from other banks" a total of $38 million.

Suddenly Penn Square also was having trouble keeping the interest-free corporate checking deposits needed to finance its lending. In the first quarter alone, about $100 million of its $227.4 million of demand deposits on hand at the end of 1981 flowed out. Banking sources speculate that the money was withdrawn by corporate customers who rebelled at attempts by Penn Square to tighten credit. The bank sought to replace the money largely by hiring money brokers, who attracted uninsured depositors by showing them Penn Square's strong year-end financial statement, audited by Peat, Marwick, Mitchell & Co.

Things got worse in June. Bank examiners from the comptroller of the currency's office began inspecting the collateral behind the bank's loans. Penn Square officers scurried to ask oilmen to secure previously unsecured loans, but often without success.

These last-ditch moves were to no avail, however. After looking at only part of Penn Square's loans, the federal examiners quickly concluded that there were more than enough losses on the bank's books to wipe out its capital, listed at $33 million on March 31. On June 30, the comptroller began talks with the Federal Reserve Board and the Federal Deposit Insurance Corp. about ways to close the bank.

The FDIC decided to liquidate Penn Square and to pay off insured depositors up to the statutory limit of $100,000 for such protection. But it was a painful decision; it meant that for the first time in the FDIC's history there were large numbers of uninsured depositors who wouldn't be paid in full. The plan is for the agency to give these depositors who had put in more than $100,000 uninsured creditors' "receiver's certificates," representing a claim on any proceeds from the FDIC's liquidation of Penn Square's assets.

The losers are legion. The uninsured depositors, mostly financial institutions, who had put $250 million into Penn Square, are expected to lose at least 20 cents on the dollar, or $50 million, provided that further losses don't emerge as a result of the current lawsuits. The FDIC already has written off $40 million to $50 million of the bank's loans as uncollectible. Longhorn's investors are trying to get out of millions of dollars of letters of credit but may fail, depending on the findings of the courts. And Michigan International is suing its $5 million back.

The biggest losers are the banks that bought Penn Square's loans. Continental Illinois Bank and Northern Trust Co. — both of Chicago — Seattle First National Bank, Michigan National and Chase Manhattan Bank have announced loan-loss provisions totaling about $450 million. Chase, as well as Hibernia National Bank of New Orleans, which was stuck with $24 million of Penn Square loans, already has sued the FDIC, seeking to mitigate the losses. Other bank suits are considered a certainty.

At the unimpressive Penn Square headquarters, near the back of a residential shopping center, only a few grim-faced people can be seen. The windowless, bunkerlike wing, with the sign "Oil & Gas Loan Division," is darkened, and two armed guards peer out from just inside the door.

D

THE PARABLE OF THE SADHU

Bowen H. McCoy

Last year, as the first participant in the new six-month sabbatical progam that Morgan Stanley has adopted, I enjoyed a rare opportunity to collect my thoughts as well as do some traveling. I spent the first three months in Nepal, walking 600 miles through 200 villages in the Himalayas and climbing some 120,000 vertical feet. On the trip my sole Western companion was an anthropologist who shed light on the cultural patterns of the villages we passed through.

During the Nepal hike, something occurred that has had a powerful impact on my thinking about corporate ethics. Although some might argue that the experience has no relevance to business, it was a situation in which a basic ethical dilemma suddenly intruded into the lives of a group of individuals. How the group responded I think holds a lesson for all organizations no matter how defined.

THE SADHU

The Nepal experience was more rugged and adventuresome than I had anticipated. Most commercial treks last two or three weeks and cover a quarter of the distance we traveled.

Harvard Business Review, September-October, 1983. © The President and Fellows of Harvard College. Reprinted by permission.

My friend Stephen, the anthropologist, and I were halfway through the 60-day Himalayan part of the trip when we reached the high point, an 18,000-foot pass over a crest that we'd have to traverse to reach to the village of Muklinath, an ancient holy place for pilgrims.

Six years earlier I had suffered pulmonary edema, an acute form of altitude sickness, at 16,500 feet in the vicinity of Everest base camp, so we were understandably concerned about what would happen at 18,000 feet. Moreover, the Himalayas were having their wettest spring in 20 years; hip-deep powder and ice had already driven us off one ridge. If we failed to cross the pass, I feared that the last half of our "once in a lifetime" trip would be ruined.

The night before we would try the pass, we camped at a hut at 14,500 feet. In the photos taken at that camp, my face appears wan. The last village we'd passed through was a sturdy two-day walk below us, and I was tired.

During the late afternoon, four backpackers from New Zealand joined us, and we spent most of the night awake, anticipating the climb. Below we could see the fires of two other parties, which turned out to be two Swiss couples and a Japanese hiking club.

To get over the steep part of the climb before the sun melted the steps cut in the ice, we departed at 3:30 A.M. The New Zealanders left first, followed by Stephen and myself, our porters and Sherpas, and then the Swiss. The Japanese lingered in their camp. The sky was clear, and we were confident that no spring storm would erupt that day to close the pass.

At 15,500 feet, it looked to me as if Stephen were shuffling and staggering a bit, which are symptoms of altitude sickness. (The initial stage of altitude sickness brings a headache and nausea. As the condition worsens, a climber may encounter difficult breathing, disorientation, aphasia, and paralysis.) I felt strong, my adrenaline was flowing, but I was very concerned about my ultimate ability to get across. A couple of our porters were also suffering from the height, and Pasang, our Sherpa sirdar (leader), was worried.

Just after daybreak, while we rested at 15,500 feet, one of the New Zealanders, who had gone ahead, came staggering down toward us with a body slung across his shoulders. He dumped the almost naked, barefoot body of an Indian holy man — a sadhu — at my feet. He had found the pilgrim lying on the ice, shivering and suffering from hypothermia. I cradled the sadhu's head and laid him out on the rocks. The New Zealander was angry. He wanted to get across the pass before the bright sun melted the snow. He said, "Look, I've done what I can. You have porters and Sherpa guides. You care for him. We're going on!" He turned and went back up the mountain to join his friends.

I took a carotid pulse and found that the sadhu was still alive. We figured he had probably visited the holy shrines at Muklinath and was on his way home. It was fruitless to question why he had chosen this desperately high route instead of the safe, heavily traveled caravan route through the Kali Gandaki gorge. Or why he was almost naked and with no shoes, or how long he had been lying in the pass. The answers weren't going to solve our problem.

Stephen and the four Swiss began stripping off outer clothing and opening their packs. The sadhu was soon clothed from head to foot. He was not able to walk, but he was very much alive. I looked down the mountain and spotted below the Japanese climbers marching up with a horse.

Without a great deal of thought, I told Stephen and Pasang that I was concerned about withstanding the heights to come and wanted to get over the pass. I took off after several of our porters who had gone ahead.

On the steep part of the ascent where, if the ice steps had given way, I would have slid down about 3,000 feet, I felt vertigo. I stopped for a breather, allowing the Swiss to catch up with me. I inquired about the sadhu and Stephen. They said that the sadhu was fine and that Stephen was just behind. I set off again for the summit.

Stephen arrived at the summit an hour after I did. Still exhilarated by victory, I ran down the snow slope to congratulate him. He was suffering from altitude sickness; walking 15 steps, then stopping, walking 15 steps, then stopping. Pasang accompanied him all the way up. When I reached them, Stephen glared at me and said: "How do you feel about contributing to the death of a fellow man?"

I did not fully comprehend what he meant.

"Is the sadhu dead?" I inquired.

"No," replied Stephen, "but he surely will be!"

After I had gone, and the Swiss had departed not long after, Stephen had remained with the sadhu. When the Japanese had arrived, Stephen had asked to use their horse to transport the sadhu down to the hut. They had refused. He had then asked Pasang to have a group of our porters carry the sadhu. Pasang had resisted the idea, saying that the porters would have to exert all their energy to get themselves over the pass. He had thought they could not carry a man down 1,000 feet to the hut, reclimb the slope, and get across safely before the snow melted. Pasang had pressed Stephen not to delay any longer.

The Sherpas had carried the sadhu down to a rock in the sun at about 15,000 feet and had pointed out the hut another 500 feet below. The Japanese had given him food and drink. When they had last seen him he was listlessly throwing rocks at the Japanese party's dog, which had frightened him.

We do not know if the sadhu lived or died.

For many of the following days and evenings Stephen and I discussed and debated our behavior toward the sadhu. Stephen is a committed Quaker with deep moral vision. He said, "I feel that what happened with the sadhu is a good example of the breakdown between the individual ethic and the corporate ethic. No one person was willing to assume ultimate responsibility for the sadhu. Each was willing to do his bit just so long as it was not too inconvenient. When it got to be a bother, everyone just passed the buck to someone else and took off. Jesus was relevant to a more individualistic stage of society, but how do we interpret his teaching today in a world filled with large impersonal organizations and groups?"

I defended the larger group, saying, "Look, we all cared. We all stopped and gave aid and comfort. Everyone did his bit. The New Zealander carried him down below the snow line. I took his pulse and suggested we treat him for hypothermia. You and the Swiss gave him clothing and got him warmed up. The Japanese gave him food and water. The Sherpas carried him down to the sun and pointed out the easy trail toward the hut. He was well enough to throw rocks at a dog. What more could we do?"

"You have just described the typical affluent Westerner's response to a problem. Throwing money — in this case food and sweaters — at it, but not solving the fundamentals!" Stephen retorted.

"What would satisfy you?" I said. "Here we are, a group of New Zealanders, Swiss, Americans, and Japanese who have never met before and who are at the apex of one of the most powerful experiences of our lives. Some years the pass is so bad no one gets over it.

What right does an almost naked pilgrim who chooses the wrong trail have to disrupt our lives? Even the Sherpas had no interest in risking the trip to help him beyond a certain point."

Stephen calmly rebutted, "I wonder what the Sherpas would have done if the sadhu had been a well-dressed Nepali, or what the Japanese would have done if the sadhu had been a well-dressed Asian, or what you would have done, Buzz, if the sadhu had been a well-dressed Western woman?"

"Where, in your opinion," I asked instead, "is the limit of our responsibility in a situation like this? We had our own well-being to worry about. Our Sherpa guides were unwilling to jeopardize us or the porters for the sadhu. No one else on the mountain was willing to commit himself beyond certain self-imposed limits."

Stephen said, "As individual Christians or people with a Western ethical tradition, we can fulfill our obligations in such a situation only if (1) the sadhu dies in our care, (2) the sadhu demonstrates to us that he could undertake the two-day walk down to the village, or (3) we carry the sadhu for two days down to the village and convince someone there to care for him."

"Leaving the sadhu in the sun with food and clothing, while he demonstrated hand-eye coordination by throwing a rock at a dog, comes close to fulfilling items one and two," I answered. "And it wouldn't have made sense to take him to the village where the people appeared to be far less caring than the Sherpas, so the third condition is impractical. Are you really saying that, no matter what the implications, we should, at the drop of a hat, have changed our entire plan?"

THE INDIVIDUAL VS. THE GROUP ETHIC

Despite my arguments, I felt and continue to feel guilt about the sadhu. I had literally walked through a classic moral dilemma without fully thinking through the consequences. My excuses for my actions include a high adrenaline flow, a superordinate goal, and a once-in-a-lifetime opportunity — factors in the usual corporate situation, especially when one is under stress.

Real moral dilemmas are ambiguous, and many of us hike right through them, unaware that they exist. When, usually after the fact, someone makes an issue of them, we tend to resent his or her bringing it up. Often, when the full import of what we have done (or not done) falls on us, we dig into a defensive position from which it is very difficult to emerge. In rare circumstances we may contemplate what we have done from inside a prison.

Had we mountaineers been free of physical and mental stress caused by the effort and the high altitude, we might have treated the sadhu differently. Yet isn't stress the real test of personal and corporate values? The instant decisions executives make under pressure reveal the most about personal and corporate character.

Among the many questions that occur to me when pondering my experience are: What are the practical limits of moral imagination and vision? Is there a collective or institutional ethic beyond the ethics of the individual? At what level of effort or commitment can one discharge one's ethical responsibilities?

Not every ethical dilemma has a right solution. Reasonable people often disagree; otherwise there would be no dilemma. In a business context, however, it is essential that managers agree on a process for dealing with dilemmas.

The sadhu experience offers an interesting parallel to business situations. An immediate response was mandatory. Failure to act was a decision in itself. Up on the mountain we could not resign and submit our résumés to a headhunter. In contrast to philosophy, business involves action and implementation — getting things done. Managers must come up with answers to problems based on what they see and what they allow to influence their decision-making processes. On the mountain, none of us but Stephen realized the true dimensions of the situation we were facing.

One of our problems was that as a group we had no process for developing a consensus. We had no sense of purpose or plan. The difficulties of dealing with the sadhu were so complex that no one person could handle it. Because it did not have a set of preconditions that could guide its action to an acceptable resolution, the group reacted instinctively as individuals. The cross-cultural nature of the group added a further layer of complexity. We had no leader with whom we could all identify and in whose purpose we believed. Only Stephen was willing to take charge, but he could not gain adequate support to care for the sadhu.

Some organizations do have a value system that transcends the personal values of the managers. Such values, which go beyond profitability, are usually revealed when the organization is under stress.

People throughout the organization generally accept its values, which, because they are not presented as a rigid list of commandments, may be somewhat ambiguous. The stories people tell, rather than printed materials, transmit these conceptions of what is proper behavior.

For 20 years I have been exposed at senior levels to a variety of corporations and organizations. It is amazing how quickly an outsider can sense the tone and style of an organization and the degree of tolerated openness and freedom to challenge management.

Organizations that do not have a heritage of mutually accepted, shared values tend to become unhinged during stress, with each individual bailing out for himself. In the great takeover battles we have witnessed during past years, companies that had strong cultures drew the wagons around them and fought it out, while other companies saw executives, supported by their golden parachutes, bail out of the struggles.

Because corporations and their members are interdependent, for the corporation to be strong the members need to share a preconceived notion of what is correct behavior, a "business ethic," and think of it as a positive force, not a constraint.

As an investment banker I am continually warned by well-meaning lawyers, clients, and associates to be wary of conflicts of interest. Yet if I were to run away from every difficult situation, I wouldn't be an effective investment banker. I have to feel my way through conflicts. An effective manager can't run from risk either; he or she has to confront and deal with risk. To feel "safe" in doing this, managers need the guidelines of an agreed-on process and set of values within the organization.

After my three months in Nepal, I spent three months as an executive-in-residence at both Stanford Business School and the Center for Ethics and Social Policy at the Graduate Theological Union at Berkeley. These six months away from my job gave me time to assimilate 20 years of business experience. My thoughts turned often to the meaning of the leadership role in any large organization. Students at the seminary thought of themselves as antibusiness. But when I questioned them they agreed that they distrusted all large organizations, including the church. They perceived all large organizations as impersonal and opposed to individual values and needs. Yet we all know of organizations where peoples' values and beliefs are respected and their expressions encouraged.

What makes the difference? Can we identify the difference and, as a result, manage more effectively?

The word "ethics" turns off many and confuses more. Yet the notions of shared values and an agreed-on process for dealing with adversity and change — what many people mean when they talk about corporate culture — seem to be at the heart of the ethical issue. People who are in touch with their own core beliefs and the beliefs of others and are sustained by them can be more comfortable living on the cutting edge. At times, taking a tough line or a decisive stand in a muddle of ambiguity is the only ethical thing to do. If a manager is indecisive and spends time trying to figure out the "good" thing to do, the enterprise may be lost.

Business ethics, then, has to do with the authenticity and integrity of the enterprise. To be ethical is to follow the business as well as the cultural goals of the corporation, its owners, its employees, and its customers. Those who cannot serve the corporate vision are not authentic business people and, therefore, are not ethical in the business sense.

At this stage of my own business experience I have a strong interest in organizational behavior. Sociologists are keenly studying what they call corporate stories, legends, and heroes as a way organizations have of transmitting the value system. Corporations such as Arco have even hired consultants to perform an audit of their corporate culture. In a company, the leader is the person who understands, interprets, and manages the corporate value system. Effective managers are then action-oriented people who resolve conflict, are tolerant of ambiguity, stress, and change, and have a strong sense of purpose for themselves and their organizations.

If all this is true, I wonder about the role of the professional manager who moves from company to company. How can he or she quickly absorb the values and culture of different organizations? Or is there, indeed, an art of management that is totally transportable? Assuming such fungible managers do exist, is it proper for them to manipulate the values of others?

What would have happened had Stephen and I carried the sadhu for two days back to the village and become involved with the villagers in his care? In four trips to Nepal my most interesting experiences occurred in 1975 when I lived in a Sherpa home in the Khumbu for five days recovering from altitude sickness. The high point of Stephen's trip was an invitation to participate in a family funeral ceremony in Manang. Neither experience had to do with climbing the high passes of the Himalayas. Why were we so reluctant to try the lower path, the ambiguous trail? Perhaps because we did not have a leader who could reveal the greater purpose of the trip to us.

Why didn't Stephen with his moral vision opt to take the sadhu under his personal care? The answer is because, in part, Stephen was hard-stressed physically himself, and because, in part, without some support system that involved our involuntary and episodic community on the mountain, it was beyond his individual capacity to do so.

I see the current interest in corporate culture and corporate value systems as a positive response to Stephen's pessimism about the decline of the role of the individual in large organizations. Individuals who operate from a thoughtful set of personal values provide the foundation for a corporate culture. A corporate tradition that encourages freedom of inquiry, supports personal values, and reinforces a focused sense of direction can fulfill the need for individuality along with the prosperity and success of the group. Without such corporate support, the individual is lost.

That is the lesson of the sadhu. In a complex corporate situation, the individual requires and deserves the support of the group. If people cannot find such support from their organization, they don't know how to act. If such support is forthcoming, a person has a stake in the success of the group, and can add much to the process of establishing and maintaining a corporate culture. It is management's challenge to be sensitive to individual needs, to shape them, and to direct and focus them for the benefit of the group as a whole.

For each of us the sadhu lives. Should we stop what we are doing and comfort him; or should we keep trudging up toward the high pass? Should I pause to help the derelict I pass on the street each night as I walk by the Yale Club en route to Grand Central Station? Am I his brother? What is the nature of our responsibility if we consider ourselves to be ethical persons? Perhaps it is to change the values of the group so that it can, with all its resources, take the other road.

E

THE CHAMPION WAY

Champion International Corporation

STATEMENT

Champion's

- Objective is leadership in the forest products industry. Profitable growth is fundamental to the achievement of that goal and will benefit all to whom we are responsible: shareholders, customers, employees, communities, and society at large.
- Way of achieving profitable growth requires the pursuit of excellence in every undertaking and by all employees

Champion

- Wants to be known for the dependability of its products and service and the integrity of its dealings.
- Wants to be known as an excellent place to work. This means jobs in facilities that are clean and safe, where a spirit of cooperation and mutual respect prevails, where all feel free to make suggestions, and where all can take pride in working for Champion.

© Champion International Statement

- Wants to be known for its fair and thoughtful treatment of employees. We are committed to providing equality of opportunity for all people, regardless of race, national origin, sex, age, or religion. We actively seek a talented, diverse, enthusiastic workforce. We believe in the individual worth of each employee and seek to foster opportunities for personal development.
- Wants to be known for its interest in and support of the communities in which employees live and work. We encourage all employees to take an active part in the affairs of their communities, and we will support their volunteer efforts.
- Wants to be known as a public-spirited corporation, mindful of its need to assist — through volunteer efforts and donated funds — non-profit educational, civic, cultural, and social welfare organizations which contribute uniquely to our national life.
- Wants to be known as an open, truthful company. We are committed to the highest standards of business conduct in our relationships with customers, suppliers, employees, communities, and shareholders. In all our pursuits we are unequivocal in our support of the laws of the land, and acts of questionable legality will not be tolerated.
- Wants to be known as a company which strives to conserve resources, to reduce waste, and to use and dispose of materials with scrupulous regard for safety and health. We take particular pride in this company's record of compliance with the spirit as well as the letter of all environmental regulations.
- Believes that the individual actions of all employees — guided by a common commitment to excellence — will ensure the company's long-term economic success and leadership position.

BACKGROUND INFORMATION

What It Is

As with organizations of all kinds, companies have their own way of doing things. They have a company personality, a mind-set, a recognizable approach to how they go about their business. In short, they have a unique "culture."

We want to build a "Champion culture" which promotes the pursuit of excellence in every undertaking and by all employees. We see this as an important ingredient in achieving our objectives of leadership and profitable growth in forest products.

The Champion Way is many things. It is an attitude supportive of our common objectives. It's an umbrella concept which covers a variety of programs, projects, and communications. It's a succinct statement of the kind of company we want to be — for use in recruiting, training, managing. In summary, it's a long-term, all-encompassing effort built around a central theme of excellence in the way we do things.

Objectives

The effort to build a Champion culture has two ultimate objectives:

- Improvement in organizational effectiveness and
- Improvement in the return on our assets.

The Champion Way is seen as an intangible partner to the many capital and other programs directed at profitable growth in forest products. The role it has been assigned is to accomplish its objectives by:

- Building an understanding of the company's operations, plans, and programs,
- Creating a sense of pride and shared interest, and
- Enhancing personal work satisfaction.

How

We have structured the Champion Way effort around seven elements — *The Champion Way Statement, Communications, Training and Development, Work Environment Tangibles, Work Environment Intangibles, Organization Structures, and Employee and Community Activities:*

- *The Statement* describes Champion's objectives and the way the company believes these objectives should be sought.

- *Communications* covers a wide spectrum of personal audio-visual, and written programs carried out at a number of levels and locations. Many of these activities already are going on.

  New initiatives will include: "direct" communications programs with a shop-floor orientation, a quarterly newsletter, and expanded use of audio-visual tools. At the core of our programs is the intent to communicate more broadly, more openly, and with more opportunity for feedback.
- *Training and Development* provide many opportunities for incorporating the ingredients of a Champion culture. In the months ahead, as we build a strengthened training capability, these ingredients will be included. Particularly important will be programs designed for first-line supervisors and their managers.
- *Work Environment Tangibles.* Providing a safe and clean workplace is the most tangible evidence of our regard and concern for the welfare of our employees.

  This element is vital in establishing bridges of trust, thus providing support and reinforcement for other aspects of The Champion Way. Conversely, neglect of the plant physical environment will easily damage other efforts at building a Champion culture of excellence.
- *Work Environment Intangibles* include most importantly the attitude and atmosphere at the plant, in the office, and out in the woods. Through actions and statements, we have to establish a feeling of mutual trust.

  Getting there consists of many things: competent and open leadership. equal opportunity, clear rules and responsibilities, no favoritism, honest labor relations, avoidance of "mickey mouse," and service awards.
- *Organization Structures.* There is an increasing utilization of shop-floor organization forms which break with traditional, task-oriented, chain-of-command structures. Even where formal structures remain traditional, techniques involving worker participation, assignment rotation, and more employee decision-making are becoming increasingly prevalent.

  These progressive organization concepts are goal-oriented and recognize the abilities and values of today's work force.

  Case histories within Champion and in other organizations will be reviewed as a basis for measured, amplified efforts to incorporate new organization structures.

- *Employee and Community Activities.* This element addresses support and encouragement of employee activities and participation in community activities, as well as direct company support of local organizations. Employees take pride in their towns, and company support of the community reflects favorably on our employees as well as on Champion.

    We see a more active involvement by our employees at the local level as a step in building a Champion culture.

    Another step is increased support for company-sponsored athletic and other programs which encourage social contacts among our employees.

Summary

Champion is committed to vigorous, profitable growth in forest products. To achieve this goal the company has laid out a strategic plan, and will implement that plan with huge investments in timberlands, plant, and equipment.

The company has also laid out a strategic plan for building a company culture of excellence. This plan — The Champion Way — is an intangible partner in the pursuit of leadership performance.

ETHICS AND BUSINESS: A PROGRESS REPORT

Kirk O. Hanson

What role does ethics have in business decisions and in the management of private and public organizations? That question has haunted thoughtful business managers throughout this century. Some have contended that business is by nature amoral and works because there is no appeal to ethics. Others, including former Treasury Secretary William Simon, have argued that ethical behavior is absolutely essential for a capitalist society and that without it, the free enterprise system would cease to function and the society would collapse.

Business schools, pressured by the events of the early 1970s, particularly corporate contributions to the political campaigns of President Nixon and the incidence of corporate bribery overseas, have sought to know how they might do a better job of preparing students to respond to ethically sensitive situations.

This article presents some initial conclusions about the role of ethics in business decisions and in management. For the past four years, Stanford Business School has studied the ethics issue, prepared new teaching materials on ethics for use in existing required courses, and developed a new elective course, *Management and Ethics*, now taken by approximately 15 percent of GSB students.

Stanford GSB, Spring, 1983. © Trustees of Stanford University.

To anyone exploring these questions, the first issue must be what is meant by ethics. Values are things or actions that are considered valuable or important in themselves. Ethics are standards of behavior that enable the individual, company, or society to pursue these values. Thus the study and practice of business ethics is concerned with norms of behavior considered proper or useful in achieving the values of the individual, organization, or society.

Unfortunately, the study of ethics uncovers not just a single set of norms that can be used in business, but many. The study of ethics in a business school, then, does not teach just one particular system of ethics. Instead, it trains students to be sensitive to situations where ethical issues lie, how to analyze the facts of a complex organizational situation, how to apply different methods of ethical analysis, and how to generate and choose among alternative courses of action.

I am convinced that unethical behavior occurs mainly because business managers do not understand the situations in which they find themselves. We share a strikingly common set of values in the United States, and given a common understanding of the facts of a situation and a correct application of analytical methods, we should arrive at similar conclusions about a "right" course of action. Unfortunately, not all business people are highly skilled and thorough in exploring the facts in complex situations or in applying ethical analysis. To ignore the impact business decisions have on those affected opens executives to the risk that the neglected areas will have bottom-line repercussions for the firm.

After studying the various types of problems business people and their critics describe as ethical, I believe we can divide the problems into three broad categories: individual, institutional, and systemic. All three should be dealt with in business education and should be understood by the thoughtful executive.

Individual ethical dilemmas are those that arise in relations between one individual and another. Such problems may be conflicts in how one ought to treat a coworker, how the credit or blame for a project ought to be shared, what one owes to one's immediate supervisor and to the company — loyalty, honesty, or whatever.

Institutional problems are those that concern the relationship between an organization and its several publics. Such problems can include how a company ought to treat its customers. For example, what level of product safety does a firm owe the purchasers of its toys or its power equipment? Other publics of the firm include its employees, its shareholders, its suppliers, the community in which it operates, the governments of the several countries it may operate in, and any other significant group affected by the way the company does business. How should the company treat each of these groups? What norms of behavior ought to govern the policies of the company toward each constituency?

Systemic questions are more global. What ethical norms should guide the economic system of which we are a part? Though we rarely are in a position to influence the basic economic structures of a nation, it is critical that we understand what values and norms guide the way we help to structure the economic system of the U.S. or other national economic systems. The study of alternative economic systems often asks such systemic ethical questions as the following: Who benefits most under this economic system — those who already have wealth or those who are willing to work hardest? How does this economic system treat those who do not have the intelligence or the physical capability to work as hard? American capitalism has traditionally been justified with such slogans as "the greatest good for the greatest number." This is a statement of ethical norm. We are contending that under a system that rewards hard work and entrepreneurialism, even the least advantaged benefit. We believe the improvement of the standard of living for the vast majority justifies the plight of those few who do not participate fully in the economy. In practice, we have used in the United States a "safety net" of welfare and unemployment programs to provide at least a minimal standard of living for those who share least in the economic system.

But a discussion of the various questions that can arise in the study of business ethics tells us nothing about the standards by which such questions ought to be resolved. The search for standards by which to make ethical decisions is a part of the history of philosophy. We cannot review that history here or even in the limits of a one-quarter course, *Management and Ethics*. We can, however, identify three primary ways in which business people think about ethical dilemmas. These in turn are consistent with the history of philosophy's search for criteria for all human decisions.

The most common way of reasoning about ethical issues in business is to consider the balance of the benefits and the costs associated with a particular course of action. If the benefits that result from a decision outweigh the costs, then the action is said to be "good." If a business person is considering a number of options, the option with the highest net benefit would be the "right" one to pursue. To pursue any other course of action, even if it, too, had a positive net benefit, would be "wrong." Such reasoning raises two problems. First, what is a benefit and what is a cost? One must stipulate what one values to use this method. Second, all of us tend to overemphasize the benefits and costs we personally enjoy or bear. The essence of ethical reasoning, however, is concern with the other individuals affected by our decisions, and thus we must weigh the costs and benefit to all parties affected by a decision our own. The net benefit then is the net benefit to *all* parties affected by a decision and not just the net benefit to the decision maker. Business people are used to thinking about benefit/cost analysis in terms of the net benefit to the client or their own firm — ethical analysis must go beyond that.

The second way of reasoning about ethical dilemmas in business is to consider what "principles" or "rights" may be affected by the decision one is considering. Such principles or rights are norms we consider absolute or close to it. The principles may be ones we learned as part of a religious tradition, such as "Thou shalt not kill," or ones that arise out of our beliefs about the rights of all human beings, rights enumerated in the U.S. Constitution or in secular philosophies. While every person's understanding of rights and principles will be somewhat different, we fortunately enjoy a common heritage of beliefs that are shared by most Americans — whether Christian, Jew, Moslem, or secular humanist. In applying this type of reasoning to a particular decision, for example, we may consider the shareholders' right to private property, the employees' right to a fair wage, to privacy, to be informed about dangers in their workplace, and the community's right to prompt and fair payment of taxes owed. The difficulty in applying this second mode of reasoning about ethical dilemmas is that there are often if not always rights and principles in conflict. The decision maker must determine which rights are more important and which exceptions to important principles and rights can be permitted and under what conditions.

The third mode of reasoning about ethical issues is known as the social justice approach. This approach asks the question: Is it fair? The concern of this type of reasoning is the distribution of benefits and costs, not just their net balance. If a business decides to close a facility and open a new one where costs are lower, there may be great benefit on balance for the corporation's shareholders and other employees, but little or none for the employees who work at the closed facility. What does the standard of fairness dictate that the corporation do for the employees of the closed facility? Does it demand that the employees be given first chance at jobs at the new facility or at other corporate operations? Does it demand that the company pay severance compensation? How much? It should already be clear that ethical reasoning does not provide ready and obvious answers. The role of ethical analysis is not to provide a single unambiguous answer, but to provide the individual a way of assessing the dictates of the values he or she believes important.

After studying corporate social behavior for over fifteen years, I am more convinced than ever that behavior considered unethical is most often the result of poor analysis and not the desire to do harm. Business people are simply not taught to think in ethical categories: they are taught, as one observer has noted, to produce the maximum personal benefit from any situation. The challenge of ethics is to get the business person thinking about maximizing the benefits to all parties affected.

How can that be done? The elective course we have introduced into the MBA program, *Management and Ethics,* has tried to develop a productive approach. Since the inception of the course, we have had the opportunity to try out many of the same techniques with executives in executive development programs, both at Stanford and for several in-house corporate management development programs. The educational approach is designed to accomplish several objectives:

- *Awareness of ethical dimensions of business decisions.* The most important first step is to help all business decision makers identify the impact of their decisions on real people. Ethics concerns nothing more than how people are affected by decisions that individual business people make. If a plant is to be closed, who really is affected and how? If the quality in a product is to be improved, who benefits and to what extent? If a new "fast track" promotional program is to be instituted, who benefits and who is hurt if some individuals have trouble getting listed among the fast track group? I believe every business decision affects one or more individuals or groups of individuals. Ethics is concerned with how they are affected, not just the effects on the manager and on the company's profits.

- *Analysis of decision options using ethical reasoning.* Once the parties who are affected by a particular decision are identified, the three types of ethical reasoning can be productively used to determine the net benefit to all parties from the proposed decision, the principles or rights of involved parties that are affected, and whether the benefits and costs of the decision are being distributed in a fair manner among all those affected. These three types of analysis may all lead to the same decision. In some complex cases, however, positive net benefits will be accompanied by severe interference with the rights of employees, shareholders, or neighbors in the community. The manager will still determine what constitutes benefit and cost, relevant rights and their relative importance, and "fairness," but at least he or she will apply these values in a thorough and deliberate manner. In practice, of course, there are a variety of pressures and influences guiding the way the manager assesses the ethical imperatives of a particular situation. What is considered a fair distribution of benefits and burdens in a plant closing, for example, will be affected by the bargaining power and the political clout of workers and the local community. Similarly, other ethical tradeoffs made by the manager must be tested in the arena of public opinion and the opinion of the manager's peers.
- *Generating creative options to further the interests of all parties.* One of the most important skills a manager can have is the creativity to search for and fashion new decision options that make the situation more of a win-win one for all parties. When rights or interests seem to be in conflict, the discovery of new alternatives may greatly relieve an apparent ethical dilemma. This skill is often called "moral creativity" or "moral imagination." The plant manager who finds a way to sell the employees the plant that is about to be closed is engaging in moral imagination by finding a solution that gives the former owners some compensation for the abandoned plant and still saves the jobs of many or all the current employees.
- *Carrying out the decision with integrity.* In business ethics, as in so many other aspects of life, good analysis and correct application of principles must be accompanied by the determination to follow through on the decision. There are many managers who know the dictates of their own values yet ignore them to protect their own interests or those of some single influential party. "I know I should not have falsified the contracts," commented one young manager,

"but my boss demanded that I do it and he would have more to say than any other person about my next promotion." Another executive commented, "I knew the payment was nothing but bribery, but it saved me from a disastrous quarter." Developing moral integrity or the personal strength to bear some cost in order to do what one has concluded is "right" is a lifelong exercise and is formed by a thousand small decisions that demonstrate commitment to personal integrity.

- *Implementing the decision effectively.* With all decisions, effective implementation is as important as determining the decision to be taken. The outcome, when implementation is neglected, is too often the opposite of what one intends. Therefore, in teaching

FIGURE F.1   *The Study of Business Ethics*

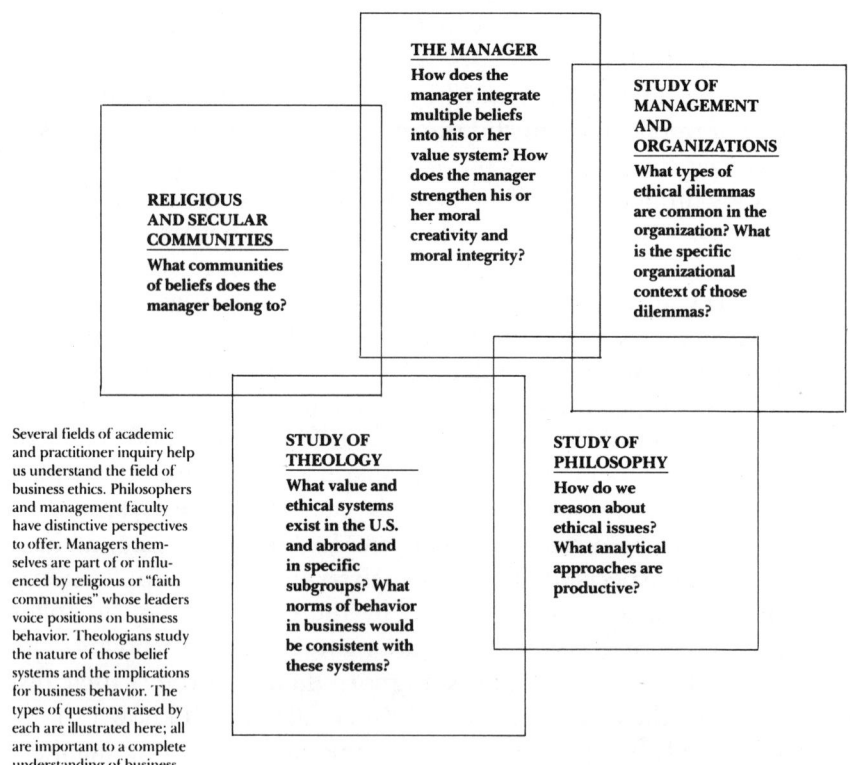

business ethics, there is considerable emphasis on implementing decisions. If a company has decided to treat its employees in certain ways, how does it formulate a policy, communicate it effectively, and monitor the compliance of several thousand supervisors? This is the domain of implementation.

We have only begun our study of ethics and its role in the management of corporations. During the next two to three years, we plan to undertake research efforts that will highlight more explicitly the ethical decisions that managers find most difficult, how ethical analysis can be refined to be of most help to managers in making those decisions, and how moral imagination and moral integrity can be effectively encouraged. We are grateful for the continuing support of individuals and foundations who show a particular interest in this field. The year 1983 is the fifth year of a grant from the Walter and Evelyn Haas Jr. Fund of San Francisco, which has been the primary sponsor of this work.

BOOKS

The following books have been published recently on the subject of business ethics. The Steckmest volume profiles the several dimensions of corporate performance that have ethical importance. The Jones volume is a guide to executive education in business ethics. The Velasquez volume is the most readable and practical single book on the subject.

Bowie, Norman E., *Business Ethics*. Prentice-Hall, Inc., Englewood Cliffs, N.J., 1982.

De George, Richard T., *Business Ethics*. Macmillan Publishing Co., Inc., New York, N.Y., 1982.

Donaldson, Thomas, *Corporations and Morality*. Prentice-Hall, Inc., Englewood Cliffs, N.J., 1982.

Jones, Donald G. (ed.), *Doing Ethics in Business*. Oelgeschlager, Gunn & Hain, Publishers, Inc., Cambridge, Mass., 1982.

Steckmest, Francis W., et al., *Corporate Performance: The Key to Public Trust*. McGraw-Hill Book Co., New York, N.Y., 1982.

Velasquez, Manuel G., *Business Ethics*. Prentice-Hall, Inc., Englewood Cliffs, N.J., 1982.

JOURNALS

These new journals address the developing field of business ethics.

Business and Professional Ethics Journal. Human Dimensions Center, Rensselaer Polytechnic Institute, Troy, N.Y., 12181.
Journal of Business Ethics. D. Reidel Publishing Company, Boston, Mass.

CASE STUDY: AETNA LIFE TRIES TO HELP A NEIGHBORHOOD

Based on an article by Robert Johnson

As part of a plan to respond to pressures from a Chicago activist group, National Peoples Action, Aetna Life and Casualty Company made the decision in 1979 to commit $20 million through local groups in seven cities to community redevelopment projects. Rather than demonstrating that Aetna was a big corporation with a heart, the projects have upset residents in three of the cities, and one on the West Side of Chicago has provoked a storm of protest.

Working through the South Austin Coalition Community Council and with its recommendation, Aetna lent $440,000 at below-market interest rates to rebuild an abandoned, boarded-up 21-unit apartment house on North Mason Avenue. The area around it was occupied by black, middle-class families, who moved in after the whites fled in the early 70's. Except for the apartment house, the dwellings are neat and well-tended. Rather than being pleased that the eyesore would be renovated, the residents of the neighborhood were incensed. Rather than helping an absentee landlord fix up his property and bring more people into the crowded area, the residents wanted the building razed and the space used as a park. At the time,

---

Based on Robert Johnson, "Aetna Sets Out to 'Do Good' for Chicago But Ends Up in Fight with Neighborhood," *Wall Street Journal,* December 6, 1982. © Dow Jones and Company

children had to cross a busy commuter train track to get to a park, while a senior citizens housing project nearby had offered to tear down the empty apartment house and turn the space into a park free of charge. Some 900 area residents signed a petition supporting the park idea and protesting Aetna's plan.

Comments one person: "Aetna or any big company that wants to help with housing should first canvass the people who live around the proposed development and see how they feel about it." The chair of Aetna's corporate responsibility investment committee says the company must rely on the judgment of the local groups it works with and that the controversy will blow over. But, as of December, 1982, the neighborhood residents showed no signs of giving up.

H

BOOK BRIEF: RONALD INGLEHART'S THE SILENT REVOLUTION

Prepared by Fred N. Twining

The primary data-base for this study is a series of intensive surveys which were conducted in the United States and European countries in the late 1960's and early 1970's. In addition to information on value preferences, data on the social background of individuals were obtained on a basis that could be related to externally measurable social conditions in each country. Inglehart takes the reader, step by step, through the analysis and interpretation of the data. He poses successive "hypotheses" about the meaning of the survey results and presents the process by which conclusions were reached. In this way he quantifies the extent of value shifts and assesses the trends of social change. He presents the phenomenon of greatly increased political awareness and "public" pressures in contemporary societies together with an analysis of the dynamics of social changes that have resulted. Clearly Inglehart's work is highly original and can help in developing a comprehensive corporate social information system.

A primary purpose of these surveys was to measure value changes, primarily between "Materialist" and "Post-Materialist" value

---

Based on Ronald Inglehart, *The Silent Revolution: Changing Values and Political Styles among Western Publics* (Princeton, N.J.: Princeton University Press, 1977).

systems. Intensive interviews classified respondents into six categories. Only the extremes — those who clearly fit the pattern — are considered to be Materialists or Post-Materialists. The remainder are in-between, with various degrees of mixed values. While only a minority of the United States respondents can be classified as "Post-Materialists," this minority is concentrated among the younger people in our society. The study shows that basic values are formed early in life and tend to remain unchanged in later years. So, it is likely that the number of Post-Materialists in our society will grow.

Materialists place higher values on Physiological Needs — for safety and sustenance:

- Strong defense forces
- Fighting crime
- Maintaining order
- Stable economy
- Economic growth
- Fighting rising prices.

Post-Materialists place higher values on social and self-actualization needs — aesthetic, intellectual, belonging and esteem:

- Beautiful cities/nature
- Ideas count
- Free speech
- Less impersonal society
- More say on job and in community
- More say in government.

Using these values as indicators, surveys in 1972/73 indicate the following results in the United States:

VALUE TYPE BY AGE GROUP IN THE U.S.

Age Group	Materialist	Mixed	Post-Materialist
19–28	24	59	17
29–38	27	60	13
39–48	34	53	13
49–58	32	58	10
59–68	37	57	6
69+	40	53	7

As might be expected, the Post-Materialists are more heavily concentrated in groups with university education:

POST-MATERIALISTS BY AGE AND EDUCATION
(Europe and United States)

Age	Primary	Secondary	University
16–24	13	22	39
25–34	8	15	37
35–44	7	13	31
45–54	6	14	20
55–64	6	9	12
65+	4	4	12

Simultaneous with changing social values is another shift. More people are acquiring political skills. Increases in educational level as well as shifting values have caused more persons, especially Post-Materialists, to become politically active. No longer is voting behavior divided along party lines, but is concentrated on the issues involved in formulating public policy. Inglehart sounds this note of warning: "The two processes of change reinforce each other. One aspect of the change in values, we believe, is the decline in the legitimacy of hierarchical authority, patriotism, religion and so on, which leads to a declining confidence in institutions. At the same time, political expression of new values is facilitated by a shift in the balance of political skills between elites and mass. Certain basic values and skills seem to be changing in a gradual but deeply rooted fashion. Undoubtedly there will be countertrends that will slow the process of change and even reverse it for given periods of time. But the principal evolutionary drift is the result of structural changes taking place in advanced industrial societies and is unlikely to be changed unless there are major alterations in the very nature of these societies."

Persons with Materialist values tend to have different job goals than those with Post-Materialist values. The Materialists place high priority on "A Good Salary" and "No Risk of Unemployment." The Post-Materialists place high priority on "A Feeling of Accomplishment" and "Working with People You Like." Dealing with divergent value systems within a corporation represents a new and growing problem of management.

The Inglehart study presents the results of surveys undertaken between the years 1970 and 1976. These data indicate that the shift toward Post-Materialist values is occurring only slowly, without dramatic changes over time. It is apparent from the data that values adopted in childhood tend to persist as a person grows older. The results of surveys at three time periods is as follows:

VALUE SHIFTS FROM 1970 TO 1976
(Six European Countries)

Ages	Percent with Post-Materialist Values		
	1970	1973	1976
15–24	24	20	20
25–34	13	13	16
35–44	12	9	11
45–54	9	7	8
55–64	7	6	6
65+	3	4	5

Of interest to multinational corporations are the measurements of social values among Western industrialized countries. The differences between countries can be accounted for, to a significant degree, by objective conditions in the history of each country. The percent of Materialists and Post-Materialists in eleven countries, in surveys taken in 1972/73, are:

Country	Materialists	Post-Materialists
Belgium	25	14
Netherlands	31	13
United States	31	12
Switzerland	31	12
Luxembourg	35	13
France	35	12
Britain	32	8
Italy	40	9
Germany	42	8
Ireland	36	7
Denmark	41	7

Inglehart carries his assessment of social change one step further — to the differences between Third World, developing countries and the Western industrialized countries. He states: "A prevailing stereotype in comparative politics used to depict the Third World as being in the process of rapid change and development, while the West was assumed to have reached some sort of end state. It seems that in many ways, the industrialized world is actually undergoing change which is more rapid and more genuinely new than what is occurring in the New Nations. But change in the industrialized world is far harder to grasp, harder to conceptualize. One tends to use familiar images because we have no model of the future. The notion that the Third World countries would come to resemble the contemporary West may have been an illusion, but it at least provided a concrete picture of where they were headed. Change in highly industrialized nations is even more of a leap into the unknown. In a confused way, one senses change in all directions — in sex roles, morals, life-styles, fashions, in the ecology, the economy, and politics."

In analyzing social change, Inglehart moves far beyond simply measuring changes in goals and attitudes of individuals involved in his surveys. His research approach moves backward along the causal chain to seek the *sources* of value shifts and forward in an attempt to analyze their *consequences*. The analytical process used starts with events in given societies, turns to their impact on what people think, and finally analyzes the consequences these intrapersonal events may have on a society. He characterizes the process used as: "The central focus is on things that exist within individuals, and these things can best be measured with survey data. But we trace their causes to changes in a society as a whole. The linkages between the individual and the system are complex. We cannot take it for granted that if increasing numbers of people hold given values, their political system will automatically adopt policies which reflect those values. It depends partly on how politically skilled those people are. And it depends at least equally on the political institutions of a given country."

Among the causes of changes in social values, Inglehart identifies the following:

- Technological innovation
- Changes in occupational structure
- Economic growth
- Expansion of education
- Development of mass communication
- Distinctive experiences of contemporary youth.

Among the consequences of changing social values, he enumerates the following:

- Changed orientation toward political issues
- Changes in social bases of politics
- Decline in support for national institutions
- Changing styles of political participation.

Out of the mass of survey data, Inglehart arrives at a significant conclusion on the relationship between changes in values and social change. In answer to the question: What goals are likely to be given greater emphasis in the post-industrial era? He states:

> The process of change is not as ephemeral as the flow of events might suggest. Instead it appears to reflect a transformation of basic world views. It seems to be taking place quite gradually but steadily, being rooted in the formative experiences of whole generation-units. Its symptoms manifest themselves in a variety of ways; sometimes they are explosive, as was the case with the unexpected student rebellions of the late 1960's. But if, as we believe, the change is a basic, long-term process, we cannot rely solely on the more blatant manifestations such as these to give an accurate picture of the scope and character of value change among Western publics. Mass survey data offer a more systematic, if less sensational, indication of what is happening. The evidence is still fragmentary, but a detailed examination of available data suggests that some profoundly important changes are occurring.

Inglehart's study strongly suggests that social values in the United States and in Western European countries have been shifting from an overwhelming emphasis on material well-being and physical security toward a greater emphasis on the quality of life. He states: "The causes and implications of this shift are complex, but the basic principle might be stated very simply: people tend to be more concerned with immediate needs or threats than with things that seem remote or nonthreatening. Thus, a desire for beauty may be more or

Appendix H / *297*

less universal, but hungry people are more likely to seek food than aesthetic satisfaction. Today, an unprecedentedly large portion of Western populations have been raised under conditions of exceptional economic security. Economic and physical security continued to be valued positively, but their relative priority is lower than in the past." This is what he calls "the Silent Revolution."

POLICY AND PROCESS: CASE AND CORPORATE POLICY STATEMENT

Prepared by Fred N. Twining and Charles S. McCoy

CASE STUDY

This case study builds on the conversation reported at the beginning of Chapter Seven. Use it as part of the case.

You are the CEO of a large, rapidly growing and very profitable manufacturing corporation. Because the company was small and family operated not too many years ago, there are many people who started out at the bottom and gradually worked their way up to very responsible positions over the years. Some continue to do well. Others get promoted beyond their ability.

One of the persons who started out as a stock clerk over 30 years ago has become head of one of the major divisions of the corporation. He is part of the senior management group that reports directly to you and with whom you work most directly in managing the company. This person, in your opinion and in the evaluation of him by his peers in the senior management group, has been promoted to a position in which he cannot perform adequately. As long as he had someone over him to sort out his good ideas and direct in a disciplined way his enormous energy, he performed superbly. Now that he must take primary responsibility for final decisions and for directing others, he seems uncertain, almost confused at times, and prone to lurch toward inferior choices. He is now 52 years old and has 34 years with the company. His inadequate performance is known by his colleagues in the senior management group and probably by many who work under him in the division. There are indications that in spite of the self-confidence he has built up over the years, he has become increasingly aware of something wrong and is feeling very insecure. Although at a more senior level than most cases, this person represents an example of a "peaked-out" employee. You know that you must develop a policy toward this group and initiate action.

A COMPANY POLICY STATEMENT: DEALING WITH INADEQUATE PERFORMANCE IN A LONG-TERM EMPLOYEE

The welfare of its employees is a key element on which the success of our Company has been built. It is the policy of the Company to manage its employees in the best interests of the entire organization.

The Company recognizes that each employee is basically responsible for his or her job performance and preparation for advancement in the Company, self-development being the most effective and enduring of the vehicles available for that purpose. However, the Company willingly accepts its own responsibility where employee performance is concerned. In the exercise of that responsibility, it attempts to utilize the skills and experience of each employee throughout his or her career in various positions that hopefully provide satisfaction to the employee while best serving the total needs of the Company. In order successfully to effect that approach, it must deal promptly and honestly with deficiencies in the performance of that employee, regardless of tenure or position.

Of special concern in the Company's shared assumption of performance responsibility is the long-term employee whose performance is inadequate. That employee is generally defined as one who is 45 years of age with a minimum of 10 years of service and who has reached a level of responsibility that he or she cannot handle in a manner acceptable to the Company after a number of years of satisfactory performance in that position or a succession of positions of increasing responsibility. It is the consensus of senior managers that in keeping with the Company's personal philosophy, those employees like all other employees should be dealt with fairly, equitably and in a manner consistent with the Company's traditional concern for its people.

This policy statement defines the Company's treatment of long-term employees experiencing inadequate performance.

1. It is the responsibility of the immediate supervisor of each such employee to recognize that there is a performance problem and to confront the situation by carrying out a performance evaluation with the employee which thoroughly reviews all aspects of the employee's work.

   In addition, it is the responsibility of the supervisor to review all the alternatives, including termination, with the employee, prior to beginning the decision-making process.

   While it is recognized that managers may inherit performance problems in the form of employees who transfer from one division to another, then display inadequate or deteriorating performance, it is understood that the manager for whom the employee currently works has the responsibility for evaluating performance and taking whatever action is necessary in connection with it. Except for unusual circumstances, there should be a minimum of three negative performance evaluations and an elapsed observation time of one year recorded before any conclusions concerning inadequacy are reached.

2. In the performance evaluation process, the employee should be asked to make a self-assessment. By eliciting an appraisal of strengths and weaknesses and likes and dislikes from the employee, the supervisor may find an approach to remedying the performance deficiency not otherwise apparent or uncover alternative job possibilities. At the very least, the self-assessment approach will promote an open exchange of ideas and aid in the employee's sense of participation and, hopefully, of cooperation.

   While it will be important to discuss positive aspects of performance, the supervisor and the employee should discuss areas of visible weakness, such as:
   a. Areas that need improvement as mentioned to the employee by supervisors, peers, friends, or others;
   b. Areas in which the employee wants and needs assistance;
   c. Tasks the employee tends to delay;
   d. Responsibilities the employee would prefer to pass on to someone else;

e. Areas of the job the employee dislikes.
3. The objective of the performance evaluation is to define the performance deficiency. The supervisor will define the nature of the deficiency by reviewing the difference between expected and actual performance and events or actions that cause dissatisfaction. The supervisor will define the dimensions of the performance deficiency and determine the employee's awareness of it and its importance.

   Definition of the performance deficiency will provide the basis for defining a solution. The supervisor will determine whether the performance problem results from a skills deficiency or a motivational cause.

   Where the problem seems rooted in a skills deficiency, opportunities for improving performance through rehabilitative or developmental training will be thoroughly explored in a conversation with the employee, using the services of the Personnel staff where appropriate. Where training is prescribed, it will be designed to overcome those specific problems encountered by the employee. An improvement schedule will be established and, whenever possible, quantitative measurement of progress will be employed.

   Where performance appraisal indicates that the deficiency is not a result of the employee's skills level and experience but results instead from a motivational problem, a personal situation, or the emotional and behavioral demands of the job upon the employee, an industrial psychologist or an appropriate member of the personnel staff, whichever appropriate, will consult with him or her to find a solution. Job performance will be closely monitored by the supervisor and an appropriate improvement time frame agreed to by the three parties involved.
4. Where it appears unlikely that the employee's performance on his or her current job will improve sufficiently to warrant retention, the next step is to evaluate other internal job alternatives. A skills analysis by the employee's supervisor and Personnel representatives, coupled with a review of the employee's experience and an analysis of his or her behavioral characteristics by the industrial psychologist, may indicate that he or she is better fitted for other positions within the organization. The Personnel Department will act as a clearinghouse for such placement activity, with personnel representatives bringing alternatives to the attention of the super-

visor and employee through their knowledge of job openings. It will be necessary, however, for the Company's informal communications network to function if placement goals are to be achieved most effectively. Lateral transfers will be considered first, then demotions. Lateral transfers will be made without changes in salary levels. Where a demotion is necessary, the employee's salary will normally be reduced to the maximum of the new job range. If the demoted employee's salary is within the range of the new job, no change will be made.

5. Where there is agreement among the supervisor, employee and Personnel representative that a sabbatical leave will be beneficial to both Company and employee and the employee holds a position in middle management or above, and is within five years of the opportunity of early retirement, the Company will make every effort to place the employee with a community or civic organization to which he or she can contribute for a period of one year. During such periods of sabbatical leave, the employee will receive full salary. Sabbaticals may be renewed from year to year where it is felt to be in the best interests of the employee and the Company. They will generally be used to bridge the gap leading to the payment of early retirement benefits, although they may be granted in other circumstances if all involved parties agree that some rehabilitative effect is likely to result and if a clear job re-entry route exists. Sabbaticals will require the approval of the President upon the recommendation of a Division/Department Head and the Vice President of Personnel with appropriate intervening approvals.

6. Where temporary leave from the Company is not appropriate and suitable placement within the organization cannot be located, the Company will assist employees with employment efforts outside of the Company. Out-placement service for employees at all levels will be offered by the Personnel Department. That service will consist specifically of:
   a. Experience and work-skills analysis;
   b. Resumé preparation;
   c. The development of presentation or interview techniques;
   d. Recognition and utilization of job sources;
   e. Introductions to selected employment agencies and executive recruiters, as appropriate.

"POLICY-AS-PROCESS" IN THE COMPANY POLICY STATEMENT

A careful reading of the company policy statement in the preceding section reveals that it embodies all of the elements of the policy-as-process approach. These are:

- The policy statement specifies how the decisions are to be made, rather than setting rules;
- The policy statement is flexible so that it may be applied to a variety of situations on a step-by-step basis;
- The policy incorporates consciously chosen social values which change from step to step;
- Each step requires consideration of certain factors applicable to the situation;
- Each step requires the exploration of certain alternatives for action with "yes" or "no" answers in a decision tree mode;
- The decision-making process can be recorded in a management control system which assures "due process" in the decisions on each individual case;
- The relationships between line and staff functions are established in each step, thus helping to coordinate actions;
- The policy statement specifies points at which higher management approvals are required, thus incorporating a system of checks and balances, under situations defined in the policy.

We believe that this kind of flexible policy statement can be effectively used for a wide variety of policies. It can serve as an effective tool for demonstrating social concerns in responsible management policy statements. The valuative aspects of the process are built into the policy statement using social value systems analysis.

J

BOOK BRIEF: CHRISTOPHER D. STONE'S WHERE THE LAW ENDS

Prepared by Fred. N. Twining

After extensive analysis, in which he draws heavily on illustrations from the business "cases," Stone concludes that the traditional market and legal strategies for controlling corporations are inadequate. Neither society nor corporate management can say that business is adequately serving society by following the dictates of the market and obeying the law. Stone catalogues the limitations of the market and the law along the following lines of argument:

The *market* is the most effective existing control over corporate behavior, but the case for the market (as well as against it) is easily and often overstated. The market plays a general allocative role, encouraging capital, labor, and other factors of production to flow to those industries and firms that can put them to the most beneficial use. One's willingness to trust in the market to fulfill this function rises or falls depending upon the response to a series of questions:

- To what extent is one willing to accept dollar values as the measure of most beneficial social use?
- To what extent are giant modern corporations freeing themselves from the forces that restrained small producers historically, allow-

---

Based on Christopher Stone, *Where The Law Ends: The Social Control of Corporate Behavior.* (New York: Harper & Row, 1975).

ing them to administer prices and manipulate their own consumer demand?

Stone concludes that few, if any, economists are satisfied that the market of itself can allocate resources adequately to fill social needs. Those who have faith that profit orientation is an adequate guarantee of corporations realizing socially desirable consumer goals are implicitly assuming (1) that the persons that are going to withdraw patronage know the fact that they are being injured; (2) that they know where to apply pressure of some sort; (3) that they are in a position to apply pressure; and (4) that their pressure will be translated into warranted changes in the corporation's behavior. None of these assumptions is particularly well founded.

The *law* is even less able to insure socially desirable behavior. Certainly it is socially dangerous for corporate managers to believe that until the law tells them otherwise, they have no responsibilities beyond the law and their impulses (whether their impulses spring from the "id" or from the balance sheet). He bases this conclusion on the following observations concerning the law as presently constituted:

- The law is primarily a reactive institution. There is, therefore, a time lag problem so that even if laws could be passed to deal with certain dangers, until they are passed a great deal of damage — some perhaps irreversible — can be done.
- The whole history of commercial law is one in which, by and large, the legislation has been little more than an acknowledgement of rules established by the commercial sector, unless there are the strongest and most evident reasons to the contrary.
- There is also the obvious fact that the laws corporations are "under" are being shaped indirectly through corporate manipulation of public opinion (which is a right guaranteed under the First Amendment).
- When we attempt to legislate in more complex areas we find an information gap; even specialized regulatory agencies, much less Congress, cannot in their rule-making capacities keep abreast of the industry.
- In many cases, there is a lack of consensus in our society on what values we want to advance through the lawmaking process. (Ex-

ample: control of resources depletion vs. the desire for material goods.)
- Difficulties in identifying who is responsible for major social problems. (Example: inner-city blight.)
- Difficulties of vagueness in laws where there is no consensus on more specific remedial measures.
- Difficulties of the web of laws and rules promulgated by regulatory agencies which threaten to choke effective action and become counter-productive to the original intent of the law.
- Laws tend to become minimums and "thou shalt nots" rather than encouraging the best aspirations of individuals or corporations. It is difficult, though not impossible, to legislate excellence.
- At some point, the cost of enforcing the law is greater than the benefits. Where laws go beyond enunciating social policy (such as employment discrimination based on sex) and undertake serious, systematic enforcement, the costs are likely to be very high unless employers believe the law is right and comply on their own.
- Delays caused by over-regulation can be costly (a cost-benefit analysis of FDA's drug overseeing estimated that the 1962 drug amendments cost consumers of drugs a minimum of 250 to 500 million dollars a year).
- Fines and other penalties against either corporations or its officers are not very effective means of controlling behavior.

Against this background, Stone examines the concept of *Social Responsibility*. Responsibility is not to be confused with altruism. In the case of human beings it is to meet far more complex and subtle needs that responsibility is developed and nurtured. Trusting in responsible behavior through some measure of self control is often a preferred solution to some of the most difficult and perhaps otherwise insoluble problems of social organization.

Responsibility can be considered according to two schemes: one emphasizes following the law, *abiding* by the rules. The second emphasizes *cognitive* process which puts a premium on autonomy and includes the following elements:

- Viewed in its cognitive aspects, responsibility involves a degree of repression. The responsible person does not immediately implement his initial desires or impulses, his "gut reaction." It is in this sense that one who, for example, simply vents his rage is not being

"responsible." Thus, reflection is always an ingredient of responsibility in this sense.
- Responsible behavior begins with perception. The responsible person observes phenomena, the irresponsible person ignores; more than this, his perceptions are stamped with moral categories. The responsible person looks for certain morally significant features of his environment: other persons, harm, pain, benefits to the social group.
- A responsible person takes measure of the full range of his freedom. It is in this sense that a man is not responsible if he adopts the posture that his decision is predetermined by forces of his environment, institutional or physical. He acts with an awareness that he will be accountable for what happens.
- To be responsible in this sense emphasizes a person's taking into account the consequences and repercussions of his actions. Thus, a person who drops a lighted match in a forest would be deemed irresponsible, not because he wanted to cause injury to others, but because he did not think of the repercussions of his action.
- He must consider and weigh alternatives.
- Being responsible involves reflection in all of the above senses, but reflection per se is not enough; the reflection must be structured by reference to the society's moral vocabulary — that is, by characterizations in terms of "good," "bad," "just," and so forth, by thinking of "obligations," "rights," and "duties."
- One must have, in addition to a moral vocabulary, a moral inclination — a desire, probably as much internalized as conscious, to "do the right thing."
- Closely related is the fact that one must be prepared to give some justification for what he is doing. Traditional ethical theories hold in common the view that to be responsible involves being prepared to explain, to give good reasons for one's actions; the responsible actor is willing to generalize the grounds for what he has done. This preparedness to justify, and especially the preparedness to do so in terms that admit of generalization (the Golden Rule, Kant's categorical imperative) is an important step towards the socialization of one's actions inasmuch as it forces awareness of the social setting and the socially sanctified grounds of behavior.

Which of these two notions of responsibility would we ideally want to implant into corporations? The answer is *both*. For where it is feasible to design relatively unambiguous rules for corporate behavior, all we want is the responsibility of the rule-following and the rule-adhering sort. But as has been stressed throughout, there is a large range of cases where rigid rules are increasingly ineffective and perhaps even counter-productive as instruments of corporate control. To meet the problems in those areas the responsibility that is needed — whether we are talking about corporations or persons — is a "mature" responsibility, emphasizing cognitive processes rather than blind rule obedience.

But what sense is there in speaking of a corporation — the entity — being responsible? What would it even mean? One aspect of responsibility is *widened information systems*. A cartoon that appeared in the *New Yorker* affords an amusing jump-off point. In the cartoon, two men, apparently public officials, have led a third, a high corporate official, to a wall of his plant which abuts and overhangs a waterway. From this prospect, the officer can look down to see three huge pipes from which his company is dumping pollutants into the water. With a look of perfectly ingenuous surprise, he remarks, "So *that's* where it goes! I'd like to thank you fellows for bringing this to my attention." Some viewers of the cartoon will interpret the corporate official's remarks cynically: surely he must have known all along. But the fact is, the intelligence gathering operations of any organization have to be limited, and, at present, the areas in the corporation's environment from which it seeks data are typically those that will inform it upon prospective sales volume, demand shifts, competitor behavior, and the like. Of its own accord, the corporation is not readily prepared to find out where, say, its pollutants are going, or to evaluate systematically what harm they may be causing over an extended period of time. Yet, if the processes through which the corporation perceives can be identified, is it not possible that the society can structure the organization's information so that the corporation will get feedback on the harm it is causing through pollution? In other words, when costs and benefits are considered, responsible self-policing — in which the company, as a first step, designs its own information network appropriately to find out where its products are going — may be part of a solution that is preferable to across-the-board, possibly futile, or even self-defeating legal measures.

The perception element of responsibility in a human being has a counterpart in problems we might want corporate responsibility to solve, and that changes in the organization's perception — its information gathering systems — would be a step, if only a first step, toward alleviating some of the problems. But there is a host of questions that remain to be answered. Are there counterparts in the organization's other internal variables — its authority structure, its reward and advancement criteria, its information channels — to the other cognizant processes that we saw to be associated with responsibility in human beings — holding action in abeyance pending an analysis of consequences, assessing contemplative behavior by reference to socially "moral" categories and the like? If so, and if the responsibility models indicate the changes in them are warranted, how can we get companies to go ahead and implement them?

New systems of corporate control are needed to insure the social control of corporate behavior. What Stone has in mind is a legal system that moves toward an increasingly direct focus on the *processes of corporate decision-making*, at least as a supplement to the traditional strategies that largely rely upon the corporate *acts*. Instead of treating the corporation's inner processes as a "black box," to be influenced only indirectly through threats, we need more straightforward "intrusions" into the corporation's decision structure and processes than society has yet undertaken. Some of his ideas are:

- Influence on policy through mandatory structural and procedural requirements is commonplace in the design of public agencies; it is only rarely and marginally used where corporations — our "private governments" — are concerned.
- Reform of the Board of Directors by eliminating inside directors in corporations of major impact, mandating that a percentage of directors should be financially disinterested, more clearly define the functions of the board, change the standards for directors' liability, provide staff for directors, and take steps to assure that certain critical information gets to the board.
- Require that certain positions be established within the organization to deal with specific social issues, and with the power to be effective.
- Extend the "probation officer" concept to corporations with a history of non-compliance.
- Define the qualifications of persons in critical positions to assure that they can carry out the assigned functions with competence.

- Impose direct requirements and controls on a company's internal information system as an effective way of influencing corporate behavior.
- Mandate that certain types of decisions be made at a high level in the organization.
- Mandate the information that must flow to government agencies and the public.
- Protect the "whistle blower."
- Specify "due process" for making critical decisions with major social impact, with a system of mandated findings.

Stone's approach is, as you might expect, primarily from a legal perspective. His case studies of selected corporations were mostly concerned with activities which are illegal or clearly unethical (*i.e.*, falsifying test data for a pharmaceutical product to obtain approval from the FDA). The controls over the decision-making process that he is suggesting here are ones that would be imposed from the outside. However, when his thesis on the "cognitive process" and "processes of corporate decision making" are considered together, they provide some valuable ideas that can be applied to the internal processes of developing corporate policy. We have designated this approach: *"Policy as Process."*

A great deal has been written recently about devising a "social audit" for corporations to supplement their traditional financial audits. Their aim would be to represent on paper the total social costs and benefits of a corporation's activities, over and above those that are now reflected in its financial statements.

The problem with the traditional statements is that they were developed to reflect the interests of the financial community. Investors — and potential investors — have no particular need for a breakdown of figures displaying, for example, how much the company has put into quality-control systems or how much it has done to increase minority worker mobility. A paper company's statement will reflect the cost of the timber it consumes; but if it uses the local river as a sewer to carry away waste, and does not have to pay for damages this causes downstream, those social costs will nowhere appear on the company's books. They don't affect earnings.

A reporting system that measured these hidden costs and benefits would be — if we had it — quite interesting. But at present, the details of how to implement it are wanting. Much of the value of a true audit, for example, is that it has a set, prescribed structure, designed to display the answers to a series of questions which are the same for all companies. This the social auditors are nowhere near achieving. And it may well be beyond their grasp.

Part of the difficulty is that many of the features that they want to reflect are not quantifiable. Moreover, even if they could agree on what internal company data were required, it would be hard to pry loose in a full and honest form. And as for the external data, the effects of any giant company's activities are almost so unimaginably complex and far-reaching that the thought of tracing out its "total social impact" seems absolutely boggling.

At present, just about the only positive reward corporations achieve is in the form of profits (or sales, or other measures of financial growth). Essentially, all other social feedback is negative — public criticisms or legal punishments for doing things badly. This need not be the case. During World War II, for example, "E" awards were bestowed on defense companies that had exceeded their allotted production. The presentation of the "E" to a qualifying corporation was the occasion of a high ceremony, at which government representatives, executives, and workers joined. The company would get a flag, and each of the workers an "E" pin. Why should not the Environmental Protection Agency, for example, be authorized to give out its own Environmental Protection "E's" to companies that accelerate beyond their "cleanup" timetables, or come up with ingenious new environment-protecting methods?

Many of the ideas in this book are provocative, but at this point they are in the "trial balloon" stage. Stone has had an important impact among those who have been placed on corporate boards of directors by order of a court. Up to this point, this procedure has been limited to a relatively few companies which have seriously breached the law or administrative regulations. Chris Stone is an articulate spokesman for his perspective on social control of corporate behavior. His ideas will probably have a broad impact on corporate decision making, even beyond the types of corporate situations which formed the case study base of his work.

CASE STUDY: BANK DEVELOPS SOCIAL POLICY LOAN COMMITTEE

Charles S. McCoy and Fred N. Twining

Senior management in a major bank operating on the national and international scene has a long history of concern for corporate social responsibility. For many years, middle management has had opportunities to contribute to policy decisions in a variety of ways, notably through a Social Responsibility Committee that reports directly to the president. Members of this committee are drawn from the operating divisions. Through "task forces" the committee carries out studies of various issues having ethical implications and develops recommendations for company policy. In twice-a-month meetings, the full committee reviews, modifies, and approves the task force recommendations, which are then transmitted to the president for integration into the bank's normal policy-making process. By rotating the membership of this committee, a substantial number of the bank's middle management group is given the opportunity to participate in shaping the bank's social policies. It also provides them training in this area and allows upper management to assess the ability of individuals to deal effectively with the social dimensions of policy, an increasingly important qualification for higher-level management positions in this bank.

Recently the bank has formed a Social Policy Loan Committee as an extension of its continuing concern with social responsibility. The idea of forming this committee emerged during a management seminar on corporate ethics involving the president and CEO, the chairman, 12 executive vice-presidents, and 5 outside members of the board of directors. The Social Policy Loan Committee is composed of the heads of the divisions dealing with loans and is charged with the responsibility for exploring social policy factors relating to the bank's lending function and to develop criteria that can be used in formulating policy about loans in all divisions.

CORPORATE RESPONSIBILITY CREED

Wells Fargo & Company

Wells Fargo & Company has a responsibility to all components of the environment in which it operates: shareholders, employees, customers, and to society as a whole, both national and international.

OUR RESPONSIBILITY TO OUR SHAREHOLDERS

We operate our company to make a profit. Profit, in an amount sufficient to attract and hold the capital of the investing public, is indispensable not only to the continuation of Wells Fargo & Company but to its ability to carry out its responsibilities to its other publics as well. We must concern ourselves with the rights and the security of that large body of citizens who have entrusted their funds to us as a sound investment. Our commitment to their best interest is unswerving.

For a longer version, see "Wells Fargo Statement of Corporate Responsibility and Case of Corporate Ethics," in Lewis E. David's (ed.) *What Every Director Should Know About Corporate Ethics*. St. Louis: Director Publications, 1978, pp. 119–138.

OUR RESPONSIBILITIES TO OUR EMPLOYEES

Our most valuable asset is our personnel. Wells Fargo & Company is committed to provide challenging and fulfilling employment in a stable and safe working environment at a fair rate of compensation. We are further committed to provide our employees with adequate opportunities for involvement in the social problem-solving process and to permit and encourage the development of meaningful social programs. With regard to our commitment to equal employment opportunity, the Company has set goals and timetables to increase ethnic minority and female employment and advancement.

OUR RESPONSIBILITY TO OUR CUSTOMERS

Wells Fargo & Company is dedicated to meeting the needs of consumers through the provision of useful goods and services in an efficient manner at a fair price. Furthermore, we will continue to strive to expand our banking and financial services to those segments of society which historically have found it difficult to secure them.

OUR RESPONSIBILITY TO OUR SOCIETY

Wells Fargo & Company is a citizen of our society. As such the Company's responsibility to society is more than the sum of its primary responsibilities to shareholders, employees, and customers. We must and do commit ourselves to a continuous re-evaluation of our relationships with governments and communities and to contributing to the solution of social problems and the attainment of social goals within a free enterprise system.

M

BOOK BRIEF: ROBERT W. ACKERMAN'S THE SOCIAL CHALLENGE TO BUSINESS

Prepared by Fred N. Twining

The Social Challenge to Business is about the corporate response to a dynamic social environment. More demanding public expectations may be forcing basic changes in the administration of large-scale economic enterprises in the United States. A quiet but profound transformation may be occurring inside the firm that is not readily apparent from a perusal of its financial statements or public statements of its executives. This book explores the dimensions of social pressure, the organizational dilemmas it causes, the way corporations have reacted, and what can be done by those who manage big companies to respond more effectively to social change.

Ackerman strongly believes that the problems posed by society's quest for socially responsive corporations are most usefully interpreted as *managerial* in nature rather than *ethical* or *ideological*. Some readers may dissent and remain firm in the conviction that the prime requirement for achieving corporate responsiveness is the ethical sensitization of top management. However, even if individual ethical conversion were a prime requirement, it would not be sufficient in

---

Adapted from *The Social Challenge to Business* by Robert W. Ackerman (Cambridge, Mass.: Harvard University Press, 1975).

itself to provoke responsive behavior in the corporation. There is a substantial internal administrative task facing even the most converted executive.

Ackerman takes a perspective from *inside* the corporation to study its responses to social demands. In particular, the answers to two questions are of interest:

- How have the managements of large corporations responded to social demands?
- What effects have efforts to implement corporate policies in areas of social concern had on the administration of the firm?

Following World War II, a great many companies embarked on diversification programs which led them into businesses employing different technologies and serving new markets. To manage these new activities, corporations adopted a divisionalized structure; they formed product divisions, each managed more or less independently of the others. Through this means, a clear distinction has been drawn between the functions of the executive at the corporate level and his functions at the division or operating level. Executives holding the top offices concern themselves with matters of financial and corporate-wide policy, while operating executives are held accountable for formulating business strategies to guide the divisions. Part of the division manager's responsibility is to plan effective responses to competitive technical and economic conditions which impinge on his particular business. He is also responsible for the profitability of the division, and his performance is regularly monitored by means of financial control systems.

Thus, corporate executives in divisionalized firms, without detailed involvement in or knowledge of operating decisions, rely more heavily on result-oriented measures than do their counterparts in single-business enterprises. Such measures have an important bearing on the process through which resources are allocated among divisions and middle managers are evaluated. Meeting short-term financial targets is consequently a matter of considerable importance to managers many levels below the chief executive.

The other phenomenon — social pressure on the business community — is perhaps more obvious. It began anew during the 1960's, after a thirty-year hiatus and after the postwar structural transformation in the large corporation had been essentially completed. Government, consumers, employees, and various interest groups have demanded changes in the conduct of business operations. The corporation has been called upon to control the environmental impact of its manufacturing processes, modify the racial or sexual composition of its work force, assume a greater responsibility for the safety and performance of its products, and exercise a greater concern for the health and well-being of its employees. In most cases, responses to these social concerns are likely to have some adverse impact on near-term economic performance, either directly because they cost money or indirectly because they take time and energy away from the traditional functions of running the business.

The convergence of divisionalization and social pressure holds two unfortunate consequences for the large corporation. First, the divisionalized structure, although proven effective in the management of the large, diversified enterprise, may inhibit flexible and creative responses to social demands. Second, efforts to incorporate social demands in the operations of the firm may have an adverse impact on its performance as a producer of goods and services. The dangers are significant. Unresponsiveness to public expectations is a clear invitation to increased government intervention in private sector affairs. By the same token an inability to generate profits sufficient to sustain investment may spell the end of an era in which exponential growth has been an overriding corporate goal.

THE SOCIAL ISSUE LIFE CYCLE

Most social issues follow patterns that, in retrospect, appear to be quite predictable. There is typically a time in which the issue is unthought of or unthinkable. In fact, social and economic sanctions are frequently applied to those who foster issues of some consequence that have no public support. However, should interest develop and be sustained, the issue passes through a period of increasing awareness, expectations, demands for action and ultimately enforcement. At the end of this period, probably measured in decades, it may cease to be a matter of active public concern. New standards of behavior may then have become so ingrained in the normal conduct of affairs that to behave otherwise would bring the social and economic sanctions formerly reserved for the contrary behavior. Thus, like the product life cycle, there is an analogous social issue life cycle.

The right to collective bargaining in the United States is an apt example. To have demanded, let alone countenanced, an independent union in the steel industry in 1890 would have been viewed as folly, if not openly subversive to the American way of life. Over the next forty-seven years, however, a great deal happened to change that attitude. The workers in the steel industry were no longer easily intimidated immigrants, the depression raised massive unemployment concerns, the rhetoric of the New Deal nurtured the awareness of social inequities, and the passage of legislation favorable to labor made unionism socially acceptable and legally enforceable.

THE ZONE OF DISCRETION

Social issues pass through an early period in which very substantial uncertainties exist in those factors of importance to the corporation in determining its response. During this period, managers have a wide variety of options available for approaching the problem. Ultimately, those options will be narrowed or even eliminated as a new standard of behavior becomes generally accepted and thoroughly enforced through regulatory or other means. This "zone of discretion," though of varying duration, is evident for each social issue. Social responsiveness entails the management of discretion. The corporation has the opportunity of setting policy to govern its relationship to emerging social expectations.

Ironically, the strengths of the divisionalized structure which have permitted diversified corporations to manage competitive conditions effectively are the sources of difficulty in the response to social demands. The dilemmas are three in number:

- Social demands subvert corporate-division relationships.
- Financial control systems are ineffective in explaining and evaluating social responsiveness.
- The process for evaluating and rewarding managers is not designed to recognize performance in areas of social concern.

It is important to recall, as these dilemmas are elaborated, that they occur as the social phenomena pass through the *zone of discretion* for corporate choice.

THE PROCESS OF CORPORATE RESPONSIVENESS

The response to a social issue changes dramatically in the corporation with time. Adaptation is forced by increasing top management expectations and a progressively more exacting social environment; old accommodations are found wanting in the face of escalating demands, and new ones are developed to take their place. As the organization struggles to adapt, learning takes place. Corporate responsiveness is evolutionary and not ad hoc as it might seem from accounts in the popular press. The evolution may not even be appreciated by managers caught up in the events of the moment, for it is neither mechanistic nor placid. It pulses with their experiences and is at times laced with conflict and crises.

In observing these machinations at close range over a period of time, a pattern can be discerned in the behavior of corporations that have enjoyed some succcess in meeting social demands. These findings suggest that the response to social demands may be more susceptible to analysis than has heretofore been recognized. If a recurring pattern can be identified and analyzed, it can also be consciously managed. If the critical decisions and the order of their appearance can be predicted with reasonable accuracy beforehand, managers may be more successful in coping with environmental uncertainties. By devoting attention to improving the *management* of the process, corporate responsiveness may be obtained with greater speed and effectiveness and with fewer unpleasant organizational side effects.

PHASES AND TRANSITIONS

As the corporation has been characterized in earlier chapters, three generic questions await management attention as it contemplates the response to social demands.

- *Policy:* What position should the corporation adopt with regard to a social demand? Specifically, should it attempt to *lead* social expectations?
- *Learning:* What has to be understood about the social demand, the alternatives available for responding to it, and the economic and organizational implications of implementation?

- *Commitment:* How is the organization to be applied to implementation in the face of dilemmas in locating responsibility, controlling and measuring performance, and evaluating managers?

In the course of responding to social demands, answers of one kind or another are found to each of these questions. The problems underlying them are not all readily visible — or at least not perceived as urgent — at the outset. They tend to arise sequentially over a period of years as the social issue and management's attitude toward it matures.

Phase 1 — Policy

In the history of a corporation's response to a social issue, a period can normally be identified that marks the issue's emergence as a top management concern. During this time the chief executive makes the critical judgment that the firm's posture on the issue deserves his personal attention. Without willingness to be assertive, the probability of early action on a corporate-wide basis appears to be practically nil.

The chief executive usually accepts the responsibility for formulating social policy without benefit of the detailed feasibility studies which generally accompany major changes in product-market policy. Under these circumstances, he quite naturally relates to the social environmental conditions as he encounters them from a *corporate perspective*, conditions which overlap, yet are distinctly different from those relevant to his division managers and their staffs. In particular, how the chief executive conceives of the company's obligations to society and his affinity for the particular issue at hand are critical determinants in the emergence of a corporate policy.

Phase II — Learning

The transition to the second phase is marked by the addition of specialists to the corporate staff, generally at the behest of the chief executive (*i.e.*, director of consumer affairs, environmental protection, minority relations, etc.). The problem is redefined as a technical one that can be attacked by isolating it and applying specialized skills and knowledge to its resolution. Justification for appointing a specialist from the chief executive's viewpoint is abundant. He typically feels someone is needed to (a) give emphasis and direction to the social policy; (b) interpret social demands and develop a corporate position on them; (c) add requisite skills to the organization; (d) coordinate the response of operating units; and (e) assist senior officers in the performance of their external duties.

The corporate response during this second phase bears the mark of the specialist. In a real sense, he is an agent of change through whom the organization learns to adapt to the social demand. He begins to inquire into alternative remedies and test their appropriateness for the firm.

The social issue specialists battle the sources of inaction evident at the end of Phase I. In doing so, they add substantive understanding, systems, and a degree of professionalism that were heretofore lacking. They are, however, largely unsuccessful in prompting changes in the standard operating procedures that governed how division-level managers make decisions impinging on the social demand. The buildup of corporate staff competence creates an unstable condition that is exacerbated by the organizational dilemmas confronting the divisionalized corporation.

Phase III — Commitment

The third phase is characterized by yet another redefinition of the impediment to responsiveness. No longer can middle managers point to the lack of policy direction or the absence of skills to apply to implementation. While far from exhaustive, sufficient effort is devoted to these areas to justify action at operating levels. Rather than a problem for specialists to segregate and resolve apart from the main-line activities of the divisions, responsiveness in the third phase is conceived as a general management concern that requires integration into ongoing business decisions. The question is posed: How can commitment for implementation be secured at middle management levels?

Acting on this redefinition of the problem, chief executives contemplate further modifications in the way responsiveness is managed, now directed squarely at the organizational dilemmas. A pattern emerges in which:

- Responsibility is firmly lodged with operating managers;
- The information system, with all of its inadequacies, is accepted as a basis for performance measurement;
- Rewards and sanctions for responsiveness to the issues are related to performance and incorporated in some fashion into the process of management evaluation.

As the social demands mature, the time-frame for mandatory response more nearly fits with the divisions' planning horizon. Division managers are now often intent on acquiring the skills necessary to direct future activities from within their units. Although the corporate specialists continue to be keyed into major developments and are called upon in specific instances, their active participation in division affairs is generally sharply curtailed. Adding specialists to the division staff presents relatively few difficulties.

In essence, the social demand is now phased in such a way that division managers handle it as they do changing competitive conditions. Response is triggered by the concerns of functional managers, who feel the weight of direct responsibility. Middle-level general managers negotiate expectations with corporate management and lend their personal influence to requests for resources or permission to institute special programs. The decision process fits progressively closely into the established pattern of corporate-division relationships. The strengths of the divisionalized organization are ultimately applied to social responsiveness rather than being subverted by it.

As the response to a social issue becomes a matter of routine, a final rather mild transition to a fourth phase may ensue. It is probable that eventually the measurement system and the associated link to performance appraisal will be found superfluous and eventually discarded. The reason lies not in the fact that continued action on the issue is unnecessary, but rather that the process for responding to it has been so institutionalized that separate accounting has little usefulness. One should not assume from this prediction that middle managers will again find their task simplified, for it is also likely that they will encounter other issues which are then in formative stages but are moving through a similar sequence.

Accommodations to social responsiveness are likely to bring changes in the administration of the firm. There will be a greater corporate interest in and awareness of the social impact of business decisions made at middle levels in the organization. Confronted by a more demanding social environment and more inquisitive superiors, operating managers may find their discretion diminished. If there is a drift in the location of effective authority over operating decisions prompted by these forces, it is certainly upward. Indeed, even the board of directors may feel compelled to assume an interest in social performance.

For operating managers, the result is likely to be more ambiguous and difficult assignments. The relationships to be managed, both inside and outside the corporation, increase with each social demand. The number of functions general managers must comprehend grows as does the complexity of the task of coordinating and balancing diverse skills and concerns. The opportunities for being wrong in somebody's eyes increase. Consequently, the tension and pressure experienced among middle managers may be expected to intensify.

It may be progressively more difficult and undesirable to rely on summary financial measures for assessing the performance of either operating units or managers. Financial controls will continue to be the dominant means for determining management effectiveness of allocating resources within the firm. Nevertheless, a greater portion of the operating manager's time may of necessity be consumed by social issues which have long-term, ill-defined payoffs. How well that job is done today may influence quite substantially the prospects for the business in the future. More sophisticated means of measuring performance will reflect the added complexity of the operating manager's assignment and the quality of the judgments he is called upon to make. Correspondingly, the dominance of financial controls may be moderated. Under these circumstances, the crispness in decision-making that accompanies clear responsibilities and simple performance measures will be eroded by numerous and often conflicting demands. Such a result may not, of course, be necessarily bad. What is lost in efficiency may be gained in more socially responsive behavior.

SPEECH TO THE ADVERTISING COUNCIL

James E. Burke
Chairman and CEO, Johnson and Johnson

Thank you, Frank Cary, Bob Beck, the officers, board, and members of the Advertising Council. There simply is no award that could mean more to me than this one . . . in part, because of my intense admiration for the work of the Ad Council.

Leverage is a favorite "buzz word" for all of us in business. . . . As a matter of fact . . . a lot of what we *do* in managing our business has to do with leverage . . . leveraging our assets . . . whether we are talking about the balance sheet . . . brand names . . . or the brain power of our people. I know of nowhere . . . that *leverage* has been practiced with such extraordinary success than by the Ad Council. . . . To take less than $2 million . . . and to leverage it into more than $700 million dollars' worth of advertising . . . and all in the interest of the public. . . . The idea itself is truly staggering.

I salute the Ad Council for what you have done for this country over the past 40 years!

And . . . try to explain the Ad Council's unique public service to someone from another country. . . . I have. . . . It's incomprehensible

---

Speech by James Burke to the Advertising Council, New York, November 16, 1983.

to them. . . . In Truth, it could not happen anywhere in the world . . . in the way it has here . . . because our capitalistic system is also unique.

And that is what I would like to comment on tonight. I would like to advance the premise that public service is not a thing apart . . . but *implicit* in the charter of every American corporation. . . . It is, in truth, its very reason for being. . . . That's what makes our enterprise system so special.

I would like to describe to you how that philosophy became *explicit* at Johnson & Johnson . . . how it has served us well for over a generation . . . and how it was dramatically tested by the Tylenol Tragedies.

But I also want to emphasize that these beliefs are not singular to Johnson & Johnson . . . but are understood by most corporations . . . and that they are understood *exceptionally* well by quite a few. . . . I have some evidence that suggests that those companies that organize their businesses around the broad concept of public service over the long run provide superior performance for their stockholders.

But first let me offer you a quotation which crystallizes these thoughts:

> Institutions, both public and private, exist because the people want them, believe in them, or at least are willing to tolerate them. The day has passed when business was a private matter — if it ever really was. In a business society, every act of business has social consequences and may arouse public interest. Every time business hires, builds, sells or buys, it is acting for the people as well as for itself, and it *must* accept full responsibility for its acts.

That was written right after World War II by a young brigadier general who had just served as head of the Small War Plants Board in Washington. . . . His name . . . Robert W. Johnson.

It was part of a preamble to a document he entitled simply . . . "Our Credo."

I have been presumptuous enough to include a copy in your programs tonight. It sounds a little pompous at first glance . . . and there is no need to read it now. . . . But essentially, what this document does is articulate our responsibilities to all of those in society who are dependent upon us.

First, to our consumers . . . doctors, nurses, patients, and mothers who buy our products and services.

Second, to our employees whose creative energies are responsible for those same products and services.

Next, to our communities . . . not just where our plants and offices are, but all of the various communities we deal with . . . including the community of man.

And finally, to our stockholders who invest their money in our enterprise.

We have often been asked why we put the stockholder last . . . and our answer has always been that, if we do the other jobs properly . . . the stockholder will always be well served. The record would suggest that is the case.

These guiding principles were disseminated among our employees in 1947.

A generation later . . . in 1975 . . . some of us became concerned as to whether, in fact, we were *practicing* what we preached.

We had become a large and complex corporation . . . with well over 100 companies around the world . . . each with its own separate mission.

In corporate headquarters we were concerned that the Credo perhaps had greater meaning to us than to those who were ultimately responsible for managing our various businesses around the world.

So we tried an experiment. . . . We invited 24 of our managers from the United States and overseas here . . . to the Waldorf, as a matter of fact . . . for a meeting to challenge the Credo.

I opened the meeting with the observation that the document was hanging in most of our offices around the world. . . . If we were not committed to it . . . it was an act of pretension and ought to be ripped off the walls. I challenged the group to recommend whether we should get rid of it . . . re-write it . . . or commit to it as is.

The meeting was a turn-on! . . . A genuine happening . . . as these managers struggled with the issues that the Credo defined.

What we discovered was that we had a set of guiding principles far more powerful than we had imagined.

This was the beginning of a series of Credo challenge meetings to include all of our key management from around the world. Dave

Clare, our president, and I chaired these sessions over the next three years. The result . . . the re-worded document in your programs tonight.

The basic philosophy is unchanged. . . . Many words stayed the same, others were changed substantively; some just modernized. Some of the responsibilities were expanded to take cognizance of a much more complicated world.

In June of 1979 we brought the managers of our 150 companies from all over the world to New York. . . . The centerpiece of that meeting was the revitalized Credo . . . a statement of purpose that everyone now not only understood, but had had the chance to contribute to.

On September 29 last year we learned with a terrifying suddenness that inexplicably someone had chosen one of our products . . . Tylenol . . . as a murder weapon.

Thus began what was to become for us "an unremitting nightmare.". . . and one that required literally dozens of people to make hundreds of decisions in painfully short periods of time.

Even when we had time for careful consideration . . . most of our decisions were complicated . . . involving considerable risk. . . . And we had no historical precedent to rely on.

As you know, we have received much praise for our handling of the "Tylenol Affair." Certainly we are proud of the heroic job done by our people at McNeil Consumer Products . . . and all of those from their sister companies who worked so tirelessly to help them during those difficult weeks.

And I would like to take this opportunity to thank our associates at Compton advertising, and at Young and Rubicam's, Burson Marsteller, our friends and associates in the trade . . . in our industry . . . in government . . . and, of course, the media.

We are grateful to all of you who helped in so many specific ways . . . and also for the outpouring of sympathy and support we felt from everyone. . . . It was a great source of strength during the ordeal.

However . . . all of us at McNeil Consumer Products and Johnson & Johnson truly believe that the guidance of the Credo played *the* most important role in our decision-making.

And here let me suggest you take the Credo home with you tonight and read it.... Ask yourselves ... with a statement like that ... if we had any alternative but to do what we did during the Tylenol tragedy.

Ask yourselves how the Tylenol consumer ... the Johnson & Johnson employee ... the public ... the stockholder ... would have felt.... What would *your* attitude today be toward Johnson & Johnson if we hadn't behaved the way we did?

And, of course, the important thing that the Tylenol affair reaffirmed is the intrinsic fairness of the American public.

A remarkable poll by the Roper organization taken 3 months after the tragedy showed 93% of the public felt Johnson & Johnson handled its responsibility either very well or fairly well.... *But* the public also gave very high marks to the Food and Drug Administration, the law enforcement agencies, the drug industry in general, *and* the media! The public knew that all of these institutions were working ... together ... and in their interest!

And what did *our* consumers do? They gave us back our business.... A year ago tonight we had but a fraction left of one of the most valuable consumer franchises ever built.... Our latest Nielsen ... taken in July-August ... shows Tylenol has regained over 90% of the business we enjoyed prior to the tragedies.

A reassuring and exhilarating outcome!

Of course, the Tylenol story is also unique.... But it dramatically reaffirms a philosophy that is not ... which is ... serving the public is what any business is all about.

That philosophy has been articulated and infused into the "cultures" by the founders and builders of many of our most successful American businesses.

Montesquieu, the French philosopher-historian, wrote, and I quote:

> In the infancy of society, the chiefs of state shape institutions; later, the institutions shape the chiefs of state.

I have long harbored the belief that the most successful corporations in this country ... the ones that have delivered outstanding results over a long period of time ... were driven by a simple moral imperative . . . serving the public in the broadest possible sense . . . better than their competition.

In preparation for receiving this award, I have attempted to find convincing evidence to support this contention. Since this was the thirtieth anniversary of this award, I decided to look at companies who had been in existence for at least that long and . . . at the same time . . . fulfilled two very rigid criteria:

First, they had to have a written, codified set of principles stating the philosophy that serving the public was central to their being.

And second . . . solid evidence that these ideas had been promulgated and practiced for *at least* a generation by their organizations.

My staff worked with The Business Roundtable's Task Force on Corporate Responsibility . . . and the Ethics Resource Center in Washington, D.C. . . . in compiling the list.

We found 26 such companies . . . quite a few of which I might add, had received this Public Service Award. . . . We then looked at the performance of these same companies . . . in terms of profits and rewards to the stockholders . . . over the 30-year period.

We had to drop 11 companies from the 26 for lack of comparable data . . . Prudential because it is a mutual company with no stockholders . . . Levi Strauss, Johnson's Wax and Hewlett-Packard because they were private corporations 30 years ago . . . McDonald's because it didn't even exist . . . and so on.

But the 15 remaining companies still deliver an impressive record.

First . . . profits. These companies showed an 11% growth in profits compounded over 30 years! (The Ad Council Award winners in the group showed exactly the same growth rate.) That happens to be better than 3 times the growth of the gross national product, which grew at 3.1% during the same period.

To understand the effect of that difference in compound rate of growth over 30 years . . . the GNP is now 2–½ times greater than it was 30 years ago . . . while the net income of these companies is 23 times greater!

And how about the stockholder?

If anyone of you had invested $30,000 in a composite of the Dow Jones 30 years ago, it would be worth $134,000 today.

If you had invested the same $30,000 . . . $2,000 in each of these 15 companies instead . . . your $30,000 would be worth over

$1,000,000! . . . $1,021,861 to be exact! (If the Dow had grown at the same rate as these companies, it would be over 9,000 . . . 9,399 to be exact.)

The results are . . . at the very least . . . provocative.

Michael Novak, in his book *The Theology of the Corporation,* talks about *democratic capitalism* as the system that has given the United States unparalleled wealth, freedom, and cultural richness. But he also says, and I quote:

> Nothing guarantees that this system will endure forever. It is an experiment. . . . Our failure to defend it well . . . with spirit and with intelligence . . . would be an unforgivable failure . . . a tragedy to the world.

I began my remarks talking about leverage. . . . and I would like to end on the same thought.

I think the lesson in the Tylenol experience . . . as well as in the record of these 15 companies over the past 30 years is the same . . . and that is . . . that we as businessmen and women have extraordinary leverage on our most important asset . . . *goodwill* . . . the goodwill of the public. . . . *If* we make sure our enterprises are managed in terms of *their obligations to society* . . . that is also the best way to defend this democratic capitalistic system that means so much to all of us.

Thank You.

TABLE N.1 *Business Summary of Corporation Responsibility*

Company Name	Document Name	Description or Essence	Originated by and Date
IBM	IBM Principles: Basic Beliefs of Company	*Primary* — respect for individual, service to customers, excellence *Secondary* — management leadership, stockholders, suppliers, corporate citizenship	Thomas Watson, Sr. Practiced since 1924 Published in 1970
Dayton-Hudson	Statement of Philosophy	Serves consumers, employees, shareholders, and communities through the common denominator of profit	Bruce and Kenneth Dayton Practiced since 1955 Published in 1967
Gerber Products	Objectives	Quality at reasonable prices to customers, employees treated fairly with pride in their management, service to communities, strive for excellence	Dan Gerber Practiced since 1943 Published in 1968

Company			
John Deere	Principles & Practices	Exists to meet needs of customers, dealers, employees, suppliers, social responsibility, quality and reliability, profits, decentralization and coordination, innovation, management development, facilities, worldwide organization.	Charles Deere Wiman Practiced since 1911 Published in 1964
Johnson's Wax	Principles	Responsible to employees, consumers, general public, neighbors and hosts, world community	H. F. Johnson, Sr. Practiced since 1927 Original publication date unknown
3M	Statement of Principles	Provide useful products and service, creating rewarding employment, adequate return on investment to investors, and contributing to a better social and economic environment for the public generally	William McKnight Practiced since 1900s Published in 1980

TABLE N.1 *Continued*

Company Name	Document Name	Description or Essence	Originated by and Date
Proctor & Gamble	Civic Responsibility	Responsible to consumer, employees, shareholders, and community	Messrs. Proctor & Gamble Practiced since founding—1837 Published in 1977
J. C. Penney	The Penney Idea	Public satisfaction, fair profit, value and satisfaction to customers, train to improve ourselves, reward performance	James Cash Penney Back to founding of company—1902 Published in 1913
Hewlett-Packard	Statement of Corporate Objectives	To test every policy, method, and act in the wise: "Does it square with what is right and just?" Most capable people, enthusiasm, working in unison toward common objectives of: profit, customers, new fields, growth, people, management, citizenship	David Packard Practiced since 1939 Published in 1957

Pitney Bowes	Business Practice Guidelines	Based on value of its products to customers and benefits derived from its operations by stockholders, employees, customers, suppliers, communities in which we operate	Walter Wheeler Practiced since 1920 Original publication date unknown
Pittsburg National	Statement of Corporation Guidelines	Service to customers, shareholders, employees, and communities	No one particular individual Practiced early 1900 Published in 1970
Levi Strauss & Co.	Social Responsibility	Tradition of social responsibility	Levi Strauss Practiced before 1900 Original publication date unknown
Kodak	Sharing & Joint Venture	To serve the best interests of shareowners, employees, customers, and the general public	George Eastman Practiced since 1880 Published mid-1970s

TABLE N.1 *Continued*

Company Name	Document Name	Description or Essence	Originated by and Date
American Can	The American Can Creed	Shareowners fair return on investment, employee treatment, customer service and quality, government and society, international community	William Woodside and William May Practiced since early 1960s Published in mid-1970s
AT&T	Statement of Policy	Responsible for services and goods, organization, customers, shareholders, employees, community, and nation	Allan von Auw Practiced since 1920 Published in 1981
Allied Chemical	General Policy Booklet	Responsible for good physical environment, quality and price, competitive wages and benefits, profitability, civic responsibilities, encourage employees to do community work	John Connors Practiced since 1960 Published in 1973

R. J. Reynolds	Commitment	The company has operated with conviction that it has an obligation to be a responsible and responsive corporate citizen.	Richard Joshua Reynolds Practiced since 1975 Original publication date unknown
Xerox	Xerox & Society	Social involvement is not only important, it is our tradition and essential to our future. He (Joseph Wilson) felt strongly that in order for Xerox to be successful as a business, we would also have to "combine the force of technology with the force of humanism."	Joseph C. Wilson Practiced for many years Original publication date unknown
Prudential	Response, Responsive, Responsibility, Responsiveness	We strive to conduct our business in a responsible ethical manner and to be helpful as we can in serving the needs of our communities and our nation.	No one person Practiced for many years Original publication date unknown

TABLE N.1 *Continued*

Company Name	Document Name	Description or Essence	Originated by and Date
McDonalds	Community Service & Social Investment Report	From the day the first McDonalds opened in 1955, we have worked to put something back into the communities where we do business. Today with the active support and involvement of our 1,300 independent local licensees, our commitment to the community has never been stronger. It is that "Spirit of Partnership" which characterizes our business.	Ray Kroc Practiced since 1955 Original publication date unknown

General Foods	Mission	It shall accept its social responsibility by conducting its business in a manner consistent with judicious corporate citizenship in the countries in which it operates. It also encourages its employees as individuals to be citizens and to take an active interest in community activities.	No one person Practiced for many years Original publication date unknown
Sun Company, Inc.	The Creed We Work By	We believe that while business cannot service if incapable of profitably, its sole obligation does not consist literally of producing profits. Instead, it must also nourish values cherished by the society of which it is a part.	J. Howard Pew Practiced Published in 1935

TABLE N.1 *Continued*

Company Name	Document Name	Description or Essence	Originated by and Date
McGraw-Hill	Code of Business Ethics	Our company has some special responsibilities beyond these. One is to be a good citizen in the community in which we work. We contribute to community as well as to national institutions and encourage employees to do so also.	No one person Practiced since 1958 Published in 1978

Coca-Cola	Commitment	There also are many opportunities where profit-making companies can go beyond business interests to share their talents and resources in a way that makes social sense. In this connection, direct financial support is given to a multitude of organizations whose programs are designed to meet the broad needs of our ever-changing society.	Robert W. Woodruff Practiced since 1920 Published in 1920
Aetna	Taking Part	As a member of the business sector, we have a stake in the overall health of the society which motivates us to perform more than a single purpose economic role.	John Filer Practiced since before 1900 Published in 1973

CASE STUDY: EASTWEST BANK LOAN POLICIES TO DEVELOPING COUNTRIES

Fred N. Twining

During the 1970's, the EastWest Bank, a large and diversified U.S. banking organization, prided itself on the achievements of its international banking division. Through this division it established a world-wide network of banking offices that enabled the bank to become a world leader in loans to developing countries. The bank's president referred to the bank's social responsibility on a global basis, citing its role in aiding the development progress of Third World countries. It was also true that these loans were typically made at high interest rates and contributed significantly to the over-all profit performance of the bank.

Early in the 1970's the bank's management developed a system for evaluating the credit worthiness of each country in which it operated. The system established "country limits" within which individual loan applications would be considered. Management decisions were made after consideration of the following factors for each country:

- Population and population growth projections,
- Loans already outstanding in the country,
- Relations between bank personnel and the country's government and central bank,

- Balance of trade, capital flow and foreign exchange reserves,
- Export/import analysis of the five most important products,
- External debt structure and past performance on debt servicing,
- Gross national product and its trends,
- Rate of inflation over the past five years,
- Monetary and fiscal policies of the government,
- Currency and exchange rates,
- The country's energy situation,
- The composition of the labor force and unemployment trends,
- A political analysis of the government and its stability, and
- The country's relations with international banking organizations.

The credit worthiness of each country was established primarily on an analysis of the above factors. However, the bank's management acknowledged that this analysis involved a considerable amount of subjectvie judgment.

In 1983, the management of EastWest Bank was faced with serious problems in its international loan portfolio. Most of the Third World countries where it had loans were faced with serious problems in living up to their loan commitments to foreign banks. The magnitude of the problem threatened the liquidity of the bank; extensive defaults could wipe out its capital and surplus.

Actually, the bank faced conditions and problems which were not foreseen at the time most of their international loans were made. Mexico is a good case in point. The bank had on its books about $4 billion in private and public sector loans, a significant portion of the $80 billion in total international loans to Mexico. Following a period of a decline in oil revenues and a drastic reevaluation of the Mexican Peso (from 25 to the dollar to 150 to the dollar) the government and private industry borrowers were unable to meet their existing loan commitments. In fact, the situation in Mexico reflected the global picture and threatened the entire world economy.

Factors in the Mexican situation that were ignored or downplayed in the bank management's analysis leading to setting of its country limits were the following:

- Mexico's population grew from 20 million in 1940 to 70 million in 1980 and another 40 million will be added by the year 2000.
- Mexico's income distribution is one of the most unequal in the world — the top 20% of the population has two-thirds of the national income; the bottom 20% has less than 3%.

- Pressures of population growth and rural poverty have caused major migrations — from the countryside to Mexico City and across the border to the United States.
- Most of the loans to Mexico have been for investment in capital-intensive industries and to large-scale export agriculture.
- The traditional small farm agricultural sector — with about 2.5 million farms — still suffers from low crop yields, which perpetuates poverty and widespread serious malnutrition.
- Government efforts to increase small farm productivity have been unsuccessful so that it has had to import about 8 million tons of cereal grains per year to feed its people, a serious drain on foreign exchange.

Knowledgeable observers believe that an unproductive small farm sector is a potential threat to the economic and political stability of Mexico. Evidence indicates that new approaches to achieving major increases in the productivity of Mexico's small farmers are needed. Following this recognition the EastWest bank, through its foundation, provided financial support to Counsultores del Campo, A. C., a non-profit Mexican organization that has developed a model for rural self-help. This model program demonstrates the effectiveness of a private sector initiative to increase the crop yields of Mexico's small farmers.

Early in 1984 the U.S. Congress and the Reagan administration were reconsidering U.S. support for the International Monetary Fund. One expressed view was that this support would, in effect, bail out the banks from excessive and unwise loans to developing countries. At the same time, negotiations were concluded with the government of Mexico that resolved their international credit crisis, at least temporarily.

This experience led the management of the EastWest Bank to reconsider its international loan policies. Should they change their methods of setting country limits to include more social factors? How far should the bank go to help developing countries solve their underlying economic and social problems? Also, should the bank join with other banks in lobbying for U.S. support of the IMF, an action that would indeed go a long way toward eliminating potential losses in their international loan portfolio?

NOTES

Chapter 1 PERFORMANCE AND ETHICS

1. Brock Yates, *The Decline and Fall of the American Automobile Industry.* New York: Empire Books, 1983 pp. 29, 240–41.
2. Thomas J. Peters and Robert H. Waterman, Jr., *In Search of Excellence: Lessons from America's Best-Run Companies.* New York: Harper & Row, 1982, p. 26.
3. Ibid. pp. 26, 51.
4. James O'Toole, *Making America Work: Productivity and Responsibility.* New York: Continuum, 1981, p. 116.
5. Ibid., p. 117.
6. Kenneth R. Andrews, *The Concept of Corporate Strategy.* Homewood, Illinois: Richard D. Irwin, Inc., Revised Edition, 1980, p. 18.
7. Ibid., p. 88, 89.
8. Thomas Donaldson, *Corporations and Morality.* Englewood Cliffs, New Jersey: Prentice-Hall, 1982, pp. 1–2.
9. Reginald Jones in *Business and Society: Strategies for the 1980's.* Washington, D.C.: U.S. Department of Commerce, December, 1980.

Chapter 2 ETHICS IN CORPORATE POLICY

1. Francine Kiefer, "Board room, classroom exploring business ethics," *Christian Science Monitor,* October 25, 1983, p. 15.

2. Quoted in Jenne K. Britell, "Ethics Courses Are Making Slow Inroads," *New York Times Magazine,* April 26, 1981, p. 44.

3. Michael Blumenthal, "Business Morality Has Not Deteriorated—Society Has Changed," *New York Times Magazine,* January 9, 1977, p. 28.

4. See Dean Acheson, "Morality, Moralism, and Diplomacy." *The Yale Review,* June 1958, pp. 481–493.

5. Darrell Reeck, *Ethics for the Professions: A Christian Perspective.* Minneapolis: Augsburg Publishing House, 1982, pp. 19–20.

6. Clarence Walton (ed.), *The Ethics of Corporate Conduct.* Englewood Cliffs, N. J.: Prentice-Hall, 1977, p. 6.

7. Bowen H. McCoy, "The Parable of the Sadhu," in *Harvard Business Review,* September-October, 1983, pp. 343, 344. This article is reprinted in Appendix D.

Chapter 3 **CORPORATE CULTURE AND MORAL AGENCY**

1. Robert C. Batchelder, *The Irreversible Decision, 1939–50.* New York: The Macmillan Company, 1961, p. 265.

2. Robert Nisbet, *The Twilight of Authority.* Quoted in William G. Scott and David K. Hart, *Organizational America: Can Individual Freedom Survive Within the Security It Promises?* Boston: Houghton Mifflin Company, 1979, p. 32. For the views of Whyte and Ellul, see William H. Whyte, Jr., *The Organization Man.* New York: Simon and Schuster, 1956, pp. 29–31 and *passim:* and Jacques Ellul, *The Technological Society.* Translated by John Wilkinson. New York: Alfred A. Knopf, 1965, *passim.*

3. Kenneth E. Boulding, *The Organizational Revolution.* New York: Harper & Row, 1953, p. xi.

4. Charles S. McCoy, Mark Juergensmeyer, and Fred Twining, *Ethics in the Corporate Policy Process: An Introduction.* Berkeley: Center for Ethics and Social Policy, 1975, pp. 5–6.

5. Richard Eells and Clarence Walton, *Conceptual Foundations of Business.* Homewood, Ill.: Richard D. Irwin, 3rd edition, 1974, p. 134.

6. *Dartmouth College* v. *Woodward,* 4 Wheat 518.636 (1819).

7. Clarence Walton, *Ethos and the Executive.* Englewood Cliffs, New Jersey: Prentice-Hall, 1979, p. 95.

8. Charles K. Wilber and Kenneth P. Jameson, *An Inquiry into the Poverty of Economics.* Notre Dame: University of Notre Dame

Press, 1983, p. 238.

9. On the issue of legitimacy in its internal and external dimensions, see the superb treatment in Edwin M. Epstein, *The Corporation in American Politics*. Englewood Cliffs: Prentice-Hall, 1969, pp. 254–292; and James Willard Hurst, *The Legitimacy of the Business Corporation in the Law of the United States, 1780–1970*. Charlottesville: University of Virginia Press, 1970.

10. Peters and Waterman, *In Search of Excellence*, p. 75.

11. James O'Toole, *Making America Work, passim.*, especially pp. 117–118.

12. C. West Churchman, *Challenge to Reason*. New York: McGraw-Hill, 1968, p. 206.

13. Philip Selznick, *Leadership in Administration: A Sociological Interpretation*. Evanston, Illinois: Row, Peterson, and Company, 1957, pp. 38–40.

14. See Charles S. McCoy, "Ethics for an Organized World" in *Ethics and Policy*, February, 1977, pp. 1–6.

15. Kirk O. Hanson, "Ethics and Business: A Progress Report" in *Stanford GSB*, Spring, 1983, p. 10. Reprinted in Appendix F.

16. Thomas Donaldson, *Corporations and Morality*. Englewood Cliffs, New Jersey: Prentice-Hall, Inc., 1982, p. 19.

17. Selznick, *Leadership in Administration*, p. 55. Burton Clark has applied Selznick's understanding to higher education and further illumined the moral dimensions of organizational agency in *The Open Door College* (New York: McGraw-Hill, 1960). John Finley Scott, in *Internalization of Norms: A Sociological Theory of Moral Commitment* (Englewood Cliffs, N.J.: Prentice-Hall, 1971) develops Selznick's perspective further in very helpful ways.

18. Edwin M. Epstein, "Societal, Managerial, and Legal Perspectives on Corporate Social Responsibility—Products and Process," *The Hastings Law Journal*, May, 1979, pp. 1303–1304.

19. Terrence E. Deal and Allan A. Kennedy, *Corporate Cultures: The Rites and Rituals of Corporate Life*. Reading, Mass.: Addison-Wesley Publishing Co., 1982.

Chapter 4 FROM SOCIAL RESPONSE TO CORPORATE ETHICS

1. John Naisbitt, *Megatrends: Ten New Directions Transforming Our Lives*. New York: Warner Books, 1982, pp. 11ff.

2. Ibid., p. 17.

3. Kenneth Boulding, *The Organizational Revolution*, p. 35.

4. Edwin M. Epstein, "Dimensions of Corporate Power, Pt. 2," *California Management Review*, Summer 1974, p. 46. See also the first part of Epstein's analysis, "Dimensions of Corporate Power, Pt. 1," *California Management Review*, Winter, 1973, pp. 9–23. Berle's views appear in a succinct form in Adolph A. Berle, Jr., "Economic Power and the Free Society," in *The Fund for the Republic*, 1957, especially p. 14.

5. See Lee E. Preston and James E. Post, *Private Management and Public Policy: The Principle of Public Responsibility*. Englewood Cliffs, New Jersey: Prentice-Hall, 1975; and John D. Aram, *Managing Business and Public Policy: Concepts, Issues and Cases*. Marshfield: Pitman, 1983.

6. R. H. Tawney, *Religion and the Rise of Capitalism: A Historical Study*. New York: Harcourt, Brace and Company, 1926; Mentor Book Edition, 1958, p. 235.

7. As quoted by Will Herberg, *Protestant-Catholic-Jew: An Essay in American Religious Sociology*. Garden City: Doubleday & Company, Inc., 1956, p. 143. See also the best-known treatment of this subject, Max Weber, *The Protestant Ethic and the Spirit of Capitalism*. Translated by Talcott Parsons. New York: Charles Scribner's Sons, 1958. Though representing a questionable historical treatment of the Reformed tradition, Weber's interpretation is a perceptive counterbalance to the exclusive emphasis of Marxists on economic factors in social causation.

8. Archie B. Carroll, *Business and Society: Managing Corporate Social Performance*. Boston: Little, Brown and Company, 1981, pp. 90–91.

Chapter 5 A COMPREHENSIVE ETHIC FOR CORPORATE POLICY

1. Kenneth E. Boulding, *The Organizational Revolution*, p. xi. On the issue of legitimacy, see also Kenneth E. Boulding, "The Legitimacy of the Business Institution" in Edwin M. Epstein and Dow Votaw (eds.), *Rationality, Legitimacy, Responsibility: Search for New Directions in Business and Society*. Santa Monica, California: Goodyear Publishing Company, 1978.

2. Milton Friedman, *Capitalism and Freedom.* Chicago: University of Chicago Press, 1962, p. 133. It ought to be noted, however, that Milton and Rose Friedman, *Free to Choose* (New York: Harcourt Brace Jovanovich, 1980) write: "Narrow preoccupation with the economic market has led to a narrow interpretation of self-interest as myopic selfishness, as exclusive concern with immediate material rewards. Economics has been berated for allegedly drawing far-reaching conclusions from a wholly unrealistic 'economic man' who is little more than a calculating machine, responding only to monetary stimuli. That is a great mistake. Self-interest is not myopic selfishness. It is whatever it is that interests the participants, whatever they value, whatever goals they pursue" (p. 27). This view is quite different from the one Friedman has espoused when writing alone, both in *Capitalism and Freedom* and in the article referred to above in Chapter 1. If this is now Milton Friedman's view, it is a vast improvement over the one he held earlier. If it is Rose Friedman's view, she is a much better thinker than her husband on these issues.

3. John Maurice Clark, *Economic Institutions and Human Welfare.* New York: Alfred A. Knopf, 1957, p. 218.

4. Henry Manne and Henry Wallich, *The Modern Corporation and Social Responsibility.* Washington: American Enterprise Institute, 1972, pp. 59–60.

5. R. Edward Freeman, *Strategic Management: A Stakeholder Approach.* Marshfield: Pitman, 1984, p. vi.

6. John Rawls, *A Theory of Justice.* Cambridge, Mass.: Harvard University Press, 1971.

7. On this point, see Brian Barry, *The Liberal Theory of Justice.* New York: Oxford University Press, 1973, p. 154.

8. John C. Bennett, "A Theological Conception of Goals for Economic Life," in Dudley A. Ward (ed.), *Goals of Economic Life.* New York: Harper & Brothers, 1953, p. 399.

Chapter 6 POLICY PROCESS AND CORPORATE PERFORMANCE

1. Philip Selznick, *Leadership in Administration,* p. 29.

2. Christopher Stone, *Where the Law Ends: The Social Control of Corporate Behavior.* New York: Harper & Row, 1975. See the Book Brief in Appendix L.

3. Charles E. Lindblom, *The Policy-Making Process*. Second Edition. Englewood Cliffs, New Jersey: Prentice-Hall, 1980, p. 4.

4. Peters and Waterman, *In Search of Excellence*, p. 76.

5. See "The Champion Way" in Appendix E.

6. Philip Selznick, "Critical Decisions in Organizational Development," in *Complex Organizations: A Sociological Reader*, New York: Holt, Rinehart, and Winston, 1961, p. 358.

7. See Charles E. Lindblom, *The Policy-Making Process;* Edwin M. Epstein, "Dimensions of Corporate Power," *California Management Review;* R. Edward Freeman, *Strategic Management: A Stakeholder Approach;* and Jeffrey Pfeffer, *Power in Organizations*. Marshfield, Mass.: Pitman Publishing Inc., 1981, for additional light on the political dimensions of policy.

8. Daniel Bell, *The Cultural Contradictions of Capitalism*. New York: Basic Books, 1976; Neil Chamberlain, *The Place of Business in America's Future: A Study in Social Values*. New York: Basic Books, 1973; George Cabot Lodge, *The New American Ideology*. New York: Alfred A. Knopf, 1976; S. Prakash Sethi (ed.,) *The Unstable Ground: Corporate Social Policy in a Dynamic Society*. Los Angeles: Melville Publishing Co., 1974; Lee E. Preston and James E. Post, *Private Management and Public Policy: The Principle of Public Responsibility;* Edwin M. Epstein and Dow Votaw (eds.), *Rationality, Legitimacy, Responsibility: Search for New Directions in Business and Society;* R. Edward Freeman, *Strategic Management;* and John D. Aram, *Managing Business and Public Policy: Concepts, Issues and Cases*. Marshfield: Pitman, 1983.

Chapter 7 SOCIAL VALUES AND POLICY ETHICS

1. Brock Yates, *The Decline and Fall of the American Automobile Industry*, p. 153.

2. Princeton: Princeton University Press, 1977. Quote below from p. 3 for a Book Brief sketching the contents of Inglehart's work, see Appendix H. For comment on the importance of scanning the environment in which organizations operate and the paucity of academic literature on environmental scanning, see Jeffrey Pfeffer and Gerald R. Salancik, *The External Control of Organizations: A Resource Dependence Perspective*. New York: Harper & Row, 1978, pp. 268–271.

3. John Naisbitt, *Megatrends*, pp. 1–2.

4. Philip Selznick, "Critical Decisions in Organizational Development," in *Complex Organizations—A Sociological Reader*. New York: Holt, Rinehart, and Winston, 1961, p. 360.

5. Keith Sward, *The Legend of Henry Ford*. New York: Rinehart, 1948, p. 199.

6. See Michael Novak, *The Spirit of Democratic Capitalism*. New York: Simon & Schuster, 1982, where this inadequate model is used. For a helpful discussion of the issue of a model for relating business and society, see Thomas M. Jones, "An Integrating Framework for Research in Business and Society: A Step Toward the Elusive Paradigm?" *Academy of Management Review*, Vol. 8, No. 4, October, 1983, pp. 559–564.

7. New York: Basic Books, 1976.

8. New York: Alfred A. Knopf, 1976.

9. New York: Basic Books, 1973.

10. Daniel Yankelovich, and others, *Work and Human Values: An International Report on Jobs in the 1980s and 1990s*. New York: Aspen Institute for Humanistic Studies, 1983.

11. This chapter is based in considerable measure on papers of the Center for Ethics and Social Policy, Berkeley, in a series on "Institutionalizing Corporate Social Responsibility." In addition to Fred Twining and me, members of the Center staff who contributed to the formulation and writing of these papers were Phil Mullins and Jim Donahue.

Chapter 8 CORPORATE PERFORMANCE: INSTITUTIONALIZING ETHICS

1. See Michael Polanyi, *Personal Knowledge: Towards a Post-Critical Philosophy*. Chicago: University of Chicago Press, 1958; and *The Tacit Dimension*. Garden City: Doubleday, 1964.

2. Books already mentioned that would be useful at various levels of management are Peters and Waterman, *In Search of Excellence;* James O'Toole, *Making America Work;* Deal and Kennedy, *Corporate Cultures;* Donaldson, *Corporations and Morality;* Preston and Post, *Private Management and Public Policy;* Freeman, *Strategic Management;* and John D. Aram, *Managing Business and Public Policy*. See

also Rosabeth Moss Kanter, *The Change Masters: Innovations for Productivity in the American Corporation.* New York: Simon and Schuster, 1982.

3. Deal and Kennedy, *Corporate Cultures,* pp. 13–15.
4. Philip Selznick, *Leadership in Administration,* p. 26–27.
5. Michael Polanyi, *Personal Knowledge,* p. 210.
6. Deal and Kennedy, *Corporate Cultures,* pp. 21, 23.
7. Quoted in Peters and Waterman, *In Search of Excellence,* p. 83.
8. Philip Selznick, *Leadership in Administration,* p. 28.
9. Jeffrey Pfeffer, *Power in Organizations,* pp. 298–299.
10. See Paul M. Hammaker, Alexander B. Horniman, and Louis T. Rader, *Standards of Conduct in Business.* Charlottesville: Center for the Study of Applied Ethics, 1978.
11. Bernard J. White, "Corporate Codes of Conduct: A Mechanism of Internal Control," in Robert K. Mautz, and others (eds.) *Internal Control in U.S. Corporations: The State of the Art.* New York: Financial Executives Research Foundation, 1980, pp. 381–82.
12. See Joanne Giunta, *Introduction to Corporate Social Responsibility Management.* Philadelphia: Human Resources Network, 1977.
13. See Raymond A. Bauer and Dan Fenn, Jr., "What *Is* a Corporate Social Audit?" *Harvard Business Review,* January-February, 1973.
14. Thomas Donaldson, *Corporations and Morality,* p. 205.
15. See *Board of Directors Manual,* Connecticut General Insurance Corporation, Hartford, Connecticut; and *Principles of Corporate Governance and Structure: Restatement and Recommendations.* Tentative Draft No. 1. Philadelphia: The American Law Institute, 1982, especially pp. 17ff. and pp. 71ff.
16. Richard T. DeGeorge, *Business Ethics.* New York: Macmillan Publishing Co., 1982, p. 137.
17. Ibid., pp. 138–140.

Chapter 9 COMMUNICATION, PARTICIPATION, AND COMMITMENT

1. Chester I. Barnard, *The Functions of the Executive.* Cambridge, Mass.: Harvard University Press, 1938, pp. 21, 71, 82.
2. Karl W. Deutsch, *The Nerves of Government: Models of Political*

Communication and Control. New York: The Free Press, 1966, p. 77.

3. Robert W. Ackerman, *The Social Challenge to Business.* Cambridge, Mass.: Harvard University Press, 1975. See the summary of Ackerman's book in Appendix O for further details on this important work.

4. *Ibid.,* p. 316.

5. Alexander B. Trowbridge, "Foreword" to Leonard Silk and David Vogel, *Ethics and Profits: The Crisis of Confidence in American Business.* New York: Simon and Schuster, 1976, pp. 8, 9.

6. This section draws heavily on a paper by the Staff of the Center for Ethics and Social Policy, Berkeley entitled "Participative Management," the Fifth in a Series of Center Papers on "Institutionalizing Corporate Social Responsibility," Berkeley: Center for Ethics and Social Policy, 1978. Fred Twining, Phil Mullins, and Jim Donahue were staff members who contributed substantively to the insights and formulation of the paper.

7. Douglas McGregor, *The Human Side of Enterprise.* New York: McGraw-Hill Book Company, Inc., 1960, pp. 33 ff.

8. Ibid., pp. 45 ff.

9. See William Ouchi, *Theory Z: How American Business Can Meet the Japanese Challenge.* Reading, Massachusetts: Addison-Wesley Publishing Company, 1981.

10. Quoted in W. Michael Hoffman and Thomas J. Wyly, *The Work Ethic in Business.* Cambridge, Mass.: Oelgeschlager, Gunn, and Hain, 1981, p. 69. See also John D. Aram, *Managing Business and Public Policy,* pp. 171ff., for further information on worker participation.

11. Rosabeth Moss Kanter, *The Change Masters.* 1983.

12. See, for example, J. D. Batten, *Beyond Management by Objectives.* New York: American Management Associations, 1969.

13. Kanter, *The Change Masters.*

Chapter 10 THE ETHICAL DIFFERENCE

1. James Burke, Speech to the Advertising Council, November 16, 1983.

2. Nancy J. Perry, "America's Most Admired Companies," *Fortune,* January 9, 1984, p. 52.

3. Ibid., p. 56.

4. Robert Levering, Milton Moskowitz, and Michael Katz, *The 100 Best Companies to Work for in America*. Reading, Mass.: Addison-Wesley Publishing Co., 1984.

5. Reginald Jones, "Managing in the 1980s," Address to the Wharton School of Business, University of Pennsylvania, February 4, 1980.

6. A. W. Clausen, "Voluntary Disclosure: Someone Has to Jump into the Icy Water First," *Financial Executive,* June 1976, p. 21.

7. For the story, see Plato, *Protagoras* 320C–323A. I am endebted to Michael Nagler of the University of California, Berkeley, for calling my attention to this item from Plato. Laura Nash of Harvard reminds me that a mischievous Plato may have woven more ambiguity into the story than appears. Hermes was not only the messenger of the gods and bringer of good fortune in business, but also at times deceitful and considered the protector of thieves.

BIBLIOGRAPHY

Ackerman, Robert W. *The Social Challenge of Business.* Cambridge, Mass.: Harvard University Press, 1975.

Aldrich, Howard E. *Organizations and Environments.* Englewood Cliffs, New Jersey: Prentice-Hall, 1979.

Andrews, Kenneth R. *The Concept of Corporate Strategy.* Revised Edition. Homewood, Ill.: Richard D. Irwin, 1980.

Anshen, Melvin, ed. *Managing the Socially Responsible Corporation.* New York: Macmillan, 1974.

Aram, John D. *Managing Business and Public Policy: Concepts, Issues and Cases.* Marshfield, Mass.: Pitman, 1983

Barnard, Chester I. *The Functions of the Executive.* Cambridge, Mass.: Harvard University Press, 1938.

Barnet, R. J., and R. E. Muller. *Global Reach: The Power of the Multinationals.* New York: Simon & Schuster, 1974.

Barry, Brian. *The Liberal Theory of Justice.* New York: Oxford University Press, 1973.

Batchelder, Robert C. *The Irreversible Decision, 1939–50.* New York: Macmillan, 1961.

Batten, J. D. *Beyond Management by Objectives.* New York: American Management Associations, 1969.

Bauer, Raymond A., and Dan Fenn, Jr., "What *Is* a Corporate Social Audit," *Harvard Business Review,* January-February, 1973.

Beauchamp, Tom L., and Norman E. Bowie, eds. *Ethical Theory and*

Business. Second Edition. Englewood Cliffs, New Jersey: Prentice-Hall, 1983.
Bell, Daniel. *The Cultural Contradictions of Capitalism.* New York: Basic Books, 1976.
Bennett, John C., "A Theological Conception of Goals for Economic Life," in Dudley A. Ward, ed., *Goals of Economic Life.* New York: Harper & Brothers, 1953.
Benson, George C. S. *Business Ethics in America.* Lexington, Mass.: D. C. Heath, 1982.
Berger, Peter L., and Thomas Luckmann. *The Social Construction of Reality.* New York: Doubleday, 1966.
Blumberg, Philip I. *Corporate Responsibility in a Changing Society.* Boston: Boston University School of Law, 1972.
Blumenthal, Michael, "Business Morality Has Not Deteriorated — Society Has Changed," *New York Times Magazine,* January 9, 1977.
Boulding, Kenneth E. *The Organizational Revolution.* New York: Harper & Brothers, 1953.
———. *The Image.* Ann Arbor: Ann Arbor Paperbacks, 1961.
Bowie, Norman E. *Business Ethics.* Englewood Cliffs, New Jersey: Prentice-Hall, 1982.
Britell, Jenne K., "Ethics Courses Are Making Slow Inroads," *New York Times Magazine,* April 26, 1981.
Bruner, Jerome S. *On Knowing: Essays for the Left Hand.* New York: Atheneum, 1973.
Buber, Martin. *The Prophetic Faith.* New York: Macmillan, 1949.
Burns, James MacGregor. *Leadership.* New York: Harper & Row, 1978.
Carroll, Archie B. *Business and Society: Managing Corporate Social Performance.* Boston: Little, Brown, 1981.
Chamberlain, Neil. *The Place of Business in America's Future: A Study in Social Values.* New York: Basic Books, 1973.
Childs, Marquis W., and Douglass Cater. *Ethics in a Business Society.* New York: Harper & Brothers, 1954.
Churchman, C. West. *Challenge to Reason.* New York: McGraw-Hill, 1968.
Clark, Burton R. *The Open Door College.* New York: McGraw-Hill, 1960.
Clark, John Maurice. *Economic Institutions and Human Welfare.* New York: Alfred A. Knopf, 1957.

Clausen, A. W., "Voluntary Disclosure: Someone Has to Jump into the Icy Water First," *Financial Executive*, June 1976.
Davis, Stanley M. *Guiding Beliefs: Managing Corporate Culture*. Cambridge, Mass.: Ballanger Books, 1984.
Deal, Terrence E., and Allan A. Kennedy. *Corporate Cultures: The Rites and Rituals of Corporate Life*. Reading, Mass.: Addison-Wesley, 1982.
De George, Richard T. *Business Ethics*. New York: Macmillan, 1982.
Deutsch, Karl W. *The Nerves of Government: Models of Political Communication and Control*. New York: Free Press, 1966.
Donaldson, Thomas. *Corporations and Morality*. Englewood Cliffs, New Jersey: Prentice-Hall, 1982.
———, and Patricia H. Werhane, eds. *Ethical Issues in Business: A Philosophical Approach*. Second Edition. Englewood Cliffs, New Jersey: Prentice-Hall, 1983.
Drucker, Peter F. *Management: Tasks, Practices, Responsibilities*. New York: Harper and Row, 1974.
———. *Managing in Turbulent Times*. New York: Harper and Row, 1980.
Eels, Richard, and Clarence Walton. *Conceptual Foundations of Business*. 3rd edition. Homewood, Ill.: Richard D. Irwin, 1974.
Epstein, Edwin M. *The Corporation in American Politics*. Englewood Cliffs, New Jersey: Prentice-Hall, 1969.
———, "Dimensions of Corporate Power: Part I," *California Management Review*, Winter, 1973.
———, "Dimensions of Corporate Power: Part II," *California Management Review*, Summer 1974.
———, "Societal, Managerial, and Legal Perspectives on Corporate Social Responsibility — Products and Process," *The Hastings Law Journal*, May, 1979.
———, and Dow Votaw, eds. *Rationality, Legtimacy, Responsibility: Search for New Directions in Business and Society*. Santa Monica, Calif.: Goodyear, 1978.
Evans, William A. *Management Ethics: An Intercultural Perspective*. The Hague: Martinus Nijhoff, 1981.
Freeman, R. Edward. *Strategic Management: A Stakeholder Approach*. Marshfield, Mass.: Pitman, 1984.
Friedman, Milton. *Capitalism and Freedom*. Chicago: University of Chicago Press, 1962.

———, and Rose Friedman. *Free to Choose*. New York: Harcourt Brace Jovanovich, 1980.

Galbraith, John K. *American Capitalism: The Concept of Countervailing Power*. Boston: Houghton Mifflin, 1952.

Guinta, Joanne. *Introduction to Corporate Social Responsibility Management*. Philadelphia: Human Resources Network, 1977.

Hanson, Kirk O. "Ethics and Business: A Progress Report," *Stanford GSB,* Spring, 1983.

Herberg, Will. *Protestant-Catholic-Jew: An Essay in American Religious Sociology*. Garden City, New York: Doubleday & Company, 1956.

Hoffman, W. Michael, and Thomas J. Wyly. *The Work Ethic in Business*. Cambridge, Mass.: Oelgeschlager, Gunn, and Hain, 1981.

Hurst, James Willard. *The Legitimacy of the Business Corporation in the Law of the United States, 1780–1970*. Charlottesville: University of Virginia Press, 1970.

Inglehart, Ronald. *The Silent Revolution: Changing Values and Political Styles among Western Publics*. Princeton: Princeton University Press, 1977.

Jones, Donald, G., ed. *Doing Ethics in Business*. Cambridge, Mass.: Oelgeschlager, Gunn, and Hain, 1982.

Jones, Thomas M., "An Integrating Framework for Research in Business and Society: A Step Toward the Elusive Paradigm?" *The Academy of Management Review,* October, 1983.

Joranson, Philip N., and Ken Butigan, eds. *Cry of the Environment: Rebuilding the Christian Creation Tradition*. Santa Fe: Bear, 1984.

Kanter, Rosabeth Moss. *The Change Masters: Innovations for Productivity in the American Corporation*. New York: Simon and Schuster, 1983.

Kiefer, Francine, "Board room, classroom exploring business ethics," *Christian Science Monitor,* October 25, 1983.

Levering, Robert, Milton Moskowitz, and Michael Katz. *The 100 Best Companies to Work for in America*. Reading, Mass.: Addison-Wesley, 1984.

Lewin, Kurt. *Resolving Social Conflicts: Selected Papers on Group Dynamics, 1935–1946*. Edited by Gertud Weiss Lewin. New York: Harper and Bros., 1948.

Lewis, Hunter, and Donald Allison. *The Real World War: The Coming Battle for the New Global Economy and Why We Are in Danger of Losing*. New York: Coward, McCann, & Geoghegan, 1982.

Lindblom, Charles E. *The Policy-Making Process.* 2nd edition. Englewood Cliffs, New Jersey: Prentice-Hall, 1980.
Lodge, George Cabot. *The New American Ideology.* New York: Alfred A. Knopf, 1976.
Lorsch, Jay, and Gordon Donaldson. *Decision Making at the Top: The Shaping of Strategic Direction.* New York: Basic Books, 1983.
Manne, Henry, and Henry Wallich. *The Modern Corporation and Social Responsibility.* Washington: American Enterprise Institute, 1972.
Mautz, Robert K., et al., eds. *Internal Control in U. S. Corporations: The State of the Art.* New York: Financial Executives Research Foundation, 1980.
McCaskey, Michael B. *The Executive Challenge: Managing Change and Ambiguity.* Marshfield, Mass.: Pitman, 1982.
McClintock, David. *Indecent Exposure: A True Story of Hollywood and Wall Street.* New York: Dell, 1982.
McCoy, Bowen H. "The Parable of the Sadhu," *Havard Business Review,* September-October, 1983.
McCoy, Charles S., "Ethics for an Organized World," *Ethics and Policy,* February, 1977.
McCoy, Charles S., Mark Juergensmeyer, and Fred Twining. *Ethics in the Corporate Policy Process: An Introduction.* Berkeley: Center for Ethics and Social Policy, 1975.
McGregor, Douglas. *The Human Side of Enterprise.* New York: McGraw-Hill, 1960.
Miller, Lawrence M. *American Spirit: Visions of a New Corporate Culture.* New York: William Morrow and Company, 1984.
Mintzberg, Henry. *The Structuring of Organizations.* Englewood Cliffs, New Jersey: Prentice-Hall, 1979.
Myrdal, Gunnar. *The Challenge of World Poverty.* London: Allen Lane, 1970.
Naisbitt, John. *Megatrends: Ten New Directions Transforming Our Lives.* New York: Warner Books, 1982.
Niebuhr, H. Richard. *Radical Monotheism and Western Culture.* New York: Harper and Bros., 1960.
Niebuhr, Reinhold. *Moral Man and Immoral Society: A Study in Ethics and Politics.* New York: Charles Scribner's Sons, 1932.
Novak, Michael. *The Spirit of Democratic Capitalism.* New York: Simon & Schuster, 1982.
Obenhaus, Victor. *Ethics for an Industrial Age: A Christian Inquiry.* New York: Harper & Row, 1965.

O'Toole, James. *Making America Work: Productivity and Responsibility.* New York: Continuum, 1981.

Ouichi, William. *Theory Z: How American Business Can Meet the Japanese Challenge.* Reading, Mass.: Addison-Wesley Publishing Company, 1981.

Perrow, Charles. *Complex Organizations: A Critical Essay.* Glenview, Illinois: Scott, Foresman, 1972.

Perry, Nancy J., "America's Most Admired Companies," *Fortune,* January 9, 1984.

Peter, L. J., and R. Hull. *The Peter Principle.* New York: Morrow, 1969.

Peters, Thomas J., and Robert H. Waterman, Jr. *In Search of Excellence: Lessons from American's Best-Run Companies.* New York: Harper & Row, 1982.

Pettigrew, A. M. *The Politics of Organizational Decision-Making.* London: Tavistock, 1973.

Pfeffer, Jeffrey. *Power in Organizations.* Marshfield, Mass.: Pitman, 1981.

Pfeffer, Jeffrey, and Gerald R. Salanick. *The External Control of Organizations: A Resource Dependence Perspective.* New York: Harper & Row, 1978.

Polanyi, Michael. *Personal Knowledge: Towards a Post-Critical Philosophy.* Chicago: University of Chicago Press, 1958.

———. *The Tacit Dimension.* Garden City, N. Y.: Doubleday, 1964.

Powers, Charles W., and David Vogel. *Ethics in the Education of Business Managers.* Hastings-on-Hudson, New York: The Hastings Center, 1980.

Preston, Lee E., and James E. Post. *Private Management and Public Policy: The Principle of Public Responsibility.* Englewood Cliffs, New Jersey: Prentice-Hall, 1975.

Rawls, John. *A Theory of Justice.* Cambridge: Mass.: Harvard University Press, 1971.

Reeck, Darrell. *Ethics for the Professions: A Christian Perspective.* Minneapolis: Augsburg, 1982

Scott, John Finley. *Internalization of Norms: A Sociological Theory of Moral Commitment.* Englewood Cliffs, New Jersey: Prentice-Hall, 1971.

Scott, William C., and David K. Hart. *Organizational America: Can Individual Freedom Survive Within the Security It Promises?* Boston: Houghton Mifflin Company, 1979.

Selznick, Philip. *Leadership in Administration: A Sociological Interpretation.* Evanston, Ill.: Row, Peterson, 1957.
Sethi, S. Prakash, ed. *The Unstable Ground: Corporate Social Policy in a Dynamic Society.* Los Angeles: Melville, 1974.
———. *Up Against the Corporate Wall: Modern Corporations and Social Issues of the Eighties.* Fourth Edition. Englewood Cliffs, New Jersey: Prentice-Hall, 1982.
Silk, Leonard, and David Vogel. *Ethics and Profits: The Crisis of Confidence in American Business.* New York: Simon & Schuster, 1976.
Steckmast, Francis W., and others. *Corporate Performance: The Key to Public Trust.* New York: McGraw-Hill, 1982.
Stevens, Edward. *Business Ethics.* New York: Paulist Press, 1979.
Stone, Christopher. *Where the Law Ends: The Social Control of Corporate Behavior.* New York: Harper & Row, 1975.
Sward, Keith. *The Legend of Henry Ford.* New York: Rinehart, 1948.
Tawney, R. H. *Religion and the Rise of Capitalism: A Historical Study.* New York: Harcourt, Brace, and Company, 1926.
Thompson, James D. *Organizations in Action: Social Science Bases of Administrative Theory.* New York: McGraw-Hill, 1967.
Twining, Fred, et al., "Participative Management," 5th in a series of Center Papers on "Institutionalizing Corporate Social Responsibility." Berkeley: Center for Ethics and Social Policy, 1978.
Velasquez, Manuel G. *Business Ethics.* Englewood Cliffs, New Jersey: Prentice-Hall, 1982.
Walton, Clarence. *Ethos and the Executive.* Englewood Cliffs, New Jersey: Prentice-Hall, 1979.
———, ed. *The Ethics of Corporate Conduct.* Englewood Cliffs, New Jersey: Prentice-Hall, 1977.
Weber, Max. *The Protestant Ethics and the Spirit of Capitalism.* Translated by Talcott Parsons. New York: Charles Scribner's Sons, 1958.
Wilber, Charles K., and Kenneth P. Jameson. *An Inquiry into the Poverty of Economics.* Notre Dame: University of Notre Dame Press, 1983.
Yankolovich, Daniel, and others. *Work and Human Values: An International Report on Jobs in the 1980s and 1990s.* New York: Aspen Institute for Humanistic Studies, 1983.
Yates, Brock. *The Decline and Fall of the American Automobile Industry.* New York: Empire Books, 1983.

INDEX

Abt, Clark, 194
Academic theory, 35, 37
Acheson, Dean, 38
Ackerman, Robert, 212–213, 215, 316
Action, 42, 65–66
    criteria for, 94, 101–102
    decision making as policy process, 130–136
    meaning and, 184–185
Advertising, 69, 154, 157–158, 183
Advertising Council, speech to, 325–331
Advisory councils, 144
Aetna Life and Casualty Company, 299–300
Affirmative action, 44, 125–126, 128–129, 170, 171. *See also* Equal employment opportunity
Alternatives:
    crises of, 81, 84–85
    developing new, 210–211
American Council of Life Insurance, 215

American Declaration of Independence, 170
Amos, 68
Andrews, Kenneth, 13
Anthropological approach to management, 63
Anti-materialism, 164
Aquinas, Thomas, 68
Aram, John D., 140
Arbuckle, Ernest, 107
Aristotle, 53, 59, 68, 104
Arts, 111, 134
Aspen Institute, 173
Augustine, 68
Authoritarianism, 139
Automotive industry, 6, 14–15, 153, 157–158, 172
Awareness, 93, 165

Bank of America, 7, 118
Banks, 7, 112
    loan policies, 141–144, 198–199, 261–265, 312–313, 342–344
Barnard, Chester, 12, 70, 204
Batchelder, Robert, 52

Bell, Daniel, 140, 162, 168, 172
Bennett, John, 115–116
Berkeley Center, 73, 108, 210–211
Berle, Adolph, 80
Blumenthal, Michael, 33
Board of directors, 195, 196–197, 309
Boulding, Kenneth, 54, 80, 87, 101
Bowen, Howard, 87
Bribery, 33, 100, 193, 180
Bruner, Jerome, 185
Buddhist ethics, 104
Burke, James, 233, 236–238, 325–331
Burns, James MacGregor, 185
Busch, August, III, 238
Business Roundtable, "Statement on Corporate Responsibility" (1981), 8–9
Business schools, ethics courses in, 31, 32, 37, 280, 281, 284–287
Business Week, 215

Callahan, Daniel, 32–33
Capitalism, 60–61. *See also* Industrialized societies, Laissez-faire capitalism; State capitalism
Capitalism and Freedom (Friedman), 260
Carnegie, Andrew, 86, 103
Carroll, Archie, 93
Cater, Douglass, 87
Ceremonies and celebrations, 65, 182, 185
Chamberlain, Neil, 140, 164–165, 168, 172–173
Champion International, 107, 132–133, 275–279
Character, corporate. *See* Corporate character
Charities, 54, 111, 258

Charters of incorporation, 59–60
Charts, organizational, 65–66
Chase Manhattan Bank, 275
Child labor, 44, 55, 105, 106, 170
Childs, Marquis, 87
Chile, 83
Chisso, 15–16
Choice, 44–47
Christian ethics, 104, 114, 116, 283
Chrysler, 153
Churches, 54
Churchman, C. West, 66
Citizens United for the Environment (CUE), 77
Clare, Dave, 337–338
Clausen, A. W., 243
Codes of ethics, 192–194, 233, 236–238, 241
Columbia Pictures, 7–8
Colonialism, 106
Commitment, 90, 222–223, 322–323
    corporate covenants and, 223–226
    development of, 180–187
    imagination and, 226–228
    innovation and, 228–230
Committees on social responsibility and ethics, 195–196, 312
Communication, 206–207
    channels of, 65
    social issue life cycle and, 212–214
    social values information in, 208–212
    social values information system, 214–217
Communist bloc, 56, 57
Communitarian social values system, 163, 168, 171–172, 211
Community, corporation as, 62–68, 182

Community activities, 88, 289–299
Conflict-of-interest, 193
Congress, 305, 344
Connecticut General, 197
Connecticut Mutual Life Report on American Values in the 80's, 17
Consequences, 135–136
Constitution, U.S., 69, 170, 283
Constitutional values, 164–165
Consumer credit, 142
Context, 131–133, 209–210, 241–242
Continental Illinois Bank, 265
Conviviality, 183
Cooley, Richard, 107, 111
Corporate character, 66–68, 70, 107–108, 240
  context and, 132–133, 209–210
Corporate culture, 50–58, 225, 239–240, 244
  of Champion International, 107, 132–133, 275–279
  context and, 131–133, 209–210
  control and, 187–189
  development of, 180–187
  dimensions of, 58–68
  rules and, 189–190
Corporate Cultures (Deal and Kennedy), 71, 181, 185–186
Corporate ethics. *See* Ethics
Corporation(s):
  as communities, 62–66
  covenants of, 223–224
  in historical perspective, 58–62
  importance of, 54–55
  as moral agents, 68–74
  organizational change in, 195–201
  power and complexity of, 80–81
Counsultores del Campo, A. C., 354
Creativity, 65, 285
Cultural Contradictions of Capitalism, The (Bell), 140, 162, 168, 172

Cultural groups, 54, 111, 134
Culture, corporate. *See* Corporate culture
Customs, 63, 64–65
Cybernetics, 206

Darwinism, social, 169
Deal, Terrence, 71, 181, 185–186
Decentralization, 95, 188
Decision making, 43, 130–136, 309–310
Decision matrix, 147
Decline and Fall of the American Automobile Industry, The (Yates), 6, 153
DeGeorge, Richard, 197–198
Delta Air Lines, Inc., 12
Deming, W. Edward, 6
Deutsch, Karl, 206
Dilemma ethics, 44
Distribution of goods and services, 55, 57
Distributive values, 165
Donaldson, Thomas, 15–16, 194–195
Drucker, Peter, 19

EastWest Bank, 352–354
Economic instability, 79
Economic justice, 115–116, 142
Education, 55, 57, 111, 165
  ethics courses, 31, 32, 37, 280, 281, 284–287
Ellul, Jacques, 52
Energy, 54, 79, 97–98
Enforcement of rules, 35, 36–37
Environmental protection, 10, 54, 57, 76–77, 78, 79, 83, 88, 91–92, 97–98, 111, 227
Environmental Protection Agency (EPA), 76–77
Epimetheus, 246
Epstein, Edwin M., 71, 80, 140

Equal employment opportunity, 83, 88, 134, 170, 213–214, 225, 227. *See also* Affirmative action
Equality, 115, 116, 165, 213
Erlach, Raymond, 263
Ethics, 240–241
   codes of, 192–194, 233, 236–238, 241'
   committees on social responsibility and ethics, 195–196, 312
   of corporate self-interest, 102–109, 117, 118, 119, 145–146, 169, 244
   crisis of policy and, 78–85
   definition of, 41–44, 225
   developing, 86–91
   developing commitments to, 180–187, 239–240, 244
   education, 31, 32, 37, 280, 281, 284–287
   Hanson on, 68–69, 280–288
   integration into corporate structures, 187–191
   integration into policy process, 191–201
   institutionalization of, 177–180
   interrelation of individual and corporate, 47–48, 51–53, 68–69, 73–74, 270–274, 281–282
   misunderstandings and problems of, 35–40
   of multiple responsibility, 109–113, 117–118, 119, 143–145
   performance and, 18–23, 239–246
   in policy formulation, 139–148
   recognition of, 40–48
   rising interest in, 31–35
   of social vision, 113–116, 118–119, 141–143
   systemic, 68, 69, 292
   see also Social values

Ethics for an Industrial Age (Obenhaus), 87
Ethics in a Business Society (Childs and Cater), 87
Ethnic groups. *See* Minorities
Europe, Western, 105, 106, 155, 294
Euthyphro, 99
Evaluation sessions, 65
Expertise, 90

Factory system, 105
Family relationships, crisis in, 81
Federal Food, Drug, and Cosmetic Act, 69
First Penn. Corp., 262
Focal values, 164
Food, 55, 142
Ford, Henry, 59, 84, 157–158
Ford Motor Company, 153, 157–158
Fortune, 238, 239
Fourteenth Amendment, 69
Fraud, 33, 100
Freedom, 115, 116
Freedom of speech, 69
Freeman, R. Edward, 110, 137, 140
Friedman, Milton, 3–4, 102–103, 104, 106, 253–260
Fuller, Stephen, 220
Functions of the Executive, The (Barnard), 204–205

General Motors, 153, 163, 220
Global society, 54, 95, 142, 156, 161, 172, 242
Government, 53, 54, 56–57, 165, 257
   expanding role of, 163–164
   regulation, 33, 57, 59–60, 106, 109, 305, 306

Haas family, 107
Handicapped, 111, 112
Hanson, Kirk O., 68–69, 280–288
Health, 55, 112, 170
Hebrew prophets, 68
Hedonism, 162
Hermes, 246
Hewlett-Packard, 107
Hibernia National Bank, 265
Hindu ethics, 104
Hobbes, Thomas, 60, 223
Holism, 164
Housing, 55, 142, 289–290
Humanitarian social values system, 168, 170–171, 172, 211
Human rights, 54, 109, 128, 129, 142, 155
Human Side of Enterprise, The (McGregor), 12, 218–219
Hunger, 79, 142

IBM, 12, 182, 186, 238
Ideology, 162–163
Implementation, 43
Income, 55
Indecent Exposure (McClintock), 7–8
Ind-Ill Company, 187–188
Individualism, 68, 163, 169, 171
Industrial expansion, 142
Industrial societies, 55, 56–57, 59, 60, 61, 294
Infant mortality, 55
Inflation, 79
"Information society," 77, 79, 156
Information systems, 57, 140, 214–217
Inglehart, Ronald, 155, 157, 291–297
Innovation, 86–91, 182, 229
  institutionalization of culture and, 189–190

In Search of Excellence: Lessons from America's Best-Run Companies, (Peters and Waterman) 11–12, 13, 62, 71, 132, 183
Integrity, 243, 285–286
Interaction, 65–66
International Monetary Fund, 344
Isaiah, 68

Japan, 56, 219
Jewish ethics, 68, 104, 283
Johnson, Robert Wood, 193, 236, 289–290, 326
Johnson & Johnson, 7, 108, 193–194, 233, 236–238, 326–329
Jones, Reginald, 19, 240
Justice, 68, 115–116, 283–284

Kant, Immanuel, 104
Kanter, Rosabeth Moss, 221, 229
Kennedy, Allan, 71, 181, 185–186
Kickbacks, 100
Knowledge theory of value, 78
Kristol, Irving, 235
Kroc, Ray, 107

Labor, 93, 105, 106
Labor unions, 54, 170, 257, 319
Laissez-faire capitalism, 56, 60, 86, 103, 104–106
Longhorn Oil & Gas Co., 261–265
Latin America, 105
Leadership, 139, 165
  development of culture and value commitments by, 185–187
Leadership (Burns), 186
Leadership in Administration (Selznick), 12, 66–67, 70, 130, 157–158, 181–182, 186
Legal profession, 54

Legal responsibility, 69–70, 227
Legislation, 106, 109, 110, 170, 213
  inadequacy of, 294, 295–296
Levi Strauss Co., 107
Lewin, Kurt, 52
Life span, 55
Loan policies, 141–144, 198–199, 261–265, 312–313, 342–344
Locke, John, 60
Lodge, George Cabot, 140, 162–164, 168, 171, 172
Luther, Martin, 68

McClintock, David, 7–8
McCoy, Bowen H., 47, 266–274
McCoy, Charles S., 298–303, 312–313
McDonald's, 107
McGregor, Douglas, 12
McNeil Consumer Products, 328
Making America Work (O'Toole), 12–13, 63, 65, 71
Management, 10–18, 23, 204–206
  anthropological approach to, 63
  appraising environment, 14–16
  awareness and, 93
  communications in, 206–217
  commitment in, 222–230
  control by, 187–189
  criteria for action, 94
  development of culture and value commitments by, 185–187, 239–240, 244
  excellence in, 11–14, 34
  institutional support, 94–95
  Management by Objectives (MBO), 262
  "Management by Walking Around," 154
  manipulation versus, 92
  operative ethics, 16–18
  participative, 95, 217–222
  political function of, 137
  science of, 70–72, 90, 129, 224
  "Theory X" and "Theory Y" styles of, 218–219
  "Theory Z" style of, 219–220
Manne, Henry, 110
Marketing policies, 83
Marshall, John, 59
Marxists, 60–61
Mass production, 55, 84
Materialism, 292–294
Mayo, Elton, 12, 70, 219
Media, 54, 57, 100
Megatrends (Naisbitt), 77–78, 155–157, 215
Mercantilism, 104–105, 169
Meritocracy, 165
Methodism, 86
Mexico, 343–344
Michigan National Bank, 265
Middle class, 59
  emergence of, 105
Miller, Arjay, 108, 110
Miller Beer, 183
Minorities, 83, 93, 106, 111, 118, 170, 213–214, 225
Monopolies, 44, 56, 106
Monroe Doctrine, 105
Montesquieu, Charles de Secondat de, 329
Moral agency, 68–74
  ethics and, 72–74
  legal responsibility, 69–70
  in social scientific perspective, 70–72, 90–91
Moralism, 38

Naisbitt, John, 77–78, 155–157, 215
National Council of Churches on Ethics and Economic Life, 86
National economy, 95, 156
National Peoples Action, 289

Negotiation, 138–139
New American Ideology, The (Lodge), 140, 162–164, 168, 171, 172
Nisbet, Robert, 52–53
Nixon, Richard, 280
Northern Trust Co., 265
Novak, Michael, 159, 331
Nuclear threat, 79

Obenhaus, Victor, 87
Organizational Revolution, The (Boulding), 54, 80, 87, 101
Organizations, 53–58, 223
  Barnard on, 205
  changes in patterns of, 195–201
  power and complexity of, 80–81
O'Toole, James, 12–13, 63, 65, 71
Ouchi, William, 219
Owens, Phillip, 177–178, 180, 192

Participative management, 95, 217–222
Patterson, Bill, 261, 262–263
"Peaked-out" employees, 149–152, 173–174, 210–2111, 298–303
Penn Square Bank, 7, 261–265
Perfectionism, 45–46
Performance, 18–23, 34
  criteria for, 20–21, 244
  ethics and, 18–23, 239–246
  evaluation of, 92, 95–96, 194–195, 238–239, 310–311
  heightened standards of, 33
  policy process and, 125–130
  profits as measure of, 5–10
  social issue life cycle and, 212–214
Personnel policies, 83, 102, 144–145, 149–152, 173–174, 185, 210–211, 298–303
Peters, Thomas, 11–12, 13, 62, 71, 132, 183
Pfeffer, Jeffrey, 189

Place of Business in America's Future, The: A Study in Social Values (Chamberlain), 140, 164–165, 168, 172–173
Plato, 53, 68, 104, 246
Polanyi, Michael, 179, 183
Policy, 29–31, 50–53
  challenge to innovate through, 86–91
  comprehensiveness and context of, 97–101, 116–120, 146–148
  crisis of ethics and, 78–85
  criteria used in, 94, 101–102
  decision making as policy process, 130–136, 309–310
  evaluation of ethics in, 139–148
  loan policies, 141–144, 198–199, 261–265, 312–313, 342–344
  organized society and, 53–58
  on "peaked-out" employees, 149–152, 173–174, 210–211, 298–303
  performance and, 125–130, 242–243
  politics of corporate policy formulation, 136–139
  relating values to policy process, 191–201
  as system in corporate communities, 66
  triadic approach to, 23, 90–91
Political economies, mixed, 104–107
Political revolution and oppression, 79, 142
Political power and participation, 55
Politics of policy formulation, 136–139
Population explosion, 79, 142
Post, James, E., 140
Post-materialism, 292–294
Poverty, 79, 105

Power, 65–66, 80–81, 90, 133–135
  politics of policy process and, 138
Prakash Sethi, S., 140
Preston, Lee, 140
Price-fixing, 50–51, 52, 100, 193
Privacy, 57
Problems, human, escalation of, 79–80
Proctor & Gamble, 108
Productivity, 10, 116, 128, 142
  in Smithian value system, 169
Profits:
  corporate self-interest and, 102–103, 106, 108–109, 128–129, 145–146
  Friedman on, 253–260
  as measure of performance, 5–10
Prometheus, 246
Protestant ethic, 162
Prudence, 104, 169
Psychological analogy of character in organizations, 66–67
Public Agenda Foundation, 173
Public interest groups, 33, 109–110
Public Policy Committee, 199–201
Public relations, 33, 129, 195
Public service, 59
Puritan temper, 162
Purposes, 63, 64–65

Quality control, 225, 226–227, 244
Quality of life, 55, 56, 79, 81
  greater emphasis on, 155, 296–297

Rawls, John, 115
Reagan administration, 344
Real estate, 52, 142, 289–290
Reason, 44
Recession, 53, 54
Reconciliation, 138–139
Reeck, Darrell, 42
Relevance, 34–35

Reflection, 43
Religion, 17, 54, 86–87, 93, 165
  history of ethics in, 104, 105
  influence of, 184, 293
Rituals, 181, 182, 185
Republic (Plato), 68
Retirement, 170
Ritual, 65, 182, 185
Robber baron, 86
Rockefeller, John D., 4, 59, 86, 103
Roman ethics, 104

Sadhu, parable of, 47, 266–274
Seattle First National Bank, 265
Self-interest, corporate, 102–109, 117, 118, 119, 244
  in policy formulation, 145–146
  in Smithian value system, 169
Selznick, Philip, 12, 66, 70, 71, 130, 133–134, 157–158
Senior citizens, 83, 111, 112
Silent Revolution, The: Changing values and Political Styles among Western Publics (Inglehart), 155, 157, 201–207
Simon, William, 290
Slavery, abolition of, 55, 105, 170
Smith, Adam, 103, 104–105, 257–258
  Smithian social values system, 168–169, 172, 210–211
Smith, Roger, 153
Social activists, 99–100, 289–290
Social audits, 194–195, 320–321
Social Challenge to Business, The (Ackerman), 212–213, 215, 316–324
Social change, 228–230
Social Darwinism, 169
Socialism, 56, 106
Social issues, 79–80
  life cycle of, 212–214, 318–324
Social justice, 68, 115–116, 283–284

Social Policy Loan Committee, 143, 144, 198–199, 312–313
Social Responsibilities of the Businessman (Bowen), 87
Social responsibility, 44–47, 76–78
 audits of, 194–195, 310–311
 committees on social responsibility and ethics, 195–196, 312
 concern for, 86–87
 crisis of, 81–83
 ethics of multiple responsibility, 109–113, 117–118, 119, 143–145
 Friedman on, 253–260
 movement to corporate ethics, 87–89
 Stone on, 316–318
Social service groups, 111
Social values, 91–96, 149–153
 changing environment of, 153–158, 291–297
 communitarian social values system, 168, 171–172, 211
 constitutional values, 164–165
 distributive values, 165
 focal values, 164
 humanitarian social values system, 168, 170–171, 172, 211
 information in communication, 208–212
 information systems, 214–217
 Smithian social values system, 168–169, 172, 210–211
 social issues life cycle, 212–214
 systems, 165–173, 210–211
 systems analysis, 159–165
 see also Ethics
Social vision, 81, 83–84, 113–116, 118–119, 141–143
Social welfare benefits, 57
Socrates, 99

South Africa, 83
Soviet Union:
 preoccupation with security in, 155
 underground economy in, 61
Specialization, 164
Stakeholders, 110, 135, 137, 196
Standard of living, 55, 56, 105
Standard Oil, 4
Stanford Business School, 280, 284–287
State capitalism, 56, 57, 61
Stone, Christopher, 130, 304–311
Storytelling, 184–185, 206
Strategic Management: A Stakeholder Approach (Freeman), 110, 137, 140
Swan, Carl, 261, 262, 263
Sward, Keith, 158
Synergism, 183

Tampon "shock-syndrome" crisis, 108
Task forces, 65, 119, 145, 312
Tawney, R. H., 86
Taxation, 60, 255–256, 257, 258–259
Taylor, Frederick, 70
Teamwork, 183
Technology, 54–55, 84, 85
 control and, 188
 social values and, 92, 156
Terminology, 39–40
Theology of the Corporation, The (Novak), 159, 331
Theory of Justice, A (Rawls), 115
Theory Z (Ouchi), 219
Third World, 56, 114, 142
 EastWest Bank's loan policies to, 342–344
 social change in, 294–295
Trading companies, 59

Trend Analysis Program, 215
Triadic approach (to policy ethics), 23, 90–91
Trowbridge, Alexander, 217–218
Truman, Harry, 52
Trusts, 44
Twining, Fred N., 219, 291–297, 298–303, 304–311, 312–313, 316–324, 342–344
Tylenol "arsenic-poisoning" crisis, 108, 193–194, 236, 237, 326, 328–329, 331

Underground economy, 61
Unemployment insurance, 170

Valence, 133–135
Values. *See* Constitutional values; Ethics; Social values
Vanderbilt, Cornelius, 86
Votaw, Dow, 140

Wallich, Henry, 110
Wall Street Journal, 215
Walton, Clarence, 43, 59

War and peace, 54, 79, 83
Washington, George, 59
Waterman, Robert, 11–12, 13, 62, 71, 132, 183
Watson, Thomas J., Sr., 182, 186
Wells Fargo & Company, 7, 107, 111, 154, 314–315
Wesley, John, 86
Weyerhaeuser Corporation, 194
Where the Law Ends (Stone), 130, 304–311
Whistle blowing, 198, 320
White, Bernard, 192
White, William H., 52
Women, 83, 105, 106, 111, 134, 170, 225
Working conditions, 55, 170, 225, 227

Yates, Brock, 6, 153
Youth protest movements, 33

Zeus, 246
Zone of discretion, 319